Classic Book Jackets

Classic Book Jackets
The Design Legacy of George Salter

Thomas S. Hansen

Foreword by Milton Glaser

Princeton Architectural Press, New York

This book is affectionately dedicated to my brother, Matthew W. Hansen.

Published by
Princeton Architectural Press
37 East Seventh Street
New York, New York 10003

For a free catalog of books, call 1.800.722.6657.
Visit our web site at www.papress.com.

Project editing: Clare Jacobson
Additional editing: Linda Lee, Megan Carey,
and Scott Tennent
Design: Deb Wood

Special thanks to: Nettie Aljian, Nicola Bednarek,
Janet Behning, Penny (Yuen Pik) Chu, Russell
Fernandez, Jan Haux, John King, Mark Lamster, Nancy
Eklund Later, John McGill, Katharine Myers, Jane
Sheinman, Jennifer Thompson, and Joseph Weston of
Princeton Architectural Press
—Kevin C. Lippert, publisher

Frontispiece: George Salter lecturing at the Cooper
Union in the 1960s. Photo by Leo Versano, courtesy
Janet Salter Rosenberg.

Photography Credits
1, 2: Stefanie Salter Kyte
3–24, 36, 37, 39, 43–46, 48–63, 71, 76, 77, 81, 82, 84–87, 90,
    91, 94, 96, 98, 99, 101–115, 124, 130, 132, 133, 136, 137,
    139, 142–148, 149, 150, 152–168, 172–174, 176, 177, 179,
    181, 184, 185–192, 197–202, 204, 207, 209, 216–221:
    Janet Salter Rosenberg
25–30, 32–35, 38, 41, 42, 64–70, 75, 78, 83, 88, 89, 97, 100,
    116–123, 129, 134, 138, 141, 151, 169–171, 175, 178, 180,
    182, 196, 203, 205, 206, 208, 210–215, 222: Collection
    of Thomas S. Hansen
31, 80: Harvard College Library
40, 47, 72–74, 92, 93, 95, 125–128, 131, 135, 140, 183, 193–195:
    Smith College Library
79: Newberry Library, Chicago, Illinois
223: Alfred E. Knopf, courtesy Janet Salter Rosenberg

Library of Congress Cataloging-in-Publication Data
Hansen, Thomas S. (Thomas Stansfield), 1947–
Classic book jackets : the design legacy of George Salter /
Thomas S. Hansen ; foreword by Milton Glaser.
    p. cm.
Includes bibliographical references and index.
ISBN 1-56898-491-x (alk. paper)
1. Salter, George, 1897–1967—Criticism and interpreta-
tion. 2. Book jackets—United States—Design. 3. Book
jackets—Germany—Design. I. Title.
NC1883.3.S24H36 2005
741.6'4'092—dc22

                                    2004008211

*This book has been set in Adobe Caslon, designed by Carol
Twombly in 1989, based on William Caslon's originals
designed and cut between 1720 and 1766.*

Table of Contents

Foreword: Milton Glaser

I was privileged to be a student of George Salter at the Cooper Union during the late 1940s. At the time, the school's commitment to the study of calligraphy and the book arts, including typography, was the centerpiece of its commitment to the field of graphic design. Calligraphy's significant educational role was propelled by an outstanding group of teachers, with George himself, Paul Standard, Leo Manso, and Phil Grushkin (his former student). Their devotion to the practice of calligraphy and good craftsmanship was never less than inspiring.

Most of us interested in graphic design studied calligraphy, letter forms, and typography for three years. One could suggest that calligraphic studies develop skills parallel to those of drawing for those interested in practicing the visual arts. They both require the replication of a form held in mind into a material object. Like playing a musical instrument, repetition and practice are essential to understand form and to produce a desired result. The neurological path from brain to hand is cleared and strengthened in this primitive and uncompromised way. Since the advent of the computer, both drawing and calligraphy have lost their central educational function, being replaced by the vocational imperatives that the new technology demands. There are signs of change in this attitude among the good design schools, although a return to studying calligraphy as a basic educational tool seems quite unlikely.

In Salter's work, illustration and letterform cannot be easily separated. They were each idiosyncratic and unique. The influence of German graphic design and the formal ideas of modernism are evident, although they are softened and made more palatable by George's literary interests and his storytelling ability.

He was a wonderful teacher and created an atmosphere of high expectations in the classroom. I must admit that although I never saw him act cruelly I feared his disapproval or, more accurately, his sense of disappointment when I did less than my best work. He was inordinately generous to his students and developed lifelong mentoring relationships with many of them.

Like another teacher of mine, Giorgio Morandi, the Italian painter and printmaker, George provided me with a model for how to be in the world. He was more urbane and culturally sophisticated than anyone I had ever met up until that time and considered his profession to have a significant social meaning as well as an aesthetic one. His middle-class European-style apartment was defined by the books that filled every available space. If the word humanist has any current meaning, George would fit the description.

This volume provides an insight into the close, almost familial, relationship I always felt toward George. We shared a connection in that George was in part Hungarian (both my parents came from Transylvania and lived some part of their life in Budapest) and that George's family were Jews who converted to Christianity in the year of George's birth. These issues never came up between us, but they might explain an affinity or recognition that we had.

When I returned from my Fulbright year in Italy in 1954, George, with his customary generosity, offered me the opportunity to take over one of his important accounts, the covers of *Ellery Queen's Mystery Magazine*. I was pleased and flattered for the opportunity and for George's belief in my ability to continue the work he had started. I designed a cover that was used for the March 1954 issue, but I immediately had misgivings about continuing. I felt, even at this early part of my career, it was not quite what I wanted to be doing. I was apprehensive and embarrassed about revealing this to George, but I finally arranged to see him. He was seated at his tiny drawing table in his apartment when I told him my concerns. He looked at me with his characteristic wry smile and said, "OK." He never mentioned the subject again. There was never any indication of disappointment about my decision, for which I am eternally grateful. He was a unique and wonderful man.

Acknowledgments

I owe thanks to many whose support and encouragement made this project possible. Professor Ronald Salter (Tufts University)—no relation to George Salter—has for years been a mentor and model for much of my work, especially for this book. The following generous people all helped with the grand plan, cheered me on, or contributed crucial details: Dr. James Fraser (Friendship Library, Fairleigh Dickinson University), Professor Alston Purvis (Boston University), David R. Godine (Boston, Mass.), Thomas Boss (Boston, Mass.), Dr. Peter Christian Hauswedell (Berlin, Germany), Dr. Steven Schuyler (North Reading, Mass.), Richard Cheek (Belmont, Mass.), Charles Rheault (Dover, Mass.), Stephen Pekich (Arlington, Mass.), Roland Jaeger (Hamburg, Germany), and James Walsh (The Houghton Library, Harvard University). Special thanks are due to Clare Jacobson (Princeton Architectural Press) for her hard work and expert guidance, and to Abby Hansen for her indispensable critical and editorial help.

Many thanks to those indefatigable librarians and archivists who helped make this research possible: Ruth Rogers (Wellesley College); Martin Antonetti, Karen Kukil, and Barbara Blumenthal of the Mortimer Rare Book Room, Neilson Library (Smith College, Northampton, Mass.); Jane Siegel (Columbia University Library, New York); and especially Paul F. Gehl (Newberry Library, Chicago), a most creative scholar-sleuth. Karen Jensen and her staff of the Interlibrary Loan Department at Wellesley College always showed me the utmost patience and perseverance. Two researchers, Amanda Zoellner (Wellesley College) and Merilee Atos (University of Texas at Austin), worked hard behind the scenes. Most of the illustrations were photographed by David Liu of DayLight Pix (Lexington, Mass.); others were made by the Mortimer Rare Book Room (Smith College). My great thanks to Janet Salter Rosenberg for permission to reproduce images of George Salter's work from the archives at Smith College and The Newberry Library.

Thanks also to experts in the field of book design who patiently answered my questions and corrected my assumptions: Alvin Eisenman (Chilmark, Mass.), Alan Powers (London, England), Paul Shaw (New York), Jerry Kelly (New York), Greer Allen (New Haven, Conn.), Jürgen Holstein (Berlin).

Many who knew George Salter personally enlightened me about the man and his work: Jeanyee Wong (New York), Milton Glaser (New York), Lili Wronker (New York), Charles Skaggs (Olympia, Washington), as well as Salter's nephew, Peter Salter (Hawaii), and niece, Stefanie Salter Kyte (Dalton, Mass.). That happy circle of The Typophiles (New York City), of which George Salter was once president, has my enduring appreciation and respect. My profoundest gratitude, however, goes to George Salter's daughter, Janet Salter Rosenberg, and her husband, Herbert Rosenberg (Dobbs Ferry, New York), whose active interest and support helped bring about this book. They gave me access to archival material and provided most of the original proofs from which the illustrations in this book come. Wellesley College consistently provided me with research time and funding. Without such a generous employer, the scholarly life would be much more difficult.

Introduction

George Salter's stature in the history of book design is undisputed. For over forty years his work stood prominently on the bookshelves of almost every educated household in the United States. Some of the once-fashionable writers his art promoted in yesterday's marketplace may never again find a reading public, but an appreciation of Salter's book jackets will rescue many recognizable names and titles from oblivion. The joy of discovering Salter's work today means encountering the strangely familiar on several levels.

Salter himself, of course, has never been forgotten, but a thorough description of his life and achievement has been lacking until now. His work must be considered alongside contemporary German book artists from his Berlin period—E. R. Weiss, Olaf Gulbransson, Paul Scheurich, and George Grosz, to name but a few. In the United States designers and illustrators like Paul Rand, Abe Lerner, John Begg, Alvin Lustig, Warren Chappell, Rudolf Ruzicka, Joseph Blumenthal, Philip Grushkin, Merle Armitage, E. McKnight Kauffer, Arthur Hawkins, Robert Josephy, Charles Skaggs, and William A. Dwiggins were active when Salter was arguably the most sought-after book artist by the best New York publishers. Many of these designers, notably Blumenthal and Grushkin, were his personal friends. Salter collaborated with Fritz Kredel on several volumes for the Limited Editions Club, including their pièce de résistance *Am Wegesrand* (1961), and with W. A. Dwiggins to produce many strikingly handsome volumes for Alfred Knopf. Salter was also known as a proficient calligrapher; he co-wrote articles on this subject with his fellow penman Paul Standard. His devotion to practice did not, however, completely prevent him from formulating theory. As an educator, Salter wrote several articles about aspects of book design, the field in which he was active for forty-five years. The students in his classes at the Cooper Union (where he taught for thirty years) and at New York University (where he briefly offered an evening course on book design) include many illustrious names in the generation of designers that followed: Jeanyee Wong, Milton Glaser, Philip Grushkin, Miriam Woods (who was also his wife's niece), Hans J. Barschel, Claire Ross, Meyer Miller, Nicholas Fasciano, Elliot Offner, and Anita Karl.

In 1939 Salter distilled his firsthand experience in the book trade in an essay that distinguished seven different jacket types.[1] He drew these types from his own work, both to present an overview of his design principles and to offer useful advice on media and techniques to students and other practitioners. His seven categories are still relevant:

1. The formal typographical or hand-lettered jacket that includes no design elements other than lettering (FIGS. 5–8).

2. The typographical or hand-lettered jacket that also incorporates elements of ornamental design but avoids pictorial representation (FIGS. 9–11).

3. The typographical or hand-lettered jacket that conveys the action or mood of the book. In this case pictorial lettering can evoke states of mind and emotional moods (FIGS. 12–14).

4. A variation on type 3, in which the primary typographical design is augmented by ornamental or pictorial details (FIGS. 15–17).

5. Pictorial design that suggests the atmosphere of a book by depicting specific details of its contents. Here the lettering supplements or explains the imagery (FIGS. 18–20).

6. Pictorial design that elicits the atmosphere of the book while not necessarily depicting concrete or realistic scenes. This category is the most suggestive and stylistically abstract, and often includes symbolic or psychological imagery (FIGS. 21–23).

7. The poster-style jacket. With directness of concrete imagery, this category relates most closely in style and intention to commercial advertising art (FIG. 24).

A broad consideration of Salter's work reveals a graphic artist *par excellence* who disciplined his talent and applied it to devising some of the best solutions to the problems posed by the genre of the book jacket. Salter had the fortunate ability to reduce the illustrated paper cover to its essential elements. He could visually evoke—by typography, calligraphy, or pictorial imagery—the atmosphere of the volume's contents. In short, by placing the highest design standard at the service of the publishing trade, he achieved the marriage of commerce and art.

George Salter's Berlin Years

George Salter's odyssey bridges two continents and cultures, spanning the severest political and military turmoil of the twentieth century. Nonetheless, nothing could halt his tireless and brilliant productivity. He survived both world wars, the rise of National Socialism in Germany, and permanent exile in a new land, and ended his days as a figure of international respect in his profession. One symbol of his adaptability was the Anglicization of his name from Georg to George in 1940, when he gained United States citizenship. Yet it would be inaccurate to portray Salter as a figure who struggled to define his identity. His life certainly included dramatic moments, but he ultimately managed to prosper without the devastating personal tragedy that marked the fates of less fortunate refugees. He was even able to help his extended family resettle in New York in the 1930s, where he married and established a family of his own.

Photographs of the man depict a calm, gentle countenance—intelligent but not stern, serene and yet engaging. Friends, colleagues, and students knew him as an affable, cultivated man with a wry sense of humor. Born with an artistic gift, keen wits, and the ability to persevere, Georg Salter was destined for success from the day he first turned his hand to the art of the book.

The official record of his life is fragmentary in places, but a vivid biography emerges from personal documents, his own statements, an unpublished interview with his widow, and memories of family, students, and colleagues. The information furnished by contemporaries who wrote articles about him before 1934 often differs from that in the personal documents.[1] Details are sometimes contradictory, or even absent on minor points, but these understandable *lacunae* result primarily from the fallibility of memory. The larger picture of the man and his work is clear, even though Salter left no autobiography.

Georg Salter was born on October 5, 1897, in the north German port city of Bremen to parents who came from quite a different part of the world, the Austro-Hungarian monarchy. His mother, Stefanie (née Klein), grew up in Hungary in a musically talented family. She and her sister both sang in the chorus of the Budapest opera. His equally musical father, Norbert (born in 1868 in Czernowitz, today in the Ukraine), studied at the Vienna Conservatory and, in his youth, played first cello in the Hamburg symphony orchestra. During his tenure with the orchestra, its conductor was no less a luminary than the young Gustav Mahler, who held this post from 1891 to 1897. Norbert Salter gave up the life of a performing musician to become the orchestra's business manager, and later expanded his interests to become a successful theater agent. As the European representative of New York's Metropolitan Opera Company, he frequently traveled between Europe and the United States.

The Salters had four children: Lili (who later studied photography with Lotte Jacobi in Berlin); Georg (the eldest son, born in 1897); Julius; and Stefan (born ten years after Georg). A fifth child died very young. In 1897, before Georg's birth, Norbert and Stephanie Salter converted to the Lutheran faith, following the path of assimilation taken by many secular Jews in Germany. As a result the Salter children were raised in the Christian faith; Georg received his certificate of confirmation at the Kaiser-Wilhelm Gedächtnis-Kirche in Berlin on March 13, 1913.

The youngest Salter child, Stefan, often accompanied his father to the U.S. on business trips. In the late 1920s, he emigrated to New York and, with the help of his older brother, Georg, became a successful book designer by the 1940s. When Stefan was in his sixties, he collected his reminiscences in a book of essays that supplies valuable biographical information on the family.[2] Stefan Salter's first chapter is a charming memoir of domestic life in Berlin that includes memories of excitement on Christmas Eve and other details of life in the Salters' prosperous household of nine (including three servants). The family enjoyed a comfortable, affluent life in the era before the First World War.

Norbert Salter's position in the international music world acquainted him with many world-renowned musicians. Visitors to the Salters' large apartment in Grunewald, a pleasant suburb of Berlin, included Enrico Caruso, Arturo Toscanini, and the young Chilean pianist Claudio Arrau, who on occasion practiced on one of the Salters' two grand pianos. Norbert Salter also counted the composer Camille Saint-Saëns among his friends.[3] In this theatrical ambience, Georg grew up playing the cello. In fact, his father thought Georg had exceptional musical talent. The combination of his environment, talent, and curiosity led Georg to develop an early interest in stage and set design. One of the two music rooms in the apartment was eventually converted into a space for a small-scale theater where he could experiment with technical elements of set design, costumes, and lighting.

In 1911 Georg received his *Abgangs-Zeugnis* (diploma) from the Werner Siemens Realgymnasium zu Schöneberg (Berlin). The document records his early grades, including, ironically, a *genügend* (satisfactory) mark in penmanship—possibly because he was left-handed at a time when schools enforced right-handedness. Salter ultimately taught himself to write and draw with his right hand. Later in life when he became a teacher, he urged his students to train their right hands.[4] In 1916, at age nineteen, Salter finished secondary school in the midst of war and immediately joined the German army. His duties included mapmaking, which further advanced his nascent skill as a draftsman. His brother Julius joined the military along with him; both survived the war unharmed and returned to civilian life to devote themselves to different aspects of the book trade.

Upon his return to civilian life, Salter began studying art with Ewald Dühlberg. At the same time he enrolled in the *Kunstgewerbe- und Handwerkerschule* (School of Applied Arts and Crafts) in Berlin-Charlottenburg, where, from 1919 to 1921, he concentrated on scene painting under Harold Bengen.[5] From 1921 to 1922 he worked at the studio for stage design at the Prussian State Opera, where he learned to apply his techniques under the tutelage of Emil Pirchan.

In 1922 Salter began to devote himself professionally to theatrical design. It has been suggested that his background and expertise in this field led him to treat book jackets as miniature mise-en-scènes of a book's theme.[6] In fact, qualities of dramatic lighting, as well as stylized angles of vision and perspective, are often apparent in his work throughout his career. Salter also worked for the then recently founded *Berliner Volksoper* where, as assistant to H. Strobach, he designed several productions, including a memorable first Berlin performance of *Boris Godunov*. When the *Volksoper* was disbanded in 1925, Salter took a job in the provinces at *Die Vereinigten Stadttheater Barmen-Eberfeld* (United Municipal Theaters of Barmen-Eberfeld). Salter designed productions in this theater for more than one hundred plays, operas, and operettas. In 1927, however, the pressure of the taxing workload finally became unbearable, and Salter returned to Berlin to concentrate on book design. His contribution to this field began in 1922, and his reputation built steadily as his virtuosity increased. The talent of one of the most famous book designers of the twentieth century did not burst forth fully formed in the first book he designed. Nonetheless, as his early jobs reveal, his mastery of the craft developed rapidly and assuredly during his first years in the business while he continued working in the theater.

Salter spent his early years of apprenticeship and professional employment as a book designer during the Golden Twenties. The phrase evokes the exhilaration, artistic freedom, and creativity of the era but ignores some harsh truths. Rather than celebrating a new era of peace after 1918, most Germans experienced a distinct postwar depression. As their defeated government experimented with shaky new democratic structures, citizens endured economic hardships. Many alleviated their despair with hedonism and an escape into the world of art and entertainment. The economic privations that marked the early years of the decade improved somewhat after 1925, but the stock-market failure and resulting unemployment of 1929 intensified them again, and the economic depression deepened. These pervasive hardships and their by-product, political extremism, were the tragic hallmarks of this decade in Germany, with sweeping consequences for all areas of life. Publishing and the book trade were no exceptions. Soon after the First World War, paper shortages and rising prices for all goods greatly reduced book production. This pressure, in turn, restricted authors' access to publishers and readers' access to new books. The implications for a young book designer were obvious. In 1923, at the height of inflation, when an American dollar would buy four trillion German marks, the presses printed plenty of paper money but very few books.[7] Later in his life Salter recalled the bizarre economic situation: the *Volksoper* paid him three times a day and gave him an hour off from work to spend the money before it devalued further.[8] This economic climate understandably drove publishers in the Weimar Republic to fierce competition. To attract readers and sell books, they turned to new marketing techniques—subscription book clubs, inexpensive series, and low-quality, mass-market paperbacks.

The lists of many publishers also reflected an awareness of international literary trends. Expressionism—the strident German artistic style of intellectual protest from the previous decade—played itself out during the 1920s. Its major proponents had either died in the war or matured beyond their youthful fervor. The passing of Expressionism from the literary scene left in its wake a void, filled by material from foreign markets. A flood of English translations reached German readers and promoted an interest in American culture that would gradually transform Europe. In the United States, war production and victory had created a world power ready to export its newfound identity. No public was more avid for new artistic and cultural trends than that of vital, cosmopolitan Berlin. The city's clubs and music halls became magnets for jazz, and the entertainment industry, especially filmmaking, blossomed. There was plenty of competition for the attention of a public voracious for entertainment. It is no surprise that the aesthetics and techniques of postwar book design also bear witness to this transformation of the zeitgeist.

Technical advances in graphic reproduction and printing methods also opened up new aesthetic possibilities for commercial art. 1922 and 1923 were watershed years for German book design, specifically for the development of the book jacket. By 1925 this medium clearly reflected new printing technology and advertising techniques. By the end of the Weimar Republic, the commercial book market was thriving, as was bibliophile publishing, evidenced by the thirty-two private presses that operated in Germany in 1932.[9]

Georg Salter's artistic career began in the interwar period. By his mid twenties he was immersed in the creative cultural ferment of ideas and stylistic trends that made the Weimar Republic so invigorating. Germany was, arguably, the cradle of twentieth-century commercial design; highly sophisticated poster art penetrated mass consciousness, and the seminal notion of branding commodities with visual trademarks was invented.[10] This artistic and commercial environment of public design, which monumentalized objects and captured universal feelings in easily decoded images, nurtured Salter's artistic imagination. In this cultural climate he learned the techniques of illustration and book design, which he later successfully adapted to book illustration and advertising texts. During this important period between 1922 and 1934, Salter worked for thirty-three German publishers—a figure that conveys the feverish competitiveness of the publishing scene of the period. For these very different firms he produced more than 350 designs, over two-thirds of which were book jackets. Once he had formed an alliance with a publisher, Salter generally received repeated commissions to produce binding and cover designs, using either illustration or typography.

After 1927 he designed several book jackets that became his trademark and greatest legacy. Success at book jacket design is estimable but not necessarily enough to ensure a major posthumous reputation. Salter, however, had the good fortune to see his designs paired with bestsellers by major writers. Furthermore, his sensitivity for literary expression made him the ideal artist to capture a book's contents on its jacket. His designs thus became signature pieces for some of the most important literary works of the twentieth century. This identification with popular literary success brought him name recognition in both literary and commercial design circles. German publishers capitalized on this ability by commissioning Salter to furnish a sort of visual branding for their books. Even rival designers paid tribute to his innovative artistic contributions.

Salter gained his earliest professional experience working for his own family's publishing firm, Die Schmiede. Four managing partners founded this business in Berlin in November 1921; among them were the brothers Julius B. and Georg Salter.[11] Because of the precarious economic climate, family support was crucial to the success of the venture. Norbert Salter not only provided capital for the firm but also placed his office at its disposal to minimize the fledgling company's overhead costs. The founders launched their company in April 1922, making a debut with titles purchased from the defunct Roland Verlag, which had not survived the inflation. Thanks to Norbert Salter's lucrative theatrical agency, Die Schmiede even managed to pay royalties to its authors at the height of the inflation in 1923. The firm's list—a program of politically left-of-center German writers and foreign literature—enhanced its cultural significance in Weimar Germany.

Georg Salter and George Kobbe independently designed some impressive covers for Die Schmiede, to create the striking, modernist look of the firm's books.[12] One of Salter's very first book designs was a pencil drawing for the cover for Hermann Kasack's book *Die Heimsuchung* [*The Ordeal*, 1922; FIG. 25]. It shows a stylized human form draped in a garment resembling a monk's habit. At the foot of the body, this garment falls into drapery with jagged lines. The vegetation in the landscape and the barely concealed rough modeling of the figure show Salter still working in the mode of stage design. By contrast, the confidently rendered, starkly aggressive title for the biography *Lenin* (1923; FIG. 26) uses a minimalist approach, which foreshadows his later calligraphic versatility. A contemporary observer noted that the essential objectivity of the red letters of this title, which could have been daubed with a bloody finger, economically conveys the threatening nature of the subject.[13]

Salter continued to work in the expressionist style through 1924, completing extraordinary covers for Joseph Roth's first book, *Hotel Savoy* (1924; FIG. 27) and for Francis Carco's *An Straßenecken* [*On Streetcorners*, 1925]. A remarkable piece from this period is the design for the small, vellum-bound luxury edition of Georg Kaiser's comedy *Kolportage* (1924), of which fifty copies were printed for private distribution. In Iwan Goll's volume of poetry *Der Eiffelturm* [*The Eiffel Tower*, 1924; FIG. 28], Salter's lettering markedly contrasts the background design by the contemporary French artist Robert Delaunay. The result vibrates with intensity.

During this period Salter also put his stamp on two popular mass-market series of reports of famous crimes as well as classics of erotic literature (FIG. 29). For each of these, he produced a distinctive cover with variations that maintain easy recognition from title to title. For example, he produced one of his early, intentionally primitive designs to establish the series that editor Rudolf Leonhard introduced at Die Schmiede. Entitled Aussenseiter der Gesellschaft [Society's Outsiders; FIG. 30] and subtitled Die Verbrechen der Gegenwart [The Crimes of the Present], the titles called for stark covers to fit the blunt reportage of some of Germany's best journalists. Another series, Die Romane des XX. Jahrhunderts [The Novels of the Twentieth Century], for which Salter designed the logo, comprised, for the most part, translations from foreign literature, and also included first printings of Joseph Roth and Franz Kafka novels.[14] Salter's cover design for one of the most important novels of the twentieth century, *Der Prozess* [*The Trial*, 1925; FIG. 31], which Kafka did not live to see, was not Salter's only encounter with this text. Later in his career, he designed an American edition of *The Trial*, which by then had become a classic.

For the most part, Salter's early work for Die Schmiede consisted of titles with sparse typographical treatment neatly stamped and centered on the covers of bound books. Most use a label format, with the names of the author and title subtly differentiated by typeface and always followed by the publisher's name printed in small capitals. This effective design not only promoted Die Schmiede, but gave the firm's books a consistently elegant appearance.

His pictorial covers and jackets, on the other hand, drew on the whole spectrum of commercially feasible styles and media. Whether incising blocks, penning letters of the alphabet, or applying colors with a brush, Salter produced distinctive work, without yet showing any hallmark of a personal style (FIGS. 32–33). His early contribution lay in a simple, down-to-earth, representational approach far removed from the organic and geometric decorations of the art-nouveau tradition that had dominated the book market at the turn of the century. His stark tonal palette and simple, almost rough, treatment of form at times seem intentionally naïve, as in the early covers for Heinrich Mann (1924; FIG. 34) Rudolf Leonhardt (1925), and Leo Matthias (1926; FIG. 35). Whatever his subject, Salter experimented freely in the 1920s, using whatever forms and media he could. It soon dawned on his contemporaries that his art represented something new. One writer, surveying five years of Die Schmiede publications, put his finger on the eclectic style of these bold designs: "Following the pressure of the times, Die Schmiede has worked its way out of its aestheticizing beginnings and today is starting to show a sharp, unsentimental, almost American face."[15] The use of the word "American" in this context of Weimar Germany metaphorically signified "cosmopolitan" or "avant-garde." Salter's work in this period draws nothing from actual American book design of the time.

Although Salter produced only two designs in his first year at Die Schmiede, and a sparse four in his second year, he designed a total of twenty-one covers by 1925.

His style matured with each passing year and his skill as a draftsman kept pace. His total output for the family firm was sixty-six designs—or roughly nine per month—while he was also freelancing for other publishers. He produced his last designs for Die Schmiede in 1928.

In 1930 Die Schmiede, like so many of its competitors, fell prey to the economy. Although the firm was forced to declare bankruptcy and sell its authors' rights, Salter was not left unemployed. The managing board had been discussing a merger with the publishing house of Kiepenheuer Verlag for years, and the two firms, in response to financial considerations, had already begun the merger process in 1927.[16] It was logical to combine the two publishing houses—now called Kiepenheuer—for they already had several authors and Georg Salter's designs in common. In fact, Salter's freelance work had visually defined Kiepenheuer's market presence. He not only designed the *Verlagssignet* (logo; FIG. 38) that the firm used from 1927 to 1933, but also eighty-eight books for Kiepenheuer between 1924 and 1934, including works by significant writers like Joseph Roth, Anna Seghers, Ernst Toller, and Arnold Zweig. Among these authors, his personal and professional relationship with the famous dramatist Georg Kaiser was unique. When the playwright moved from Kiepenheuer Verlag to Die Schmiede for personal reasons, legal conflicts with Kiepenheuer ensued. But these, ironically, paved the way toward the contractual union between the two firms.

As a freelancer for Kiepenheuer, Salter's created his first designs for Georg Kaiser's plays. These were simple typographical covers using an image of a winged lion to achieve a feeling of a loosely defined series. This unifying emblem became so closely identified with Kaiser that it was used on Hugo Koenigsgarten's 1928 scholarly book about the playwright. Kaiser's importance to Kiepenheuer—based on strong sales and his cordial relations with the managers—led to a pleasant friendship with Georg Salter. Kaiser wrote several humorous postcards to Salter between 1924 and 1926, when Salter was working as a stage designer at the City Theater in Barmen (now Wuppertal, in North Rhine-Westphalia).[17]

Salter's work for Kiepenheuer opened new vistas for book design. His particular blend of innovative typographical covers and atmospheric illustration had never before been seen on books. Particularly effective were covers for which he used two or more typefaces to produce textual articulation. One brilliant example of this technique is the design for Marieluise Fleisser's collection of stories *Ein Pfund Orangen* [*One Pound of Oranges*, 1929; FIG. 39], which plays on the tradition of the printer's broadside of type specimens. The six contrasting typefaces combine visually to suggest that this is a collection of different stories that nonetheless form an organic whole.[18]

His solution for the cover of François Villon's *Balladen* [*Ballads*, 1930; FIG. 40] uses an eye-catching, off-center arrangement that mingles roman type with brown bands of Villon's own text lettered in a medieval manuscript hand. Such pictorial word play is typical of Salter's best work, for it lets him comment on the poet's name and historical period through the use of archaic lettering, while also foregrounding the text of the ballads themselves. Bertolt Brecht, another collaborator involved with this remarkable cover, wrote an aggressive sonnet especially for this piece. On the back of the Villon jacket, Brecht challenges the reader to spend three marks on this book rather than on cigars (a well-known Brechtian indulgence). Salter's creatively eclectic jacket thus links literary history with contemporary book production, both as aesthetic composition and marketing strategy for Kiepenheuer's volume.

Equally complex in design and allusion is Salter's typographic cover for *Quer durch* [*Straight through*, 1930; FIGS. 41–42], by the notable Kiepenheuer author Ernst Toller, who was for a time a political fugitive. Salter plays with types and layout conventions as he wraps Toller's collection of pro-Communist texts and revolutionary broadcasts in an imitation of a wanted poster.

Salter designed two Joseph Roth novels for Die Schmiede in the 1920s, but it was not until he produced the later Kiepenheuer jackets for *Hiob* [*Job*, 1930; FIG. 44] and *Radetzkymarsch* [*Radetzky March*, 1932; FIG. 45] that he designed best-sellers for the author. For these titles he chose visual treatments completely unrelated to earlier designs. The concept for *Hiob*, the story of a modern Job, uses a typographical solution rich in descriptive text. The jacket was selected as one of the fifty best book designs of 1930. *Radetzkymarsch*, on the other hand, combines text with a scene of autumnal bleakness in muted tones to evoke the melancholy spirit of the end of the Austro-Hungarian Empire. Salter's cover for another novel about Austrian history, Alexander Lernet-Holenia's *Die Standarte* [*The Regimental Colors*, 1934; FIG. 46], evokes the subject with greater élan, showing the unfurled flag of the Habsburg double-headed eagle.

Of all the businessmen with whom Salter allied himself during the Weimar years, Eric Reiss, a fine-press publisher, released the most sophisticated titles. He founded his firm, Erich Reiss Verlag, in 1910, around the same time as Kiepenheuer, but with a very different philosophy. Reiss, who had true bibliophilic taste, published not only exquisite volumes for connoisseurs, but also beautiful books at low prices. To this end he hired well-known graphic artists, illustrators, and designers, like Walter Tiemann. In 1930 he hired the freelancer Georg Salter, who left his creative mark on the firm's trade titles. Erich Reiss Verlag was thus known not only for his cosmopolitan list—like Die Schmiede, it had a strong emphasis on Jewish writers and literature in translation—but also for its recognizable designs. Salter produced a total of sixteen covers for Reiss, the last of which appeared in 1933.

One of Reiss's best-selling authors was the Prague-born journalist Egon Erwin Kisch, whose journalistic reports from exotic corners of the globe found an eager readership. Salter's cover art for these books was groundbreaking in its astounding freedom of experimentation and wit. In some cases, lettering alone conveys a sense of the book's contents. For example, the nervous calligraphy, primitive in its oversized proportion, on the cover of *Schreib das auf, Kisch!* [*Write that Down, Kisch!*, 1930; FIG. 47] captures the haste and fear behind the act of recording this wartime journal. The combination of bold text and delicate background watercolor images for *China geheim* [*Clandestine China*, 1933; FIG. 48] suggests hidden truths behind the headlines. Salter's designs for Kisch showcased his most innovative side. The poster style of *Paradies Amerika* [*Paradise America*, 1930; FIG. 49] matches the colors of the American flag with *Schablonenschrift* (stencil lettering) to create a visual message that mixes the ideas of commodity and politics and implicitly makes ironic the notion of paradise. German script for Marieluise Fleisser's *Die Mehlreisende Friede Geyer* [*The Traveling Flour Saleswoman Friede Geyer*, 1931], for which Salter designed two covers (FIGS. 53–54), uses very different images, both personal and somewhat eccentric, to communicate the author's essence. The photomontage for the German translation of *Die Junggesellin* [*The Bachelorette*, 1932; FIG. 55] communicates its contents with images. Salter employed a striking photograph, which suggests a psychological study of the modern woman.

While he was working for Erich Reiss, Salter was also one of three eminent and very different designers associated with the publishing firm of S. Fischer. Emil Rudolph Weiss worked in the classic manner of traditional, refined taste; Hans Meid produced delicate designs for works of fiction. Salter's wide-ranging talents and eclectic styles, however, made him the artist of choice for texts expressing a sense of contemporary urgency. Of the three designers, Salter was the most influential during the late 1920s in defining S. Fischer's public face.[19] As a gesture in recognition of the importance of book design, Fischer's brochure advertising inexpensive *Verlagsprospekt für Sonderausgaben* (special editions) named not only the author of each work but also its designer.[20] Salter produced seventy-seven designs for Fischer between 1926 and 1934, including three covers for the annual *Almanach* (FIG. 56), an advertising booklet, and the logo for the series S. Fischer Bücherei. The bulk of his output, clustered in his last years in Berlin (1930–1933), exhibits the breadth of his talent, a spectrum that included photomontage, pictorial narrative scenes, wood-block prints, and virtuoso calligraphy. Two of his jackets for novels by Bernhard Kellermann stand out for their brilliant execution and vivid images. *Der*

Tunnel [*The Tunnel*, 1931; FIG. 57] is a masterpiece; its style embodies the aesthetic called "streamlining" and is reminiscent of the best posters by Adolphe Cassandre.[21] Its strong diagonals and exaggerated perspective echo the tradition of the best German advertising art to convey power and speed. *Die Stadt Anatol* [*The City of Anatol*, 1932; FIG. 59] uses a very different stylistic vocabulary to depict an explosion in an Anatolian oil field. In this design, the shapes and patterns of the black clouds relate to the similarly airbrushed cover of Saint-Exupéry's *Nachtflug* [*Night Flight*, 1932; FIG. 60]. This delicate, soft-focus technique remained a hallmark of Salter's art throughout the rest of his long career.

The most distinctive and probably best known of Salter's covers for Fischer's books was his design for Alfred Döblin's expressionist novel *Berlin Alexanderplatz* (1929; FIG. 61). This signature piece from the Weimar years represents the apex of Salter's ability to find visual correlatives for the written word. If designers are to books what architects are to buildings, then this cover promised book arts what the Bauhaus offered cities: a completely new modernist aesthetic. Salter's innovation is a collage of text and image that superficially resembles a child's rebus but is actually a very sophisticated recapitulation of Döblin's own literary technique. The concept is completely harmonious with the text. Its jarring, multicolor raggedness conveys the conflict that the novel portrays through the voice of the naïve narrator. Rather than proclaim its own wit and detract from the novel, Salter's jacket serves Döblin's text by drawing the viewer as reader to the characters and plot before the book is even opened. This is, arguably, the most significant book jacket for a work of German literature in the twentieth century. Published in October 1929, it sold 50,000 copies by December 1932. Five months later, Döblin's name was on the regime's blacklist, and he was forced to emigrate. Politics put an end to any future possibilities that Salter's magnificent design portended.

In the year following the success of *Berlin Alexanderplatz*, Salter produced a remarkable cover in the graphic tradition of poster art for the German translation of John Dos Passos's *The 42nd Parallel* [*Der 42. Breitengrad*, 1930; FIG. 62]. This design is another superb demonstration of his grasp of the relationship between content and image. He used the aesthetics of the practitioners and theorists of New Typography (artists like El Lissitzky, Lazlo Moholy-Nagy, and Jan Tschichold) to present Dos Passos's modernist prose. Bright colors, oversized numerals, rules, and strong, Bauhaus-inspired asymmetry accompany the rhythmical alternation of large and small sans-serif letters. The associations with industry and urbanization make this functionalist aesthetic appropriate to notions of America. Salter's panoramic design goes a step further and solves a problem inherent in the object itself by spreading images across the back of the book that advertise its identity whether it be open or closed.

The 1920s brought experimentation with photomontage—though Salter used the medium sparingly. Traditionalists who disapproved of photography as a typographic method rejected it as machine-age technology, foreign to fine printing and the elevated art of the book. In 1928, however, Jan Tschichold began promoting photography as an avant-garde medium of commercial design. By adding photography to his own artistic repertoire, Salter followed this course, which was dominated by his brilliant contemporary John Heartfield, then working for Malik Verlag. Heartfield had made photomontage so prominent in book jacket design that no serious designer could ignore it. He used this technique aggressively, and often with propagandistic content, whereas Salter's temperament and style dictated otherwise. Salter's own photomontage for the most part avoids partisan political content, focusing on attracting book buyers rather than promoting any special political agenda. For example, the gray-toned cover for the Heinrich Hauser title *Feldwege nach Chicago* [*Byways to Chicago*, 1931; FIG. 63] evokes a dusty trek through the American Midwest. The license plate diagonally covering the blurred cityscape conjures up the gritty atmosphere of the open road and generally evokes urban conditions during the Depression.[22] Despite these successful forays into photographic representation in the 1920s and '30s—and occasional use of the technique in later years—Salter remained fundamentally a draftsman faithful to the hand-drawn image.

Salter's extensive work for Germany's larger publishers should not eclipse his memorable projects for smaller firms. His designs for the Dietrich Reimer Verlag included a redesigned cover for the monograph series Junge Kunst [Young Art].[23] His wonderful covers for the novels of Jack London for Universitas in the mid 1920s are both eye catching and artistically subtle (FIGS. 64–65). His images fit the content of the novels—lively scenes of men drinking and gambling—but his figures float in space supported by bold title lettering. His angles are dramatic, even cinematic, while his austere watercolor technique advertises the rough-hewn atmosphere of the books.

Salter executed ambitious designs for the publisher Grote for Wilhelm Raabe's classic nineteenth novel, *Die Chronik der Sperlingsgasse* [*Chronicle of the Sperlingsgasse*, 1931; FIG. 66]. The book included six illustrated scenes (FIG. 67) from the stories—atmospheric vignettes that have a narrative function within the text and that generally show greater scenic detail than Salter's cover designs.[24] Salter also designed jackets for Julius Stinde's novels, beginning with *Die Familie Buchholz* [*The Buchholz Family*, 1930, 1933; FIG. 68]. For these books, he produced bindings and very colorful, painterly jackets using traditional German blackletter (*Fraktur*) lettering.

Salter's logo designs for various publishing firms constitute an important part of his work in this period. Hölscher's seminal essay on Salter from 1930 contains twelve such designs, including a number of prototypes that were never implemented.[25] Salter used his own monogram on a few jackets and also produced ones for clients; notably, Transmare Verlag, Gustav Kiepenheuer, S. Fischer Verlag, and a series logo for Klinkhardt & Biermann.

Salter's Berlin years show astonishing development. During this period he matured from an imitative young draftsman of the early 1920s to the most distinctive and technically proficient German book designer of the 1930s. He did not have to be converted to modernism; the influence of the Russian constructivists on commercial design, which was in turn mediated by the Bauhaus, constituted an essential element in his artistic training. Unlike some adherents of the new typography, he was not so much a dogmatic avant-gardist as an open-minded experimenter.

German book design of the Weimar period, like all commercial art of the age, showed a remarkable plurality of forms. The traditional, decorative covers of designers like E. R. Weiss, Emil Preetorius, Walter Tiemann, and Hugo Steiner-Prag coexisted in the marketplace with the experimental, modernist work of men like Rudolf Geyer, George Grosz, Fritz Löwen, John Heartfield, Paul Urban, and Jan Tschichold.[26] Correspondingly, Salter's designs from these Berlin years drew sustenance from the eclecticism of his age. He was free to play with any style that appealed to him—traditional, constructivist, realistic—and with all media, from woodcut to photomontage. As a result, his work in this period defies easy categorization. He was devoted to neither abstract representation nor the avant-garde, though his early use of expressionist design forms does show him working in that aesthetic. Nor was he a pure traditionalist promoting popular notions of realistic representation. While his covers show romantic watercolor images, they also overlay these with bold typography. The German modernism that nourished Salter synthesized many design approaches and permitted the widest possible variety of solutions.[27] The result was that at times he used appealing images to advertise a book, while at others he produced purely functional covers that simply labeled the contents. Similarly, his achievements in the category of lettering encompass spare, sans-serif fonts (favored by adherents of New Typography) as well as the ornate *Fraktur*, a classic German letterform into which Rudolf Koch had breathed new beauty. In this rich eclectic mix of modernist possibilities, even the apparent conservatism of *Fraktur* permitted innovative experimentation; Salter exploited the rough, calligraphic beauty inherent in this typeface (FIG. 75).[28] By the time he had reached his late twenties, Salter was master of all such aesthetic possibilities but slave to none. Throughout the 1930s his contemporaries praised the resourcefulness and objectivity of his work. They also noted his stylistic self-sufficiency and transcendence over any particular design school.[29] His mastery of different media and styles makes him the quintessential hybrid modernist.

From Berlin to New York: The 1930s and 1940s

In 1931 the calligrapher and typographer Georg Trump recognized Georg Salter's talent and hired him to direct the Commercial Art Department at the Höhere Graphische Fachschule (Institute of Graphic Arts) in Berlin. Trump had reorganized this institute from the earlier Kunstgewerbeschule Berlin-Ost (School of Applied Arts, Berlin East).[1] He and Salter would come to share a profound mutual respect as colleagues and friends.

Salter was naïve about the political climate that followed Hitler's seizure of power in January 1933. In the early days of the new regime, a knife-carrying student in a National Socialist uniform accosted Salter in his classroom and challenged his presence there on racial grounds. Salter, raised from birth a Lutheran, was so shocked by this hostility that he never again set foot in a classroom in Germany. This incident was but one small, public display of what would become official policy. Trump, as head of the Institute of Graphic Arts, had the unpleasant duty of dismissing his protégé from this state institution. Trump himself despised the arrogance of the National Socialists and soon left the capital, Berlin, for Munich. Eventually Trump had to enlist and was later badly wounded in the war. By that time Salter was well established in the United States, but his friendship with Trump remained strong. After the war the two men corresponded again and eventually reunited when Trump visited New York in the 1950s.

The pain of public intimidation erased any delusions of personal safety that Salter might have cherished. Although he was actively planning his emigration strategy, he could not immediately sever his ties to the profession in which he had achieved prominence, even as his commissions ceased. Salter's papers from this period preserve some curious sketches for a revised edition of the one-volume reference book, *Knaurs Konversations-Lexikon A–Z* (FIGS. 78–79), edited by Richard Friedenthal, which he had designed in 1932. Six of these preliminary designs use *Fraktur* (blackletter) lettering, and four employ the startling color combination of black, red, and white—colors associated with National Socialism. These designs leave a confusing impression: were they meant as parody? Did he intend this color scheme to make the book design acceptable to a publisher friendly to the new regime? Whatever the point of this exercise, Salter consigned the designs to his files and never submitted them to Knaur. He could not possibly have been flirting with reactionary politics or the design principles of the society that had rejected him, for he had already set his sights outside the German market. This is obvious from the first job he completed for a foreign publisher during this period—a job with particular cultural significance. Salter designed a sober cover for the German exile periodical *Die Sammlung* (FIG. 80), published in Amsterdam by Fritz Landshoff's Querido Verlag.[2] *Die Sammlung* was the most respected voice of the intellectual opposition to Hitler, and Salter's work for the journal placed him squarely in the anti-Nazi struggle.

After losing his teaching position, Salter soon left the capital that had celebrated and rewarded his talents. He first moved to Baden-Baden, Germany, in May 1933, and worked briefly for a dog breeder while awaiting an American visa.[3] His visa finally came through the consulate in Stuttgart on October 1, 1934, with help from his brother Stefan, who had submitted an affidavit in support of Georg's emigration. As a farewell to Berlin, he visited the city for a week before proceeding to Hamburg and Cuxhaven, from where he left Germany.[4] Twenty-seven of his designs nonetheless appeared on the German market in 1933. Eight that he finished that year appeared in the market in 1934, after he emigrated. Among these were a literary almanac for S. Fischer, *Almanach: das 48. Jahr; S. Fischer zum Gedächtnis* [*Almanac: the Forty-Eighth Year; in Memoriam S. Fischer*]. The famous cover for *Der Tunnel* was still in print in 1935. In 1937, three years after Salter's emigration, Kiepenheuer reprinted Hans Reimann's *Vergnügliches Handbuch der deutschen Sprache* [*Lighthearted Handbook of the German Language*]; the new design bore significant modifications from the 1931 original (FIG. 81).

Just as Salter's impact upon the style of German book design approached its zenith, the political climate prevented him from teaching and barred him from freelance employment. When he emigrated to the U.S., he took with him talent and reputation, but little else. These were enough to change the face of the American book. Salter's emigration put him among the first wave of refugee artists and intellectuals to leave Germany. This group included illustrious book designers, illustrators, and typographers such as Jan Tschichold, Fritz Kredel, Fritz Eichenberg, Josef Albers, Imre Reiner, John Heartfield, Herbert Bayer, Jan van Krimpen, Hugo Steiner-Prag, Hans Alexander Müller, Josef Scharl, Richard Floethe, Hermann Kosel, Robert Haas, and Berthold Wolpe.[5]

Salter made a safe departure from his homeland, sailed on the *S. S. Albert Ballin*, and reached New York early in November 1934. A family story recounts that he arrived with four words of English and four dollars in his pocket.[6] Unlike many of his fellow refugee artists and intellectuals, Salter did not suffer hardship for long. He fled a culture that prized commercial art and found another where the industry was booming with opportunity. The first five assignments that he received in the U.S. from Simon & Schuster had been arranged before his arrival. This meant that the émigré who arrived in New York on Friday was earning money by Monday. Good fortune of this order usually depends upon guardian angels working behind the scenes. In Salter's case, Hellmut Lehmann-Haupt, Robert Leslie, and Ernst Reichl all played significant roles in easing his transition.

Lehmann-Haupt had come to the U.S. in 1929. He was curator of the Department of Rare Books at Columbia University from 1930 to 1937 and a historian of the American publishing trade. His position gave him unique opportunities to promote new talent and to foreground European artists and illustrators. He had organized an exhibition of fifty book jackets by Georg Salter at Columbia University in November 1933. Salter thus arrived in New York with a reputation already established.[7] The relationship between the two men ran deeper than patronage. Not only did Lehmann-Haupt include a passage on Salter in the first German edition of his book on the history of American publishing (Leipzig: Hiersemann, 1937), but he and his family hosted Salter for a brief period during his transition to an unfamiliar culture. Salter even stood as godfather to one of their three sons, Carl.

Salter's first residence in New York was an apartment he shared with his brother Stefan, who had been in America since 1928. Stefan was still struggling to establish himself and was earning only $8.00 per week in 1933. Georg, who never felt the poverty of the Depression, began helping his brother financially as soon as he arrived. He taught Stefan about book design and found him employment at H. Wolff.[8] Georg eventually left Stefan's apartment to stay with the Lehmann-Haupts in Riverdale (a suburb of New York City) and subsequently moved to an address near Gramercy Park in Manhattan. When his mother and sister arrived as refugees (his father had died in Hungary in 1936), he moved to 40 East Tenth Street in Greenwich Village and renovated an apartment so that they all could have privacy in their new quarters.

H. Wolff Book Manufacturing Company on West Twenty-Sixth Street was Salter's first workplace in the U.S. There he established himself once again as a freelance designer and jacket artist. H. Wolff was one of the most important binderies for the American book trade. The company employed a professional staff that included the type and book designer Ernst Reichl, who soon became Salter's close friend. Salter and Reichl made the company's design department famous at the book industry's annual exhibitions, where many of their efforts won honors for the firm.[9] Salter's contributions to H. Wolff were so great that in 1938, when Paul Standard published a retrospective of the H. Wolff bindery, he praised Salter's presence at the firm. Noting the positive influence of new blood from Europe, he said of Salter: "The force of his quiet example has in a few short years helped to advance American jacket design and lettering. His work has a rightness that proceeds from restraint."[10]

These first years at H. Wolff were marked by vigorous creative activity. Simon & Schuster gave Salter his first commissions, ten of which appeared in 1935. One of the most striking was the poster-style cover for Frank Buck's *Fang and Claw* (FIG. 24). Three early projects for Viking saw him designing jackets for literary works by Hermann Broch and Stefan Zweig (FIGS. 82–83), thereby solidifying his links with German exile culture.[11]

In 1936 while still working from his office at H. Wolff, Salter executed his first Thomas Mann volume for Alfred Knopf, a subdued design for an anthology clad in a monochrome typographical jacket. His earlier German cover for Mann's *Königliche Hoheit* [*Royal Highness*, 1932; FIG. 75] for S. Fischer had marked his first association with the German Nobel laureate in literature, but the titles for Knopf set him on course to become the premiere designer of Mann's works in America. He produced covers for ten different Knopf authors in 1936 and, in the same year, also illustrated a charming children's book for Oxford University Press entitled *Do Not Disturb: The Adventures of M'm and Teddy* (FIG. 84). This was the first of his three forays into illustrated juvenile books.[12]

Salter's informal but fruitful association with H. Wolff provided a superb introduction to the design departments of all the major New York publishers. He had found the ideal place to hang his hat while he improved his English, adjusted to his new homeland (where, to the amusement of colleagues, he rejoiced in paying taxes, the symbol of belonging in his new country[13]), and established his reputation before striking out on his own. While his English was still rudimentary, his brother Stefan would often read him the books for which he had to design jackets. But he learned rapidly and mastered very idiomatic English. He later looked back with amusement at early misunderstandings, such as expecting a pastry when ordering sweetbreads in a New York restaurant, or once urging his design students to use "acute angels" in their sketches.[14]

Salter's arrival on the New York literary scene made a splash among book designers. One of two issues of the trade journal *PM* (*Production Manager*) for which Salter designed covers included a congratulatory note inside the back cover from the printer of the magazine, greeting Salter as "A New Star."[15] Dr. Robert L. ("Doc") Leslie, head of the Typophiles and editor of *PM*, wrote a brief promotional article in 1935 in which he included examples of four of Salter's recent jacket designs and an illustration done for H. Wolff. Leslie's praise for this European transplant reads like a herald of a new age in American book design: "He draws a tree, a streamlined train, or a street scene with the absorption and delight of a youngster with his first set of watercolors. Yet, he [...] knows his materials and has complete control of them."[16] The short piece documents the respect Salter commanded among his American colleagues, who marveled at his artistic spontaneity, innate sense of style, and meticulous work methods. Printers and photo engravers, likewise, acquiesced to the tough demands he placed on them to reproduce his designs to high standards of quality. Such publicity established his reputation in New York and paved the way for a teaching contract at the Cooper Union in 1937 where he began to offer courses in calligraphy and lettering.[17] During his time as adjunct member of this faculty (1937–1967), Salter was able to recommend Paul Standard, Leo Manso, Charles Skaggs, and Philip Grushkin (his former student) for teaching posts.[18]

In addition to his academic duties and ambitious jobs produced for large New York publishers, Salter also took on modest commissions. One such project was for the National Home Library Foundation in Washington, D.C., an idealistic publisher of inexpensive reprint editions that advertised its books on the radio. The first series of thirteen titles with cloth covers and jackets retailed for twenty-five cents each. Salter created separate jackets for each book in the series—a departure from his approach to German series designs in the 1920s. His diverse designs for books from *Hamlet* (FIG. 85) to *Hans Brinker* were united by their high-contrast, black-and-white images and individualized by stylish title lettering.[19] A second series on which Salter left his mark employed a different solution to the problem of series design. The twelve slim volumes of Headline Books (published both in boards and soft covers for the Foreign Policy Association between 1935 and 1937) presented a difficulty: how to enliven a series of covers using titles but no other visual imagery. Salter met the challenge with creative lettering. Of a more ambitious nature was the set of four simplified piano scores for Simon & Schuster in 1936 entitled *Operatic Masterpieces* (FIG. 88). Rather than focusing on typography, Salter returned to the familiar visual world of stage design and painted highly theatrical scenes in soft-focus airbrush technique.

Among some of Salter's finest color work from the 1930s is the remarkable cover for William Faulkner's novel *Absalom, Absalom!* (Random House, 1936; FIG. 89). Here the airbrush achieves an eerie effect as the dynamic lettering projects a nebulous psychological state. Such lettering became one of Salter's calligraphic signatures for expressing uncertainty, fear, and emotional disturbance. The jacket for Arnold Zweig's novel of the First World War, *Education Before Verdun* (Viking, 1936; fig. 90), points the way toward Salter's later war scenes, which are always personal in tone. In this view of no-man's-land, a soldier stares into the distance to draw the viewer's gaze and thoughts into the scene. The pose owes much to the visual tradition of German Romantic painting in which such figures—often with their backs to the viewer—convey isolation and introspection. Here the soldier meditates on death and glory, as represented by the ghostly hero's cross. The airbrush technique, a Salter hallmark, softens lines and shadows for these dreamlike, psychological states. In the same year, Salter designed a witty anthology of quotations, *Ex Libris* (New York Times, 1936; FIG. 91), compiled by Christopher Morley. Ernst Reichl's ingenious binding for the book stamped the names of the featured writers in gold. The first printing had a two-color title page, which was later replaced by one in black ink. Because the printer produced too few copies of Salter's four-color jacket, a glassine one was substituted in later printings.

Salter's cover for Nicolai Gubsky's autobiography, *Angry Dust* (Oxford University Press, 1937; FIG. 95), is a striking example of his successful reuse of earlier material. The cover visually quotes his epoch-making design for Döblin's *Berlin Alexanderplatz* (S. Fischer, 1929; FIG. 61). The composition retains its virtuosity in this second incarnation but is less appropriate to this text than to Döblin's. As a result, perhaps, it never achieved the same fame. In the same year Salter designed the cover for Ignazio Silone's *Bread and Wine* (Harper, 1937; FIG. 96) a multilayered image that contrasts the gray-toned background of a shadowy, allegorical struggle with the symbols of salvation, bread and wine, elevated and set off in color.

One of Salter's most significant designs from this period—a design he later called his favorite project[20]—was for Kafka's classic novel *The Trial* (Knopf, 1937; FIG. 97). This was his first design for a work by Kafka since the three bindings he executed during the Weimar years. After Salter's death, the volume *Kafka—The Trial of Six Designers* appeared, which featured this 1937 design in addition to five others by contemporary designers.[21]

One small mystery about the design for John Steinbeck's *Of Mice and Men* (Covici-Friede, 1937) remains to be solved. The first edition of this novel, designed by Robert Josephy, was issued in several different printings with a jacket version that bears an uncanny resemblance to Salter's work. Josephy was certainly not the artist. It is, however, an illustration that bears no signature—a rare, but not impossible, occurrence in Salter's career. However, Salter did log this Steinbeck title into his list of commissions, confirming that he executed a pictorial binding for the book and strongly suggesting that he also designed the first (preliminary) jacket. He even underlined the code for "binding." Salter's binding design for *Of Mice and Men* (FIG. 98) was brought out in a very small production run between the first and second printings of the novel. It seems that this was a trial design, early in the production process. This interim edition was not seen again after Josephy's lettered binding and jacket became the standard. The copies with this variant Salter binding show details that correspond with subsequent printings, which also have certain pages reset and words removed.[22] Is it possible that the publisher Pascal Covici requested a binding different from Josephy's first design—one that was more in keeping with book jacket? He would naturally have turned to Salter for such a variation. It is possible that Josephy made some objection to Salter's design, which is why so few of the alternative designs survive. Most probably, only a few experimental copies were bound (with reset pagination) as sample pieces for the relevant decision makers.[23] Very few, if any, of these books reached the market, which explains why bibliographers of Steinbeck have not acknowledged them as part of the official publishing history of the novel; they are simply too rare. Viking Press, which bought Covici-Friede, reissued a pale version of the original jacket design on their Compass Edition of the novel in 1963. The slightly altered text of this jacket identifies the author as the winner of the Nobel Prize for Literature but does not acknowledge any designer.

Despite his frequent association with Nobel Prize–winning authors, Salter did not work solely in the service of serious modern literature. One of his cleverest images is a mystifying cover on a chapbook for the Typophiles (the New York circle of designers and typographers), *Left to Their Own Devices* (Typophiles, 1937; FIG. 99). Salter's work appeared in several of the club's publications, but this cover (one of two he completed for the Typophiles) was particularly witty. It takes the form of a brainteaser for a collection of devices based on the letter T. Salter contributed one of these devices as well as the cover. The imagery of a truncated leg with speech balloons creates associations on many levels, such as a rebus, implying perhaps that all this imagery is a form of "leg-pulling."

In the 1930s Salter established himself in different areas of book jacket design. His first covers in the detective-mystery genre (for Knopf in 1935 and 1937) led him by the end of the decade to an association with the publisher Lawrence Spivak. Spivak had a small empire of inexpensive detective and science fiction serials. In 1939 he appointed Salter as the art director of Mercury Publications, which published Spivak's various series in digest format. Despite this time-consuming professional commitment, which he maintained until his death, Salter designed twenty-five additional book jackets in 1939.

In the 1930s Salter also established close associations with contemporary American writers such as Robert Nathan, for whom he created six designs; Nora Lofts, five jackets in the 1930s; William Faulkner, three jackets between 1934 and 1940; and Frederic Prokosch, a novelist for whom Salter produced some of his most accomplished work. Publishers' art directors also took advantage of Salter's background by consistently assigning him jackets for English translations of German and Austrian writers in exile. This reinforced a cultural alliance with important refugee writers of his generation.[24] Many of his covers designed for New York publishers reflect the political threat from Germany by using imagery that captures the concerns of a generation on the brink of war.

The decade of the 1940s brought Salter continued professional advancement as well as major changes in his private life. From his arrival in the U.S. to the end of 1940, he produced approximately 185 book jackets and at least thirty magazine covers—more than one per week. He registered his income in 1940 as $5,000—a clear reflection of the market opportunities that had opened to him.[25] The most significant personal event of the year was his naturalization as American citizen on September 19, 1940. Forever after this day, he signed his name as "George Salter."[26] In the same year he was also able to help his brother and sister-in-law, Julius and Käthe Salter, escape from Paris, although their presence in New York seems to have brought more family discord than pleasure. Salter had to support his brother, whose demands were considerable, by getting him work at H. Wolff bindery, as he had with Stefan years earlier.[27] A happier change followed with his marriage to Agnes Veronica O'Shea (of Northampton, Massachusetts) on July 22, 1942, after a two-year friendship. In 1946 they adopted their daughter, Janet.[28] The new family continued to live at the same address in Greenwich Village. Work was steady and life tranquil for Salter. His reputation increased steadily.[29]

An early triumph in this decade came when his design for Paul Gallico's *The Snow Goose* (Knopf, 1941; FIG. 116) was chosen as one of the fifty best books of the year, which firmly linked his name with a popular best-seller. The wartime subject of Gallico's book was typical of many of Salter's commissions from these years. Between 1939 and 1942, for example, he created twelve covers and the company logo for Alliance Book Corporation, the publishing firm of the German exile Fritz Landshoff (FIG. 117). This venture focused strongly on topical issues and works by German exile writers.[30] The first of these was by the refugee historian Konrad Heiden, *The New Inquisition* (1939; FIG. 118). For this book Salter's jacket quoted images from Albrecht Dürer's woodcut *The Four Horsemen of the Apocalypse* to convey the terrors of National Socialism. By contrast his design in poster colors and a schematic pictorial style for Emil Ludwig's *Quartet* (1939; FIG. 119) conveys tranquility. The cover for Norbert Muhlen's *Schacht, Hitler's Magician* (1939; FIG. 120) uses lettering and imagery that work together to communicate the bloodstained statistics of Hitler's regime. A particularly noteworthy cover for Alliance from 1941 helped to market the harrowing exposé *Out of the Night* (FIG. 121), by Richard Krebs under the pen-name of Jan Valtin. This pseudonym added to the mystery surrounding the seven hundred–page first-person narrative about the cruelties of Nazi prisons and Stalinist reprisals. Salter's jacket art, which honors the dignity of individual suffering, helped make Valtin's account a marketing sensation that sold 300,000 copies in the first month.[31]

Salter's work for Alliance marshaled his talents firmly in service of the Allied war effort. An even more profound association with the firm of L. B. Fischer made him the most effective commercial artist for a German-exile publishing house.[32] Since 1936 Gottfried Bermann-Fischer (son-in-law of the firm's founder, Samuel Fischer) had been playing a dangerous game, staying just steps ahead of the German authorities by moving his business first from Frankfurt to Vienna, and then to Stockholm. Throughout this journey he sought access to English-speaking markets, and by 1940, fearing the imminent occupation of all of Scandinavia, he gained a foothold in New York with Alfred Harcourt's financial assistance. His partner was Fritz Landshoff (who had founded the German section of Querido Verlag, Amsterdam); the "L" and "B" in L. B. Fischer stood for Landshoff and Bermann. They kept in close contact with their Stockholm office, where the German texts were published, but the goal for New York was to print works by important American authors and only a few translations of German literature.

Nonetheless, the intellectual status that Fischer had enjoyed in Europe derived from the prestige of authors like Thomas Mann and Franz Werfel. Books by such refugee writers allowed Fischer to become the most important German-language publisher outside the country's borders. Bermann-Fischer's encounter with Salter in New York awakened memories of successes from the Berlin days. Salter was living proof that one of their former principal designers could carry his prestige intact to the New World and add luster to their list. The first announcement, which appeared on February 14, 1942 in *Publishers Weekly*, proudly stated: "All the book jackets for our entire spring list were designed by GEORGE SALTER."[33] Although the firm was short lived, Salter created thirteen covers as well as other designs for this venture. All but two were from 1942, its first year.[34]

The 1940s were busy for Salter. With many of his younger peers in uniform, he often had more commissions than an artist of even his diligence and energy could handle. At times, with permission from the appropriate art directors, he subcontracted jobs to Miriam Woods, his personal assistant, with the clear understanding that her work would always bear her signature.[35] Salter designed the brochure for L. B. Fischer's new list, including the exquisite, calligraphic fish logo (FIG. 123), as well as all titles for the company's first year, which covered an impressive intellectual spectrum. For Otto Zoff's *The Huguenots* (1942; FIG. 126)—one of the most frequently translated German books of the 1940s—Salter integrated an historical woodcut into his design. By contrast, his elegant lettering for the anthology *Heart of Europe* (1943; FIG. 127) presents an honors list of émigré culture.

One legal barrier stood between L. B. Fischer and potential American profits. Alfred Knopf insisted on exercising his American option rights to the works of their former author Thomas Mann. Without the rights to Mann's books, L. B. Fischer did not own enough intellectual properties to compete in the American market. This resulted in the firm's bankruptcy in 1945, though some of its titles appeared for two more years under the imprint.

L. B. Fischer's demise did not severely damage Salter's career. His covers for Thomas Mann's works were central to Knopf's list in the 1940s. The war in Europe produced a steady stream of books for which Salter's jackets provided powerful marketing tools. His scene for the cover of F. C. Weiskopf's *The Firing Squad* (Knopf, 1944; FIG. 129) is a good example, for it combines a chilling narrative quality with the promise of serious political content. Salter's airbrush technique dramatized the iconic monumentality of the Arc de Triomphe on Ilya Ehrenburg's *The Fall of Paris* (Knopf, 1943) and created an introspective mood for David Ormsbee's *Chico Goes to the Wars* (Dutton, 1943; FIG. 131). The cover of the latter is a psychological depiction of war showing the experiences that crowd the mind of the protagonist, whose face is rendered in lifelike detail. One element of this cover directly relates it to contemporary events—the image of the falling soldier quotes Robert Capa's famous photograph from the Spanish Civil War, *Death of a Nationalist Soldier*. Salter used an open eye on his covers, as in that for Ormsbee, to symbolize personal insight. He included another striking open eye in the very spare design of *East of Midnight* (Knopf, 1946; FIG. 132). The simplicity of color and detail here create a very different effect, both alluring and sinister.

In several designs from the postwar years, Salter experimented in new areas of the publishing market. Among his commercial projects is a charming anomaly, the hand-lettered volume of selections from Henry David Thoreau's writings entitled *What I Lived For: From Walden* (Archway Press, 1946; FIG. 138). The volume was one of six titles commissioned by prominent calligraphers for a series called The Scribe, which was the brain-child of Ernst Reichl.[36] This little book is a striking document of Salter's lettering skill. In 1984 Salter's colleague and younger contemporary Charles Skaggs wrote an article that surveyed American calligraphy of the period when Salter was at his peak. The piece is not only a good overview of the subject, but a critical appreciation of Salter's calligraphy:

> [His] experiments in style, color, and background textures (too often with airbrush) covered an extraordinary range—primarily for novels, detective stories, and science fiction. A Salter jacket usually had a surprise or new kick, as he sought to expand his own metier and jacket concepts in general. But his penwork was a dead giveaway. His most characteristic writing was a scratchy, nervous italic of low horizontal sweep. This was often combined with rather naïve line illustrations, such as those he did for the novels of Franz Kafka. No artist derived more joy from book work or was granted more intellectual independence by publishers than Salter. He was a vocal advocate of smaller sizes of titles and authors on jackets. Amidst surrounding blatancy, George's designs spoke in eloquent *sotto voce*, with bright colors as a foil. His virtually self-taught calligraphy was as uniquely recognizable as any we have seen—all conceived and produced in a Manhattan studio as orderly and antiseptic as a dentist's office.[37]

At the opposite end of the spectrum of fine book design are the six covers that Salter conceived in 1946 for Penguin Books in New York. Penguin titles during this period in Britain were easily recognized by their typographically elegant simplicity, whereas mass appeal in the American market called for looser, more eye-catching aesthetic formulas.[38] In keeping with this demand, Salter's covers were more schematic and less refined than his classic jackets for hardback books. Instead of showing exquisite complexity or sophistication, they used simple draftsmanship that fit the inexpensive format of the mass-market paperbacks themselves. Between 1941 and 1945, Salter also updated the designs of four covers for Pocket Books. These titles included an illustration for Felix Salten's *Bambi* (1942; FIG. 139) that echoes the Walt Disney animation of the same year, and a very somber design for the memorial tribute to Franklin Delano Roosevelt (1945; FIG. 140). This was probably the first "instant book," for it was produced and sold as an edition of 300,000 copies within six days of the president's death.[39]

Salter's work for The Limited Editions Club began in the 1940s and included some of his finest designs in a medium other than book jackets. This publishing venture, founded by George Macy in 1929, marketed well-made books to a discriminating group of subscribers. The best designers, printers, and illustrators of the day (including Pablo Picasso) produced signed and numbered volumes on fine paper in decorated slipcases. Between 1941 and 1967, Salter worked on eight different books for The Limited Editions Club. At times he designed every aspect of the volume; in some cases he collaborated with other artists or did only the typography. The acclaimed *Poems of Heinrich Heine* (1957) is a beautiful example that shows Salter's talents united with the illustrations of Fritz Kredel. These two outstanding artists worked together on four titles for The Limited Editions Club, as well as on the two-volume set of Lewis Carroll's Alice books (Random House, 1946), which Salter designed and Kredel colored. This association opened the way for their collaboration on the fine limited edition, *Am Wegesrand* (1961).

The 1940s brought not only commissions for political and belletristic covers, but also included mystery novels, which Salter approached with characteristic vigor and for which he developed a distinctive style. For *The Scarf* (Dial, 1947; FIG. 19), the first novel written by Robert Bloch, author of *Psycho* (1959), Salter's abstraction avoided a realistic crime scene, which would have better served the pulp market or *Mercury Mystery Magazine*. Among Salter's papers is a note, jotted to himself before he began to sketch this cover: "Psychological murder story. Young writer suffers from compulsion to kill, kill, kill. His instrument is a maroon scarf, a legacy from his old-maid school teacher who had fallen in love with the boy.—Notice evil eye, concentration, compulsion [represents] state before deed."[40] The result is a disembodied image of the scarf surrounded by vibrating shock waves that evoke tension.

Among the greatest of Salter's works from the late 1940s is the jacket for Elias Canetti's *The Tower of Babel* (Knopf, 1947; FIG. 142), where he combines a psychological style with powerful geometric patterns. Salter was proud of this piece, which he described thus: "The strained emotional tone of the book is fused with the jacket style in *The Tower of Babel*. Its exciting pattern and strident color are highly charged with the discords of psychological tensions [in Canetti's text]."[41] Such statements reveal Salter's desire to couple marketing image with literary intent. The jacket for Thomas Mann's

Doctor Faustus (Knopf, 1948; FIG. 143), which Fischer had published in German the previous year in Stockholm, was visually less ambitious, but similar in approach. For *Doctor Faustus*, he captured a complex novel of ideas with suggestive abstraction in order to convey its themes of justice and music. The reader must interpret the complex geometric form—based on Dürer's engraving *Melancholia*—and relate it to Mann's novel. The inspiration for this design must have come from reading Mann's text.

A quiet triumph, and a departure from his customary work, came in 1948 with Salter's binding for McGraw-Hill's enormously successful introductory economics textbook by Paul A. Samuelson, a professor at the Massachusetts Institute of Technology. The designer of the book, Alvin Eisenman, managed the art department at McGraw-Hill from 1945 to 1950. Eisenman hired Salter specifically to produce a binding that looked, as he put it, more like a classics textbook than a work on economics.[42] Everyone involved during the production stage of this venture observed carefully while the text was market-tested among undergraduates at MIT. It was later revised for clarity based on the results of this test. McGraw-Hill executives feared that an economics text that came from an engineering school might appear too "techie" for mass appeal. Salter's green binding, undersized gold lettering, and subtle design probably contributed to catapulting Samuelson's book to its enviable position as the best-selling textbook of the twentieth century. Once the first edition had consolidated its market niche, the art department experimented with new designs in subsequent editions.

By the end of the 1940s, the influence of pulp fiction had significantly transformed the art of the book jacket. Many saw this new aesthetic, associated as it was with the low end of the publishing industry, as a lamentable decline in quality. The emerging paperback market, in particular, peddled sensationalist literature with lurid images of sex and violence. In 1947, in reaction against this perceived decline in artistic standards for trade books, several designers formed The Book Jacket Designers Guild. George Salter was chairman and members included Leo Manso, Meyer Miller, Jeanyee Wong, and Miriam Woods. The group held annual exhibitions dedicated to recognizing and rewarding good taste and high quality in book covers.[43] The six catalogs of the Guild's shows bear Salter's stamp throughout. He not only designed the monogram logo for the group, but also created the format and typography of the first volume, which determined the look of subsequent catalogs. As the preface to the first exhibition catalog in 1948 stated, the purpose of the Guild was to stimulate interest in the book jacket as a creative form and "elevate the artistic level" of its design. Certain designs were explicitly disparaged, for example, those "all too *conspicuous top-heavy ladies in undress*."[44] The sixth and last catalog makes this and other points even more forcefully:

Rejected was the stunt jacket that screams for your attention, and then dares you to guess what the book is about.

Rejected was the jacket that is born of the assumption that if the book has a heroine; or if the author is a woman; or the author's mother a female; the jacket must say SEX.

Rejected were the burlap backgrounds, the airbrush doilies and similar clichés as well as the all too many good illustrations that were stretched, squeezed, tortured and mutilated to fit a jacket format with just enough room left for an unrelated title.[45]

Despite the tone of alarm, this manifesto is not merely a puritanical rejection of nudity. This prestigious group of New York designers—who were responsible for most American book design of the day—belonged to a generation that saw dramatic technological and aesthetic changes in their industry, as well as in society at large. Salter and his colleagues were not simply being ornery or disaffected, but were protesting the toxic interaction among bad writing, cheap production techniques, and low artistic standards—mass-market forces that combine to trivialize literature and debase public taste. For these seasoned designers, the gratuitously lurid scenes on paperback covers represented painful departures from high standards of presentation, to which the Guild remained devoted. The group disbanded after eight years. Its efforts may have elevated the status of the cover artist, but its goal of halting the publishing industry's penchant for risqué and titillating designs was a losing proposition.[46]

Designs of the 1950s and 1960s

In the 1950s George Salter's American career reached its halfway point. He had spent sixteen years working successfully in his new country and would remain productive there until his death seventeen years later. He was at the top of his profession, although even he faltered when jobs dried up briefly in the middle of the decade. Nonetheless, professional colleagues continued to hold him in the highest esteem and publishers still coveted his book jackets for their annual lists. Salter's election to membership in the New York bibliophile Grolier Club in 1951 attested both to his character and status among book professionals. In 1957 the designer Joseph Blumenthal listed him among the designers and printers he most admired.[1]

By this time Salter's name was virtually synonymous with the book jacket, and he was the highest paid designer of hardback book covers in New York. In 1960 he generally charged $250 per job; it was not until 1970 that such a fee became the market average. Salter was able to conceptualize a job quickly and usually complete it after just one preliminary sketch. He was therefore able to supplement his steady work with jobs that needed to be completed on short notice.

Earlier in the twentieth century, the paper book jacket, for all its fragile and ephemeral nature, became the primary marketing tool of the book industry. Not all designers, however, embraced the development readily. The illustrious W. A. Dwiggins, for example, foresaw the potentially cheapening effect that flashy, undistinguished book jackets could have on the industry. He preferred that publishers preserve traditional methods and produce beautifully decorated bindings instead.[2] Dwiggins's objection typifies the tension that existed between the traditional trade of bookbinding and the emerging one of graphic design. Yet the formal division between the binding and the jacket ultimately made it possible for the paper cover to evolve into a separate art form. By the midtwentieth century, book jackets often complemented decorated bindings, thus resolving the opposition.

Covers designed before 1950 often diverged stylistically from the contents of their books.[3] Salter, however, rarely made this mistake, in part because he frequently used the design principle he described in his category six, which advocates allusive techniques of symbolic imagery to suggest content.[4] Salter's intellectual approach sometimes raised eyebrows. One Massachusetts bookseller, who relied on the clarity of a book jacket's message to sell his products, labeled the sort of interpretive imagery that Salter favored the "Guess-What Jacket." Without naming the designer, he criticized one of Salter's designs in the pages of *Publishers Weekly* for including a Latin conjugation on its cover (FIG. 149). Instead of clearly promoting the contents of the book, he argued, such details merely puzzled bookseller and buyer.[5]

Salter took up the gauntlet in the following issue of *Publishers Weekly*.[6] He explained that imagery can work powerfully through connotative details, rather than solely by literal representations of a story line. Simplistic visual imagery, he argued, was often an inadequate merchandising tool for books of substance; challenging works of literature deserve more sophisticated designs than detective fiction. The cover of a more complicated book, on the other hand, has the potential to arouse curiosity in educated readers who care about style as well as content and stimulate a potential buyer to learn more about the book. For this purpose, image and jacket text must work together to whet the appetite, whether for knowledge or entertainment. Hardcover books sell differently from the mystery digests on the newsstand, Salter asserted. Because their content is simple and quickly consumed, mysteries and pulp paperbacks can rely on simple pictures to signal their contents, which is not the case with more challenging fiction.

Being a literate man who would have felt dishonest designing a cover before reading the text, Salter was committed to conveying a book's essence graphically. Unlike most designers, who relied solely on summaries from outside readers, Salter found his design ideas in the manuscripts themselves. To do otherwise would have meant compromising the author's work. "No designer," he wrote, "can supersede the manuscript and make it a tool for his own notions."[7] His allegiance to a book's subject matter, however, did not preclude the possibility of alternative interpretations.

Salter's designs for Alfred Knopf are among his greatest accomplishments. The quality and quantity of these commissions distinguish this particular professional association as the apex of his career. The close collaboration between artist and art department at Knopf set this experience apart from his work with other publishers, as did the cordial attention that Salter received from the urbane, aesthetically sophisticated Alfred Knopf himself.[8] Unlike most publishers, Knopf cared greatly about the appearance of his books. John Tebbel, in his survey of American publishing, states: "It was no wonder that Knopf design excelled. The staff designer was Harry Todd (in later years, Atheneum's vice-president of production), and design services were regularly provided by W. A. Dwiggins, Warren Chappell, Herbert Bayer, Charles Skaggs, and George Salter—a formidable team."[9] Salter also had a close personal friend at Knopf in Sidney Jacobs, the head of Knopf's art department. Some publishers did not permit jacket artists to sign their work, but Knopf celebrated his designers by giving them extensive credit both in colophons and advertising. Salter happily produced 178 designs for Knopf between 1935 and 1967, many for the Borzoi imprint. He himself noted the unique flair of what he called "the Borzoi style," which often placed his book jackets in combination with decorated bindings of Dwiggins, a major force behind this elegant style.[10] This felicitous collaboration is particularly evident in the nine Thomas Mann titles that Salter worked on for Knopf. Dwiggins's bindings were usually black-stamped cloth with gold lettering and ornate spine decoration, whereas Salter preferred two colors, stamped gold monograms and—in the case of *The Transposed Heads* (1941; FIG. 146)—a richly decorated pen-and-ink drawing that echoes the book's jacket. Salter found it particularly satisfying to work on Thomas Mann's books. This relationship appealed to his sense of historical continuity, which had its roots in designs he had first created for the great German publisher Samuel Fischer in 1932. In Alfred Knopf he felt that he had found a publisher of the same stature.

Salter's achievements for Knopf included books by the most prominent European and American writers of the day: Kay Boyle, Albert Camus, Elias Canetti, Friedrich Dürrenmatt, Paul Gallico, John Hersey, Franz Kafka, H. L. Mencken (with bindings by Dwiggins), Robert Nathan, and others. Among the most successful jobs from this period is one of his signature pieces, the jacket for *The Wall* (1950; FIG. 156), John Hersey's novel about the Warsaw ghetto. A complex and demanding project, *The Wall* required painstaking draftsmanship. Salter kept several proofs, all heavily marked up with detailed instructions to the printers. The final version shows an outline of a ghostly image, a formula in Salter's visual vocabulary for rendering imagined or recalled characters, such as the dead. The figure of the writing man is an unusual literary touch; he is the narrator who has pieced this account together from an archive that survived the historical events. Salter's design decisions seem to have sprung from a powerful personal, intellectual, and literary response to the work. In a letter of condolence to Salter's widow at her husband's death, Alfred Knopf commented: "There are some books which, without his help, would have taken a good deal longer to make the public grade. And there were others, like 'The Wall' and 'The Last of the Just' that seem to have been written so that George could design them."[11]

Symbolic representation rather than realism is also central in his work for *The Quest* by Elizabeth Langgässer (Knopf, 1960; FIG. 157) an ambitious job for which Salter produced the comprehensive design, including line-drawn vignettes for each chapter head. The art department at Knopf judged the final work a masterpiece. This greatly pleased Salter, especially since the extensive time he devoted to the project had effectively reduced his hourly fee to minimum wage.[12]

Critics and readers alike admired Salter's covers that used symbolism to suggest historical relevance. Such designs were often both intellectually stimulating and visually appealing. The huge, two-volume novel *The Demons* (Knopf, 1961; FIGS. 164–165), by the Austrian Heimito von Doderer, is a good example of one such job. The pictorial slipcase, dominated by an ominous spider web, depicts the writer illuminated in a tiny corner. A literary production of such daunting size needed plenty of marketing text to encourage potential buyers. Salter printed promotional blurbs on the plain jackets of each volume. The red cloth bindings of the books themselves are the visual high point of the project, for they repeat the web motif from the slipcase with additional human figures. The bold color screen on the title page echoes this binding and creates a coherent transition from the external visual imagery to the literary experience of the book.

Salter experimented with richly decorated bindings and often paired them with jackets of very dissimilar styles. Margaret Jordan's story of village life, *Miracle in Brittany* (Knopf, 1950; FIG. 168), uses a window on the jacket that opens onto a depiction of the whole village on the cover. Not every job went smoothly, however. Robert Nathan, for whose books Salter designed six very successful jackets, insisted on being consulted at every stage of the design process of *The Weans* (Knopf, 1960; FIG. 166). When Nathan took exception to the preliminary illustrations and designs, Salter revised and simplified his visual ideas in an effort to make them more acceptable to the author. After that commission, he received no further titles by Nathan.[13]

A few of Salter's most effective book jackets deserve special mention for their creative use of visual effects. William Styron's *Lie Down in Darkness* (Bobbs-Merrill, 1951; FIG. 169) breaks up the visual field into different bands that each convey an aspect of the contents, from the symbolically dark storm cloud above to the broken magnolia flower below. Moody and suggestive imagery also worked well for Salter's Kafka designs. The American discovery of the works of Franz Kafka in the 1950s prompted Knopf to bring out two Kafka titles in that decade, one of which, *The Trial, Definitive Edition*, used an expanded reissue of Salter's 1937 design with a changed color scheme. The new edition uses the eerie vignettes from the jacket drawing on the title page and chapter openers to capture the novel's foreboding atmosphere. Similarly, the allegorical jacket for the definitive edition of Kafka's *The Castle* (Knopf, 1954; FIG. 170) shows a lone wandering figure engulfed by a wintry landscape. The stylized maze on the front cover reinforces the existential message, which intrigued the postwar reading public.

Salter's pictorial jacket for *Lord of the Flies* (Coward-McCann, 1962; FIG. 178), William Golding's novel of marooned English schoolboys' encounter with elemental evil, takes an approach different from the one he used for the Kafka novels. The colorful, panoramic jacket introduces the ominous motif of the sharpened stick, which is repeated on the binding where the sharpened points are colored blood red. The anthropomorphic trees on the jacket of *The Garden of the Finzi-Continis* (Atheneum, 1965; FIG. 192) suggest a strong psychological attachment to a place, while the design for Julio Cortázar's postmodern novel *Hopscotch* (Pantheon, 1966; FIG. 21) features hot colors and jagged wedges as a jarring background for the hopscotch game, hinting at the nonsequential order in which the text should be read. As typical of Salter's work, these pictorial jackets are full of allusions to literary content. They are not miniature posters that beg to be purchased; rather, they ask to be examined. By contrast, the lettered covers for Oswald Spengler's *Decline of the West* (Knopf, 1962; FIG. 8) and Hermann Hesse's *Demian* (Harper & Row, 1965; FIG. 5) use powerful, declamatory lettering to make an unambiguous presentation. Salter knew that some books' covers required a typographic style to attract the most attention.

When he worked on books for a particular imprint, Salter naturally adapted his ideas to its overall format. For example, he produced about fifteen jackets for the Modern Library between 1940 and 1964. From 1917, to the ascendancy of the paperback, these well-made, hardbound volumes provided inexpensive reprints of classics for a broad reading public. With these Modern Library commissions, Salter kept good company: Joseph Blumenthal and E. McKnight Kauffer also designed jackets for the series. The jobs did not offer a great range of possibilities, but for each one Salter produced fine lettering, sometimes augmented by elements of ornamental design or abstract devices that correspond to the second category of his book jacket design principles.[14] All these efforts preceded a complete redesign of the Modern Library in 1967, the fiftieth anniversary of the series. Unfortunately, this effort neither produced the hoped-for improvement in sales nor forestalled the cancellation of the series. The Modern Library hardback finally ceded the field to the paperback market in 1970.[15]

Not every Modern Library design was free of problems. In 1965 Salter wrote to Sidney Jacobs at Knopf to criticize the lack of attribution to the designer in two Modern Library titles: Kafka's *The Trial*, which he had found in a bookstore, and Spengler's *Decline of the West*. The former volume, which was essentially a reprint of his own 1957 design, did not mention his participation as designer or illustrator. The latter was a reworking of Salter's 1961 Knopf design, reduced in size, without his signature on the jacket. Salter was understandably distressed about the abandonment of the Knopf tradition of crediting the designer on the colophon page. He argued that the designer's name could surely be printed on the title page. The issue behind this correspondence was not one of copyright or payment, but of respect and fairness to the book artist.[16]

In December 1961 the New York gallery The Composing Room dedicated an exhibition to Salter entitled *A Third of a Century of Graphic Work*. Meyer Miller chose 150 items to display, eighty-seven of which were illustrated in a catalog designed by Philip Grushkin. This chronological presentation not only showed mastery of all seven of Salter's book jacket categories, but also conveyed the unity of a period style. When viewed as a group, the covers all show Salter's signature composition: strong colors, bold lettering, and well-defined fields that create structural order and clarity. But the covers are more than just concise, they are painterly, as opposed to merely "designed." Salter's panoramic views, symbolic allusions, natural forms, and striking visual details, constantly show that art and craft are inseparable at the most sophisticated levels. Salter's work is ultimately rooted in the medium of easel painting; his preference for detailed hand work and his relative indifference to new technologies underscore this background. With the exception of some portrait photography on the jackets of a few memoirs and biographies (and a few of his last mystery magazine covers), the camera played no role in his late work. His best designs avoided flat realism, which he felt belonged most properly to this newer medium.[17]

Salter's attachment to traditional techniques and aesthetics could make him a tough critic of contemporary book art. As a famous master and teacher, he was often asked for his opinion. In his interview for "50 Books of 1965," he was candid about the strengths and flaws he found in some of the representative submissions.[18] His objection to the stultifying conformity of modern textbook design still rings true, as does his observation that trends do not necessarily amount to true innovations. Salter's criticisms leave the impression that he had witnessed a decline in craftsmanship that often accompanies technological advances, and had recognized the connection between cheaper color reproduction techniques and lower design values. He never ceased to raise his voice in support of diligent attention to details in his craft.

Salter applied his high standard of craftsmanship to what is widely considered the finest book designed by German exile artists. In 1961 he allied his talent with that of his friend Fritz Kredel (they had previously collaborated on several projects) to produce *Am Wegesrand* [*By the Wayside*; FIGS. 193–195]. Although conceived, lettered, and illustrated in the United States, this slender volume was produced in Germany in a limited edition of 150 copies. Kredel's hand-colored woodcuts of delicate flowers echoed the illustrations in his first successful flower book, *Das Blumenbuch* (*Flower Book*), designed by Rudolf Koch for the Insel Verlag in 1929–1930. For this new joint venture, Salter produced delicately lettered texts of German poetry to accompany Kredel's fine illustrations. *Am Wegesrand*, and the earlier *Blumenbuch* were both among the volumes that the Grolier Club included in the one hundred most significant books of the twentieth century.[19]

Publishers and art directors relied upon Salter's images to lend intellectual respectability to their products. For this reason, his book covers have a proud place in his oeuvre. But they are only part of the story, for Salter also left his stamp on magazine design. He designed covers for American mystery magazines in the 1940s and '50s, and for science fiction magazines in the 1960s. In fact, his overall contribution to this market segment was immense. In addition to his magazine designs, the few illustrated covers that he created in the 1940s for Pocket Books and Penguin Books of New York attested to his flexibility. Without lowering his standards, Salter could appeal to a mass market with eye-catching designs. Although his reputation rests most solidly on designs from publishers like Alfred A. Knopf, whose serious books called for thought-provoking and sophisticated jackets, he could produce mystery digests for a different target audience. After all, he did not disdain mass appeal, only vulgarity and poor workmanship. Nonetheless, his work for Mercury Publications remained a sideline endeavor.

Salter's involvement with Lawrence Spivak's Mercury Publications gave these popular paperbacks a cachet no other publisher could claim. The venture was an offshoot of Spivak's magazine, *The American Mercury*.[20] Salter, who had a good working relationship with Spivak, produced about 750 covers for various Mercury Publications, many of which were detective stories. In fact, his covers for literary works by Franz Werfel, Rudyard Kipling, Don Marquis, and Nicholas Monserrat appeared in the two Mercury series, Mercury Library and Mercury Book. In 1938 when Spivak launched the Bestseller Library, Mercury Publications titles were appearing at the rate of one per month. By March 1940 the Bestseller Library series split, creating Mercury Mysteries (FIG. 199) and Bestseller Mysteries; Spivak began publishing *Ellery Queen's Mystery Magazine* in 1941 (FIGS. 200–209), and in 1942 it added a new imprint, Jonathan Press Mysteries. Salter came to Mercury Publications as art director in 1938 to help manage the venture. He designed the various series to give each a distinctive look within the so-called "digest" format of 128 pages. He did this by varying the font size on the double column pages, which were somewhat wider than those of the standard paperback. For a long time the Mercury Mysteries bore Salter's two-color scenes within a postage stamp frame, with distinctive hand lettering in the center of the cover. Eventually they were changed to resemble the wittier, more colorful Ellery Queen covers. Salter preserved the series identity by using a bold stencil font at the top of the cover and printing the author's name (or author plus title) below the illustration.

In all his mystery magazine designs, Salter remained closer to the style of highbrow publishing graphics than to pulp fiction. His tacit loyalty to the tradition of fine art lent the mystery genre a degree of respectability. A certain taste and deliberate restraint set Salter's mystery covers apart from the lurid excesses of many contemporary paperbacks—those that today, ironically, are appreciated for their camp effects. These jobs for Spivak presented Salter with few intellectual challenges. His task was essentially to represent either a corpse or a person in imminent danger of becoming one. Although he firmly believed that the cover should reflect the contents of the book, he did not enjoy reading mysteries, and so he collaborated with his wife, Agnes, who read the texts and suggested material for these designs.[21] Salter then depicted bloody corpses, disheveled vixens, and unsuspecting victims, but his images are never quite as undraped or sadistically mangled as on the covers of so many Dell, Pyramid, or Avon paperbacks of the same period. Regardless of the content, the pictures are detailed paintings, sometimes completed with the airbrush. True to form, Salter managed to capture mournful gazes, alluring physical traits, puzzling visual ambiguities, and finely rendered objects. These covers give quick impressions that hint broadly, if not always quite accurately, at the plots of the books. Upon close inspection they reveal Salter's private enjoyment of the fine technical points of even this sort of illustration. Thanks to his experience, and continued presence, in the world of book publishing, these covers strike a wonderful balance of text and illustration that gives the mystery magazines a look that allies the pulps with hard-cover books.[22]

Salter stepped down from his position as art director of Mercury Publications in 1958 but continued to design covers for the firm. During the 1960s, toward the end of his career, his illustrations were gradually supplanted by photography. For several of these illustrations he posed female employees of Mercury Publications as models.[23] He did not consider the introduction of this new technology, which coincided with his advancing age and declining health, as an improvement over the artistry of the hand-drawn cover. He always believed that the quality of the image on paper outweighed the method of getting it there, and the more artisanship involved in the job, he reasoned, the better the final product.

During his long and prolific career, Salter produced several designs unrelated to book covers—a few commercial advertisements in Germany in the 1920s, some beautifully lettered broadsides for the AIGA (American Institute of Graphic Arts) in the 1940s, packaging for Conté Castile Shampoo in 1953, and a dial for General Electric Clocks in 1954. He also accepted many private commissions for bookplates and letterheads. In addition, he created handsome wine lists for the New York wine merchant A. N. Luria in 1938 and 1939, each with eight wood-cuts of wine-growing scenes. He also shaped the masthead for *Eve Magazine* in 1945, lettered two different series of art books published by Harry F. Abrams, and created the popular Book of the Month Club subscriber bookplate (FIG. 211). In 1950 he made gift and Christmas cards for several magazines and for the television show *Meet the Press*, another venture that Lawrence Spivak launched and hosted. In 1962 Salter designed one of the most popular UNICEF Christmas cards (FIG. 213), and, during the last year of his life, he lettered the record jacket covers in the Time-Life series The Story of Great Music.

As in his early days in Germany, Salter was in demand as a designer of trademark logos. American publishing houses for which he designed logos include American Mercury (FIG. 214), Basic Books (FIG. 215), Columbia University Press (FIG. 216), Alliance Books, L. B. Fischer, Atlas Magazine, Simon & Schuster, and World Publishing Company. He also designed the device for the Twentieth Century Fund (FIG. 217) and the stylized windows on the graphic trademark for Lincoln Center for the Performing Arts (FIG. 218). For binding designs he consistently stamped authors' monograms on the front board—Thomas Mann's titles for Knopf being a prime example. This convention not only connected the author's identity from the jacket to the title page but, as Salter well knew, also flattered the author's ego.

As a designer Salter was keenly aware of the role of typefaces in book production. "Typography is an instrument; it must be played like one," he once wrote.[24] He respected the artistry of contemporary typographers, both in Europe and the U.S. In 1953, with Paul Standard, he promoted the work of F. H. Ernst Schneidler in a New York exhibition that helped revive interest in this designer. Then in old age, Schneidler had founded Juniperus Press in 1921 and was the chief figure of the Stuttgart School of Design, which trained superb typographers and calligraphers (among them, Georg Trump) from the 1920s through the postwar period.[25] Through their correspondence in the mid-1950s, he and Salter (who never met in person) developed a deep friendship. Salter paid homage to the great calligrapher in the Sixth Annual Exhibition of the Book Jacket Designers Guild (1953), a celebration of the graphic beauty inherent in the alphabet.[26]

As early as the 1930s, Salter put his dedication to typography into practice by venturing into the realm of type design. The result was Flex (FIGS. 221–222), a so-called ribbon font named for its flowing, calligraphic line. Continental Typefounders Associates of New York manufactured Flex and had it cast in the Netherlands in sizes from thirty to sixty point.[27] Salter believed that typography should derive from handwriting, and thus designed this display face as a broad-stroke, cursive hand. Flex was introduced in the December 1936 issue of *PM*, where it was used for several headings. A note explains that Salter conceived the idea in 1935 when working on an advertisement for glassware: "He wanted to get the effect of luminosity and transparency characteristic of glass."[28] Although essentially a display font for commercial advertising, Flex also found occasional use in book design. Robert Josephy employed the type on two of his books: Lawrence Watkin's *On Borrowed Time* (Knopf, 1937) and Christopher La Farge's verse novel *Each to the Other* (Coward-McCann, 1939). What this typeface lacks in subtlety, it makes up for in panache, with its liquid line racing along the page like a spool of unwinding film. Nonetheless, Salter was never quite satisfied with the result.[29]

Salter's influence on German and American book design was profound. His own words written in 1935 about his personal standards for book jackets—the medium he virtually defined and with which he will always be associated—best appraise his achievement:

> A good jacket must be more than a record or a report. It must transmit
> a mood. It must appeal to the imagination. It must be in perfect accord
> with the literary quality of the book. It must be even more if it is to
> function as an important sales factor, if it is to "stop" the eye of the
> person passing by—yet within the limits of good taste, within the
> restrictions of good art.[30]

Judged by his own criteria—good taste and good art—Salter's designs are successful. At worst, some of his covers may seem dated, but this is hardly a condemnation. Artistic vision always reflects a generational style, and Salter's achievement inspired imitation among his contemporaries and students.[31] His aesthetic was certainly not the only option in the industry, but it reflected its highest standards. During his early years in Germany, while his skill as a draftsman grew in strength and confidence, his work had already achieved a striking maturity of style. During these early years as a professional bookman, he mastered his trade. He was working in all media across the entire range of expressive possibilities; his creativity flourished, whether his subject matter was shocking or idyllic.[32] Remarkable, too, was his seamless transition and continuous evolution from Berlin to New York. Yet stylistic change is evident in this odyssey. Salter's lettering became more developed during his New York years, and his range of styles more differentiated, while he also tempered his style to the tastes of his new American audience.[33] His American oeuvre contains fewer bold experiments, fewer modernist echoes, and more pictorial scenes, and places greater emphasis on consistency of craftsmanship. This is partly due to the inevitable process of maturation, but it is also a response to the demands of publishers' art departments. In response to these market forces, Salter's New York covers developed a personal style that encourages a dialogue about the contents of the book between the designer and the viewer.

The commonality among great designers has less to do with shared styles than with technical excellence. Each artist brings a unique approach to the problem of translating idea into image. Like the best of his generation, Salter found his own formulas. At its most pictorial, his style reflects the strong palette and symbolic realism of easel painting. At its most literal, it explores the infinite visual possibilities inherent in the alphabet, which his pen animated in myriad forms. By the 1960s, technological advances in typesetting and photo-offset printing gradually began to render such techniques outmoded. Nonetheless, the heart of Salter's work fulfills the mission of modern design, for he skillfully translated personal inspiration into public message. His once brashly innovative style had become virtually ubiquitous by the 1960s—so well known that it seemed classic and, as a result, conservative. For example, during this decade he never adopted the so-called psychedelic style, a short-lived fashion that he left to a younger generation. Nor did he follow the surrealist direction of E. McKnight Kauffer—a territory he had explored in his youth. He did not produce modernist abstractions like Alvin Lustig's witty variations on Paul Klee's linearity, or find much in common with the geometry of Paul Rand's commercial montages. The hard-edged pictorial realism of New Deal art, from which Norman Rockwell had come, never resonated deeply with him. He preferred to entice and intrigue rather than show and tell. He remained true to a signature style that made him celebrated, varying his expressive possibilities without ostentation or affectation within the categories of the book jacket that he had defined for himself.[34] With meticulous craftsmanship, and an uncanny ability to coordinate a marketing image with a book's content, Salter designed book jackets that, to paraphrase another designer, give timeless pleasure after other designs contemporary to the period have become merely "contemporary."[35]

George Salter died on October 31, 1967, in New York City. He is buried beside his wife Agnes O'Shea Salter (1901–1989) in Cummington, Massachusetts, in the Hampshire Hills where the family used to spend their summer vacations.[36]

FIGURE 1. Stefanie and Norbert Salter with baby Georg and older sister, Lili.

FIGURE 2. Georg Salter at the cello with his older brother, Julius (ca. 1905).

FIGURE 3. Salter hiking in the Alps, ca. 1927. From this date forward he produced book jackets almost exclusively and was hailed by contemporaries as one of the most innovative designers in the industry.

FIGURE 4. Georg Salter (ca. 1940) when he was just establishing a name for himself in New York City. Salter and his family had known the émigré photographer Lotte Jacobi-Reiss, who took this portrait, from their days in Berlin.

1

2

3

4

THE DESIGN LEGACY OF GEORGE SALTER

In 1939 Salter defined seven categories of the book jacket. Figures 5–8 represent the first of these, the formal typographical or hand-lettered style, which includes no design elements except lettering.

FIGURE 5. Harper & Row, 1965.

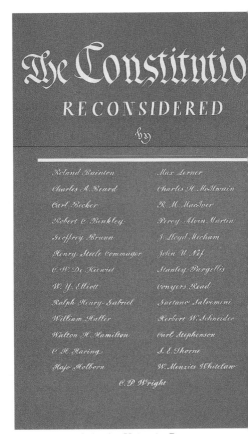

FIGURE 6. Columbia University Press, 1938.

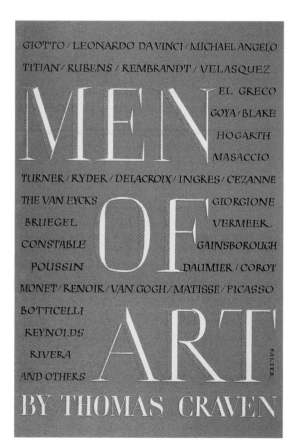

FIGURE 7. Knopf, 1962.

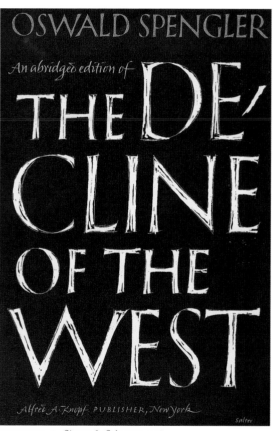

FIGURE 8. Simon & Schuster, 1936.

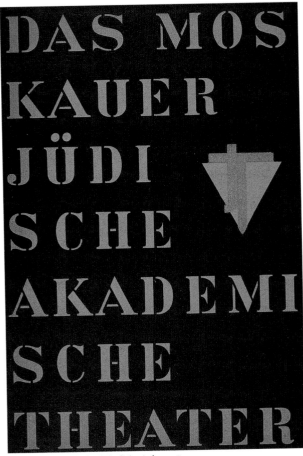

FIGURE 9. Verlag Die Schmiede, 1928.
A collection of essays on the Jewish Theater of Moscow.

FIGURE 10. Knopf, 1939.

The second category of jacket (FIGS. 9–11) is the typographical or hand-lettered style that adds elements of ornamental design to lettering but avoids pictorial representation.

THE
Thomas Mann
READER

Selected, Edited, and with Introductions,

by JOSEPH WARNER ANGELL

TRANSLATIONS BY H. T. Lowe-Porter

A representative cross-section of Mann's writings:
two short novels; selections from BUDDENBROOKS,
THE MAGIC MOUNTAIN, JOSEPH AND HIS BROTHERS,
DOCTOR FAUSTUS; four short stories; five character
portraits and essays; and four political essays.
    The editor supplies a general introduction and
    valuable prefatory notes to each section.

Salter

FIGURE II. Knopf, 1950.

Goodbye

JAPAN

BY JOSEPH NEWMAN
Tokyo correspondent of the New York Herald Tribune

salter

FIGURE 12. L. B. Fischer, 1942.
This cover, which was designed after the bombing of Pearl Harbor, implies the Japanese military presence in the air without resorting to propaganda.

The typographical or hand-lettered jacket (FIGS. 12–14) conveys the action or mood of the book by evoking states of mind and emotion.

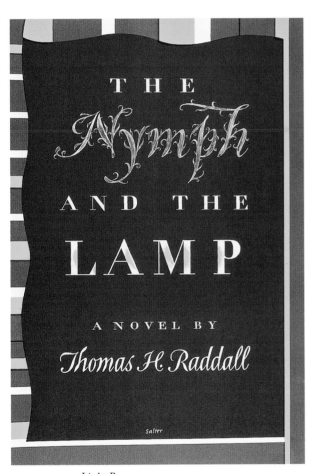

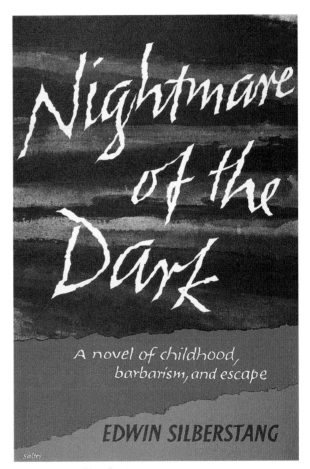

FIGURE 13. Little, Brown, 1950.
Organic lettering here transforms the word *nymph* itself into the sylvan creature it signifies.

FIGURE 14. Knopf, 1967.
The frantic quality of this lettering is all the more ominous against its stygian background.

Figures 15–17 are a variation on the previous type, in which the primary typographical design augments ornamental or pictorial details.

FIGURE 15. Knopf, 1944.

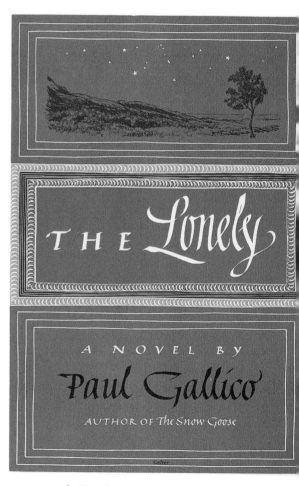

FIGURE 16. Knopf, 1949.

FIGURE 17. Knopf, 1938.

57   THE DESIGN LEGACY OF GEORGE SALTER

FIGURE 18. A. A. Wyn, 1945.

58   CLASSIC BOOK JACKETS

In this category (FIGS. 18–20) atmospheric pictorial design suggests specific details of the book's contents, while the lettering supplements or explains the imagery. These very different street scenes show the scope Salter brought to the imagined cityscape.

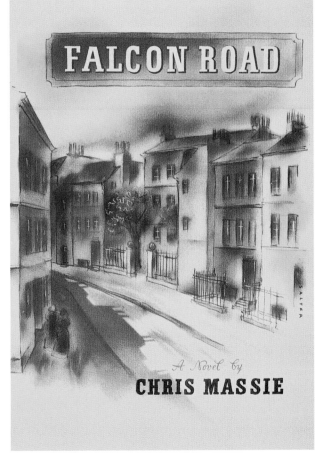

URE 19. Knopf, 1943.

FIGURE 20. Longmans, Green, 1936.

These covers (FIGS. 21–23) elicit the atmosphere of the book without necessarily depicting concrete or realistic scenes. Their imagery is symbolic or psychological in an abstract style.

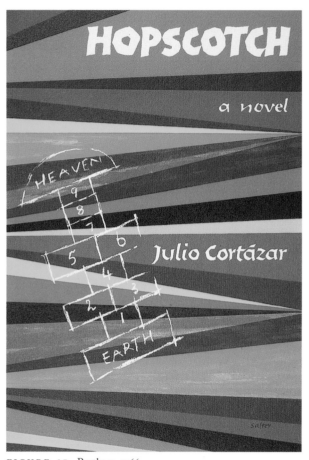

FIGURE 21. Pantheon, 1966.
The contrast between the apparently naïve children's game and this jarring, aggressive background prefigures the disquieting literary experiment inside the covers.

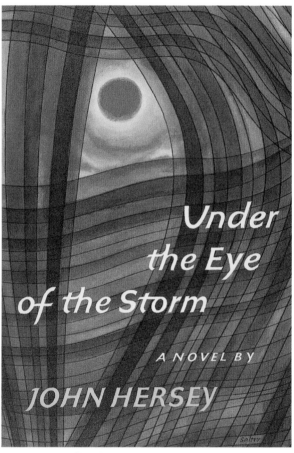

FIGURE 22. Knopf, 1967.
The image of a central eye focuses the design as it rivets the viewer's attention.

FIGURE 23. Dial, 1947.
For this first novel by the author of *Psycho*, Salter chose a suggestive, disembodied image rather than a violent or psychologically disturbing one. He jotted a note to himself as he planned the design: "Psychological murder story. Young writer suffers from compulsion to kill, kill, kill. His instrument is a maroon scarf, a legacy from his old-maid school teacher who had fallen in love with the boy.—Notice evil eye, concentration, compulsion [represents] state before deed."

FIGURE 24. Simon & Schuster, 1935.

The poster-style jacket, the last of Salter's seven categories, uses direct, concrete imagery and is more closely influenced by advertising styles than the other types. This, the second cover Salter finished in the U.S., proclaims its origins in the bold German poster art of the 1920s, the so-called *Sachplakat*. Its powerful, unaffected lettering is more slogan than title. Salter has here transferred the elements of a successful poster—a central figure, simple, concentrated imagery, flat colors—to make a striking cover.

FANG
AND
CLAW

SALTER

BY

FRANK BUCK

WITH FERRIN FRASER

FIGURE 25. Die Schmiede, 1922.
Salter's first figural cover design was a pencil drawing in the expressionist style executed when he was twenty-five. The lone figure towering prophetically over the landscape has a dramatic quality that matches the rhetorical pathos of Kasack's prose.

FIGURE 26. Die Schmiede, 1923.
This remarkable visual gesture has the nonchalance of graffiti, as if scrawled in blood on a blank wall. It is an early triumph of Salter's minimalist design that implies the content of Lenin's life.

FIGURE 27. Die Schmiede, 1924.
This anthropomorphic building on the cover of Joseph Roth's first book dramatizes the haunting memories of an ex-soldier who has suffered the horrors of war and found refuge in the Hotel Savoy. Salter exploits the contemporary expressionist style, which by the mid-1920s is in danger of becoming banal.

FIGURE 28. Die Schmiede, 1924.
Effective lettering can paint visual pictures, as the cover for Goll's dissonant, urban poetry of the avant-garde demonstrates. In keeping with the functionalist aesthetic that exploits both sound and image in the printed word, Salter's vivid, freehand letterforms build an Eiffel Tower with the book's title to produce a coherent architectonic design.

29   30

FIGURE 29. Die Schmiede, 1923.
Another youthful pencil drawing, this time for maxims about love.

FIGURE 30. Die Schmiede, 1924.
Salter created a unified look for the fourteen titles in the series
Aussenseiter der Gesellschaft (Society's Outsiders). The roughly stylized outlines scratched in ghostly silhouette on colored background
fields introduce contemporary reportage about a gritty subject.

FIGURE 31. Die Schmiede, 1925.
Salter's design for this simple book label is typical of many covers that
he produced in the 1920s. Later in his career he designed an American
edition of *The Trial*, which became a classic.

Salter's designs for bindings without pictorial jackets are often wonderful visual experiments, as these abstract shapes and freehand letterforms demonstrate.

FIGURE 32. Die Schmiede, 1925.

FIGURE 33. Die Schmiede, 1926.

FIGURE 34. Die Schmiede 1924.
The slightly irregular capitals and simple central design in two colors lend an uncomplicated, hand-crafted look to Mann's collection of essays proclaiming the "dictates of reason."

FIGURE 35. Die Schmiede, 1925.
Book jacket design is closely allied with poster art, as in this unabashedly commercial image with its hot, tropical colors and informal letterforms for a travelogue about Mexico. 1925 marks a watershed in Salter's development, when he begins to abandon modernist forms for more traditional, representational designs.

FIGURE 38. Logo *(Verlagssignet)*
for the publisher Kiepenheuer.

FIGURE 36. Die Schmiede, 1926.

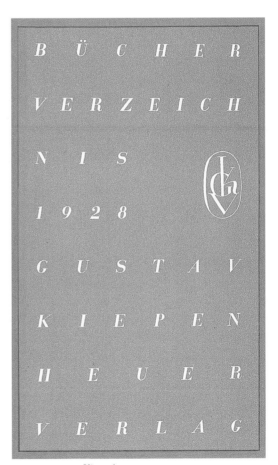

FIGURE 37. Kiepenheuer, 1928.
Restrained classicism organizes the cover of Kiepenheuer's 1928 title
list. Salter's lettered roman capitals create a subtly proportional grid
that is juxtaposed with the offset logo he designed for the firm.

EIN PFUND
Orangen
und 9 andere
GESCHICHTEN DER
Marieluise Fleisser
AUS INGOLSTADT

G. SALTER

GUSTAV KIEPENHEUER VERLAG

39

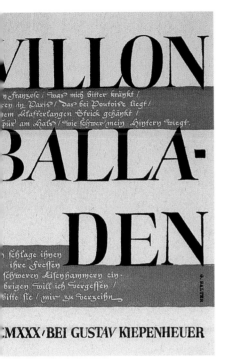

40

41

42

FIGURE 39. Kiepenheuer, 1929.
The convention behind this eye-catching cover for *A Pound of Oranges* is a page of printer's type specimens. Salter produces the titles of a collection of short stories in contrasting lines of blue and red, and sets off the author's name in cursive script. This visual effect conveys the variety of the book's contents. Note Salter's monogram on the right.

FIGURE 40. Kiepenheuer, 1930.
Between the imposing roman capitals on this collection of ballads appear Villon's own texts in a calligraphic, medieval hand. Bertolt Brecht wrote a poem (printed on the back of the jacket) proclaiming his debt to Villon and urging the buyer to spend money on this book rather than on cigars.

FIGURES 41 AND 42. Kiepenheuer, 1930.
The Communist activist and writer Ernst Toller played a role in the 1919 Munich revolution, which put a price on his head. Typography juxtaposes with photomontage on the jacket to simulate a wanted poster for the autho.

FIGURE 43. Kiepenheuer, 1930.

For this novel, which fictionalizes the rise of National Socialism in Germany, Salter has the title, *Success*, loom in huge, ominous letters across the world. The small inset map of Bavaria reveals the site of Hitler's early gains.

FIGURE 44. Kiepenheuer, 1930.

Salter's hand lettering in combination with typeset text presents Roth's novel about a simple man—the allegorical Job of the title.

FIGURE 45. Kiepenheuer, 1932.

Muted black and yellow tones (the colors of the Habsburg dynasty) capture the nostalgic mood of the end of the dual monarchy. Schönbrunn Palace stands desolate behind a barren tree, which casts a shadow (visible beneath the printed text) of the double-headed imperial eagle. In later editions this text was removed from the cover to reveal the eagle.

FIGURE 46. Kiepenheuer, 1934.

For this novel of the First World War, the Habsburg black and yellow combine with cursive calligraphy to present the story of an Austrian regiment.

47

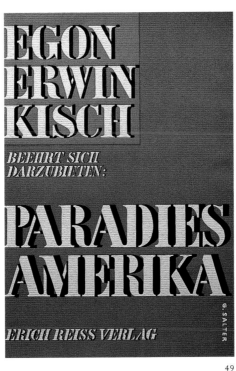

48

49

50

FIGURE 47. Erich Reiss, 1930.
Salter's best lettering plays visually with words while conveying an emotional sense of a book's contents. The terror of Kisch's wartime journal is conveyed by the blood-red background and nervously scrawled, oversized calligraphy that collides with the edges of the cover.

FIGURE 48. Kiepenheuer, 1933.
Salter's airbrush technique lets the background figures fade behind the title, which promises to reveal "clandestine China."

FIGURE 49. Erich Reiss, 1930.
Stencil lettering implies commercialism as it advertises Kisch's journalistic reports from America. Salter cleverly reverses the color fields of the American flag.

FIGURE 50. Kiepenheuer 1930.

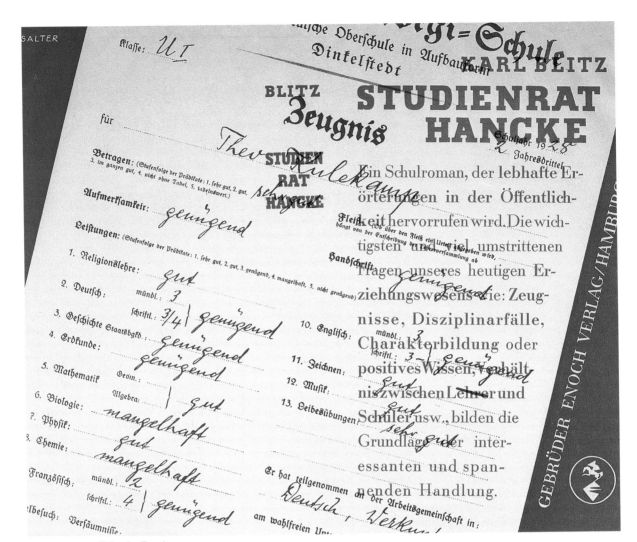

FIGURE 51. Gebrüder Enoch, 1930.
Salter invented the style of book jacket that boldly combines diverse letterforms
for their visual and linguistic content, transforming the viewer into a reader. The
text beneath Salter's title (in red, the color of a correcting pencil) set against a
diagonally printed report card, introduces the story of a schoolteacher.
Publishers eventually relegated such text to the flap copy.

FIGURE 52. *BDG Blätter* 6, 1930.
Visual effects with typography are Salter's specialty. This cover for the journal of
German commercial artists cleverly uses color to differentiate three large initials
from their background. What at first glance seems to be an illusion, produces
perfect legibility.

mitteilungen des bundes

deutscher gebrauchsgraphiker e. v.

als manuskript gedruckt

jahrgang 1930. heft 6

BLÄTTER

g. salter

53

54

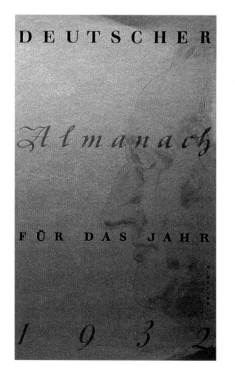

56

FIGURE 53. Kiepenheuer, 1931.
For this story of a traveling saleswoman, Salter uses six different letterforms, which he unites by a coherent color scheme. The playful images represent both the sacks of flour she sells and her mode of transport.

FIGURE 54. Second cover design for the same work.

FIGURE 55. Erich Reiss, 1932.
This appealing photograph for a novel entitled "The Bachelorette" is a fitting image for a study of modern woman.

FIGURE 56. Reclam, 1931.
In 1932 many German publishers marked the centenary of Goethe's death. Salter reproduced this famous profile for Reclam's literary almanac.

FIGURE 57. S. Fischer, 1931.
One of Salter's most striking book covers of the 1930s promotes this novel about a subaquatic, transatlantic train. This style is typical of the machine age aesthetic that extols progress and technology with sleek, aerodynamic images and streamlining.

FRANZ KAFKA

BEIM BAU DER CHINESISCHEN MAUER
Ungedruckte Erzählungen und Prosa aus dem Nachlass

G. SALTER

Martin Buber, André Gide, Hermann Hesse
Heinrich Mann, Thomas Mann und Franz Werfel geben diesem Band folgendes Geleitwort

*Immer deutlicher wird in Deutschland wie in Eng-
land und Frankreich die besondere Bedeutung Kafkas
erkannt. Haben die aus dem Nachlaß edierten drei
Romane in Kafka, den man vorher als einen Sprach-
meister und Meister der kleinen Form bewunderte, den
nur mit den Größten vergleichbaren Romancier, den
unerbittlichen Gestalter und Deuter der Zeit sehen
lassen, so steht die weitere Überraschung bevor, daß
die persönlichen Dokumente des Nachlasses den streng
und vorbildlich kämpfenden Menschen in der ganzen
Tiefe seines religiösen Bewußtseins aufzeigen.*

58

59

FIGURE 58. Kiepenheuer, 1931.
Typographic design can be simple and monolithic, as in this cover for a
collection of Kafka's stories.

FIGURE 59. S. Fischer, 1932.
The ominous cloud of airbrushed smoke that billows from a burning oil well
advertises this novel of petroleum exploration and intrigue in Anatolia. The
contrasting color fields and jarring textures demonstrate Salter's pictorial
imagination, which will emerge with more clarity during the decade.

FIGURE 60. S. Fischer, 1932.

FIGURE 61. S. Fischer, 1929.
Salter's outstanding design undoubtedly helped Döblin's novel of Berlin's seamy
underworld become a best-seller. He combines naïve elements of a child's rebus
with a calligraphic summary of the plot line. The result is the most famous book
jacket for a work of twentieth-century German literature. Never before had book
design achieved such a powerful fusion of word and image. The author supplied
extra text specifically for this jacket.

Alfred Döblin
BERLIN ALEXANDER-PLATZ
DIE GESCHICHTE VOM FRANZ BIBERKOPF
S. Fischer Verlag
Von einem einfachen MANN wird hier erzählt, der in BERLIN am ALEXANDERPLATZ als Strassenhändler steht. Der MANN hat vor anständig zu sein, da stellt ihm das Leben hinterlistig ein Bein. Er wird betrogen, er wird in Verbrechen reingezogen, zuletzt wird ihm seine BRAUT genommen und auf rohe Weise umgebracht. Ganz aus ist es mit dem MANN FRANZ BIBERKOPF. Am Schluss aber erhält er eine sehr klare Belehrung:
MAN FÄNGT NICHT SEIN LEBEN MIT GUTEN WORTEN UND VORSÄTZEN AN, MIT ERKENNEN UND VERSTEHEN FÄNGT MAN ES AN UND MIT DEM RICHTIGEN NEBENMANN.
Ramponiert steht er zuletzt wieder am ALEXANDERPLATZ, das Leben hat ihn mächtig angefasst.
G. SALTER

61

63

FIGURE 62. S. Fischer, 1930.

Salter's whimsical map for *The Forty-second Parallel* shows an amusing collection of clichés: the three cityscapes are all versions of New York; a trademark cowboy is placed in Georgia; and a balletic baseball player strikes a pose that could never occur to an American. The powerful diagonal of the sans-serif title shouts modernity, while at the far Pacific end of this panoramic cover—wrapping around to the back of the jacket—solid blocks of eye-catching color show the spectrum.

FIGURE 63. S. Fischer, 1931.

The Texas license plate from the year of the book's publication lends a gritty, local authenticity to this photomontage. Salter's cover is one of the many from the Weimar period that reflects the German fascination with America. Here, however, wanderlust for the "byways to Chicago" is overshadowed by the forbidding gray background of the city stockyards.

64

FIGURES 64 AND 65. Universitas, 1926.
Powerful lettering and stylized figures animate the covers
Salter designed for Jack London's novels.

FIGURES 66 AND 67. G. Grote, 1931.

Salter's blackletter font, here rendered in red, conveys the historical atmosphere of this nineteenth-century chronicle of life on an urban street. The detailed houses on the left contrast with those on the right, which are left white and unfinished, suggesting loss and longing for the past. Salter created six illustrations for Raabe's novel. Here the narrator at his open window records the sights and sounds of life around him on the street, the Sperlingsgasse.

FIGURE 68. Grote, 1930.

One of Salter's famous street scenes, this time of *Biedermeier* Berlin in the first quarter of the nineteenth century.

66

67

68

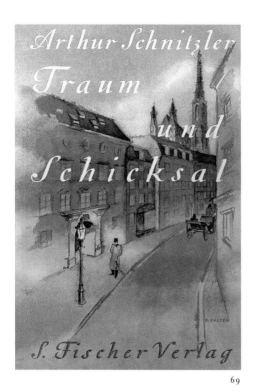

69

70

71

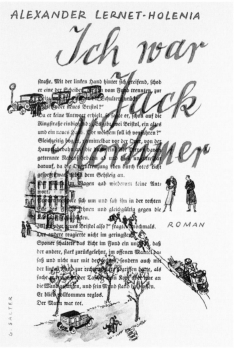

72

73

74

75

FIGURE 73. Kiepenheuer, 1932.
Design reveals, more subjectively than one might suppose, the ponderous and
pessimistic nature of this huge tome on sex and character.

FIGURE 74. Fischer, 1932.
Steuermann's story about "man on the run" is one of those prescient, late-Weimar-
era works that thematizes an existential exile before the political reality that forced
thousands, including author and designer, to leave Germany.

FIGURE 75. S. Fischer, 1932.
For his first Thomas Mann cover, Salter hand letters an elegant, red *Fraktur* to
echo the eighteenth-century version of this type. It is a far cry from the heavy
blackletter version, which carries political connotations.

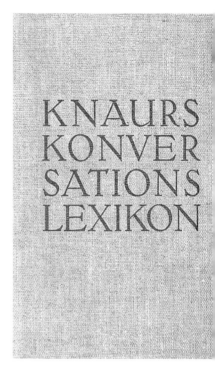

76
77

FIGURE 76. Zsolnay, 1933.

FIGURE 77. Engelhorn, 1933.
Endless roads and open sky beckon anyone who seeks "the American adventure."

FIGURE 78. Knaur, 1932.
Salter never aligned letters arbitrarily. This block of type lends sedate coherence
to the disparate entries inside the lexicon.

FIGURE 79. Salter's files contain six sketches for a new jacket design planned
for the 1934 revised edition of figure 78. He emigrated in 1933 and never
submitted the work, but his ideas are nonetheless curious. The use of heavy
blackletter seems to exploit the design aesthetic of National Socialist propaganda
to the point of parody.

The word that best fits Georg Salter is "versatility." He mastered the entire spectrum of book jacket techniques, from calligraphy to photomontage, airbrush, watercolor, and pen and ink. Throughout, Salter adhered to a design ideal that always foregrounded the commercial function of his art. In order to stimulate imaginations and entice potential readers to buy, his covers awaken visionary images of the contents that are typically more suggestive than concrete.

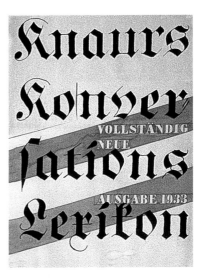

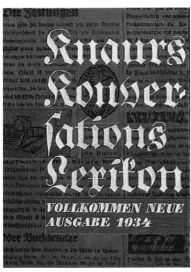

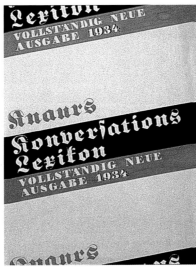

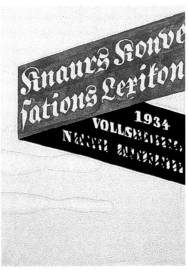

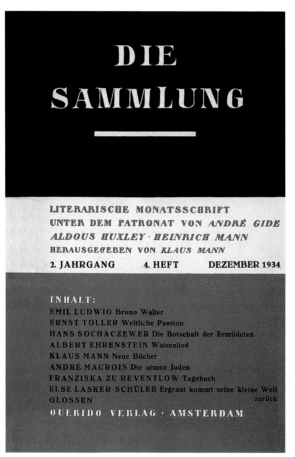

DIE
SAMMLUNG

LITERARISCHE MONATSSCHRIFT
UNTER DEM PATRONAT VON *ANDRÉ GIDE*
ALDOUS HUXLEY · HEINRICH MANN
HERAUSGEGEBEN VON *KLAUS MANN*
2. JAHRGANG   4. HEFT   DEZEMBER 1934

INHALT:
EMIL LUDWIG Bruno Walter
ERNST TOLLER Weltliche Passion
HANS SOCHACZEWER Die Botschaft der Ermüdeten
ALBERT EHRENSTEIN Waisenlied
KLAUS MANN Neue Bücher
ANDRÉ MAUROIS Die armen Juden
FRANZISKA ZU REVENTLOW Tagebuch
ELSE LASKER-SCHÜLER Ergraut kommt seine kleine Welt
GLOSSEN   zurück
QUERIDO VERLAG · AMSTERDAM

80

FIGURE 80. Before leaving Germany in 1934, Salter designed this cover template for the most prestigious journal of German exile culture. It is a straightforward, typographic approach with a bright color field that varied from issue to issue. Fritz Landshoff, the editor, would have liked to hire Salter for his publishing house in Amsterdam, but Salter had already set his sights on the United States.

FIGURE 81. Kiepenheuer, 1931.
A text-heavy cover for a lighthearted manual of style. The fine calligraphy conveys clearly the idea that the buyer will literally write better after reading this.

Hans Reimann

Vergnügliches

Handbuch der

deutschen

Sprache

Vergnüglich! Nicht allein, weil das Schulgeld für diesen Kursus nur Reichsmark 3.50 ausmacht, sondern auch, weil es wirklich ein Vergnügen ist, endlich einmal der deutschen Sprache auf so unterhaltsame und spassige Weise teilhaftig zu werden. Mancher lernt's nie, und auch dann noch unvollkommen. – Aber hier kann es ein jeder spielend erreichen. Gustav Kiepenheuer Verlag.

G. SALTER

81

FIGURE 82. Viking, 1935.
One of the first covers Salter designed in the United States.
The design hints that "the unknown quantity" is love.

FIGURE 83. Viking, 1939.

Stefan Zweig

BEWARE OF PITY

The First Long Novel
by the Author of "MARIE ANTOINETTE" etc

Do not
disturb

Salter

by Elizabeth Luling

FIGURE 84. Oxford University Press, 1936.
The teddy bear's story is illustrated in crayon, an appropriate
medium for the target audience.

FIGURE 85. National Home Library Foundation, 1935.
Salter produced separate images and lettering for each jacket in
this inexpensive series of literary reprints.

FIGURE 86. Salter's original sketch for *The Court of Fair
Maidens* included an architecturally elaborate, aristocratic interior.

FIGURE 87. Simon & Schuster, 1936.
The published design.

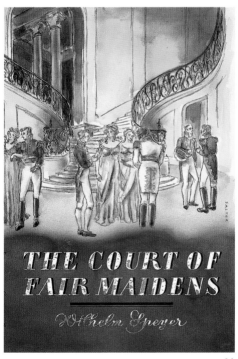

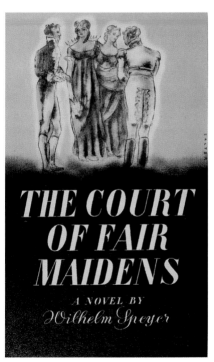

85

86

87

FIGURE 88. Simon & Schuster, 1936.
The piano scores in this series called on Salter's training as a stage designer to depict ambitious opera sets.

FIGURE 89. Random House, 1936.
Salter's signature airbrush technique creates an eerie view of a house through foreground foliage.

FIGURE 90. Viking, 1936.
This atmospheric cover conveys a psychological drama by pulling the viewer's and soldier's gaze alike into no-man's-land to contemplate a hero's death.

88

89

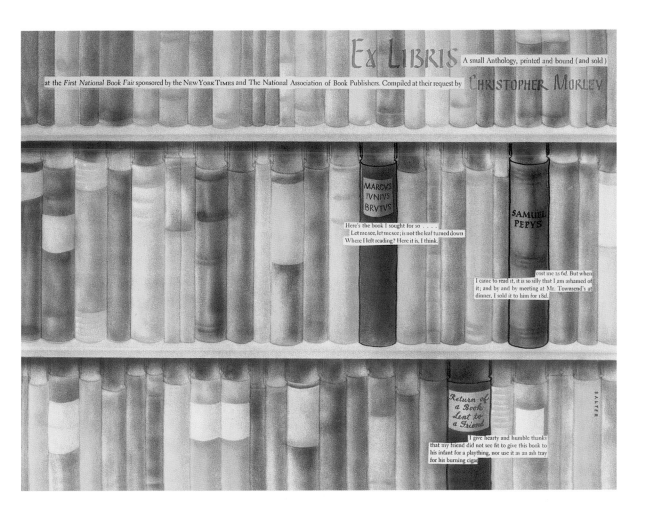

FIGURE 91. New York Times, 1936.
Images of books cover a collection of quotations about
books and reading.

FIGURE 92. Triangle, 1936.

FIGURE 93. Oxford University Press and Methuen, 1937.

FIGURE 94. Knopf, 1937.
Salter's selection was crucial to his visual message. In this
example details of human form alone convey the drama.
Identities are erased, but the viewer senses a struggle.

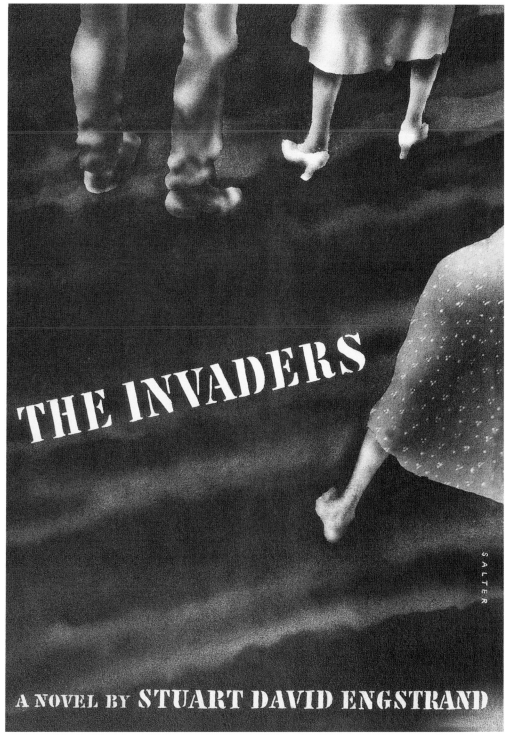

94

95 96

FIGURE 95. Oxford University Press, 1937.
For this design Salter reaches back to his great success of 1929, *Berlin
Alexanderplatz* (FIG. 61). This concept, although exquisite, was wasted on
a lesser book.

FIGURE 96. Harper, 1937.
A multilayered, symbolic scene evokes both the mystical and historical
connotations of Silone's antifascist novel.

FIGURE 97. Knopf, 1937.
Salter was proud of his American design for Kafka's novel. His illustrations
suggest the ambiguity between the protagonist's reality and the surreal
events he experiences.

OF MICE
AND MEN

John Steinbeck

—

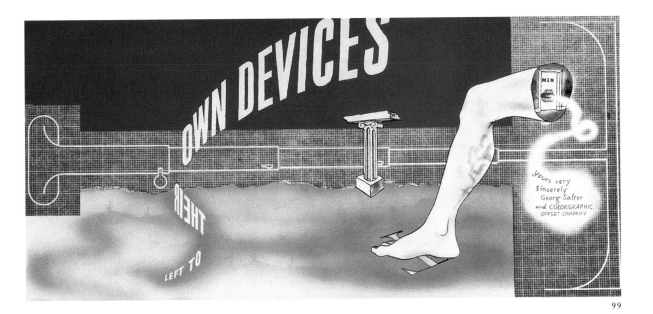

FIGURE 98. Covici-Friede, 1937.
Salter's trial binding design for *Of Mice and Men* is a true rarity. Published in a very small number between the first and second printings, this interim edition was discontinued after the standard binding and jacket were issued.

FIGURE 99. The Typophiles, 1937.

FIGURE 100. Title list for Borzoi Books, 1937.
Alfred A. Knopf published some of his best-designed books under the Borzoi imprint. The freehand fluidity of Salter's lettering matches the speed of the trademark wolfhound.

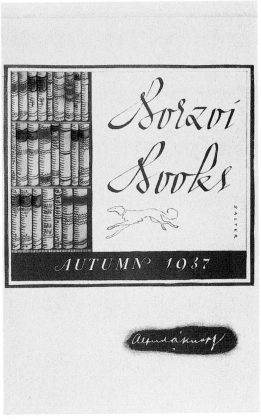

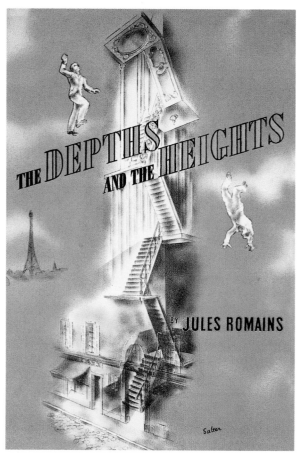

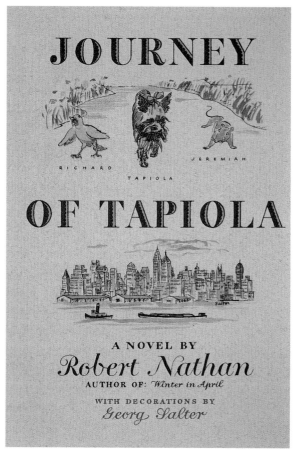

FIGURE 101. Knopf 1937.
By this period Salter was able to use a technique called "dropout," or lettering done on a second, white sheet. The final cover combines negatives of both the text and art so the letters are "reversed out" on the colored background. With this system the artist does not have to letter directly over the airbrush work.

FIGURES 102 AND 103. Knopf, 1938.
The jacket and binding for these canine adventures offer a visual invitation to follow the dog on its travels.

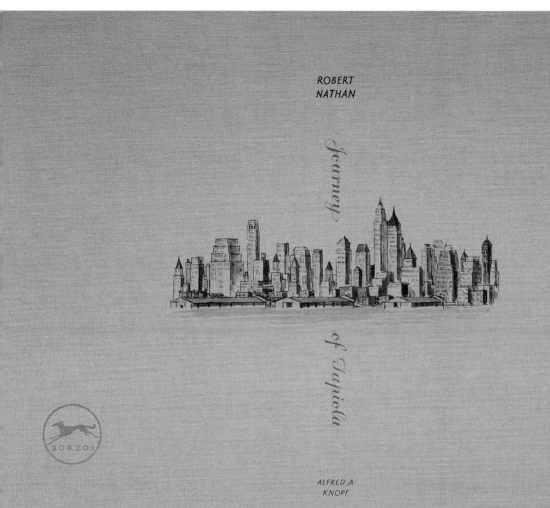

ROBERT
NATHAN

Journey

of Tapiola

ALFRED·A·
KNOPF

104

105

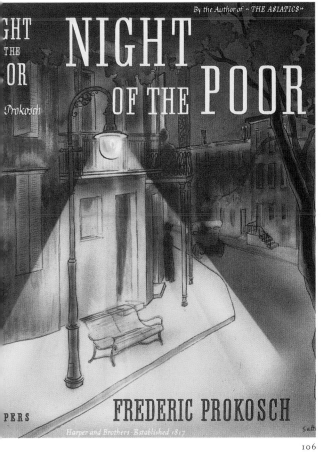

106

107

FIGURE 104. Knopf, 1938.

FIGURE 105. Simon & Schuster, 1936.
A cover designed to span front and back has a panoramic effect that proclaims the contents even when the book is lying face down—a position that otherwise renders it visually anonymous.

FIGURES 106 (Harpers, 1939) and 107 (Harpers, 1941).
Salter did some of his best pictorial covers for books by Prokosch, a novelist and gifted travel writer.

The Missing Miniature

The
Missing
Miniature

by
Erich Kästner

Alfred·A·Knopf

Those who read for pleasure
will find plenty of it in this rare
combination of joyous comedy
and wildly exciting mystery.

by Erich Kästner

WILLIAM LYON PHEL
"It is an absolutely ench
book. The ingredients of
and excitement are perfe
mingled. The humor is
spontaneous, graceful, de

For a fuller description of th
tale see the back of the wrapp

FIGURE 108. Knopf, 1937.
One always has to inspect the entire cover to appreciate Salter's effects.
For this humorous mystery tale he has placed an enigmatic observer
inside the front flap.

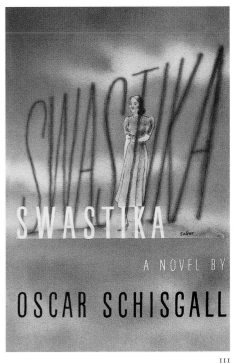

109

110

111

FIGURE 109. Simon & Schuster, 1937.

FIGURE 110. Knopf, 1938.
The former chancellor of Austria, who was unsuccessful in preventing the German annexation of his country in 1938, was imprisoned by the Nazis after the *Anschluss*. As the focus for his design, Salter uses the crutch cross, party symbol of Schuschnigg's pro-Fascist *Vaterländische Front*.

FIGURE 111. Knopf, 1938.

*Two examples of original designs that gained
greater coherence through simplification.*

FIGURE 112. Salter's original sketch for Graham Greene's novel is much
more detailed and complex than the published version.

FIGURE 113. Viking, 1938.
The final design omitted the disturbing eye, which may have seemed an
incongruous companion to the gramophone.

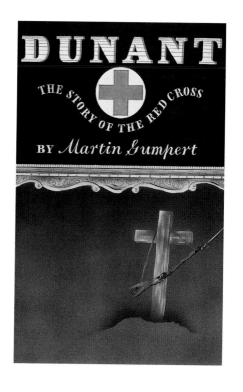

FIGURE 114. Original design.

FIGURE 115. Oxford University Press, 1938.
The vibrant color scheme and central design of Salter's final version have a
direct message.

FIGURE 116. Knopf, 1941.
The graceful flourishes of Salter's lettering echo the bird in flight. The Book
Jacket Designers Guild chose this design as one of the fifty best jackets of 1941.

THE DESIGN LEGACY OF GEORGE SALTER

117

FIGURE 117. Publisher's logo for Alliance (N.Y.)

FIGURE 118. Alliance, 1939.
Salter draws on Albrecht Dürer's woodcut of the *Four Horsemen of the Apocalypse* to make a statement about National Socialism. Below the great symbolic juggernaut the real people suffer.

FIGURE 119. Alliance, 1939.
Between 1939 and 1942 Salter designed twelve covers for Alliance Book corporation. Many of the volumes were topical works by German exiles.

FIGURE 120. Alliance, 1939.
The blood-stained balance sheet of Hitler's banker makes the connection between finance and militarism.

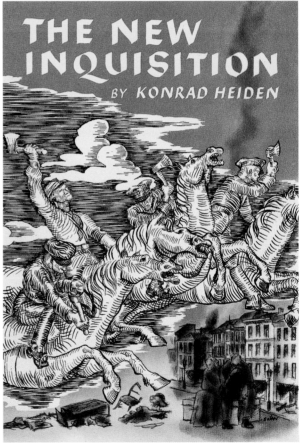

118

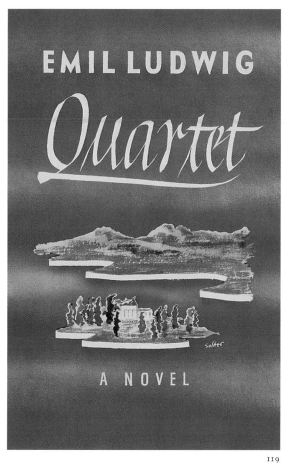

119

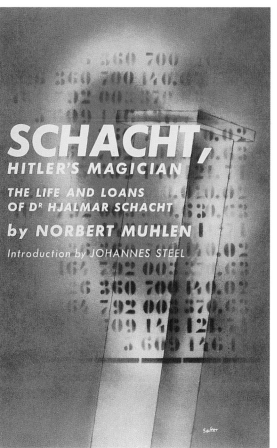

120

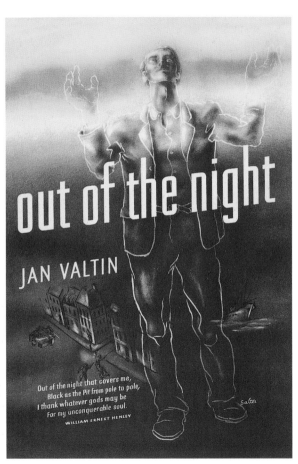

FIGURE 121. Alliance, 1941.
This 700-page best-seller is a harrowing exposé of Nazi prisons and
Stalinist reprisals. By capturing the dignity of individual suffering,
Salter's jacket art helped fuel this marketing sensation.

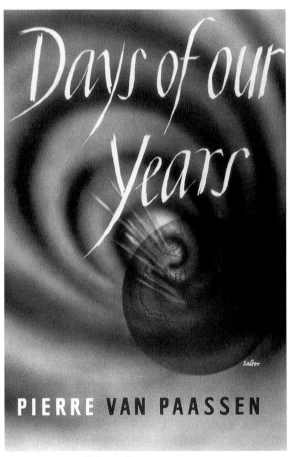

FIGURE 122. Hillman-Curl, 1939.

FIGURE 123. Logo for the publishing house L. B. Fischer (New York). When Gottfried Bermann-Fischer and his partner Fritz Landshoff gained a foothold in New York, they named their firm for the *L* in Landshoff and the *B* in Bermann, while paying homage to the publishing house of S. Fischer. Salter designed an elegant calligraphic rebus for the new firm.

FIGURE 124. American Mercury, 1940.
The oversized figure with his swelled head is an apt visual metaphor for the pupil who has outgrown his teacher.

FIGURE 125. Columbia University Press, 1940.
An understated, schematic representation of the destruction of Rotterdam.

FIGURE 126. L. B. Fischer, 1942.
Salter used a historical woodcut in his design of this book, which was one of the most widely translated German works of the decade.

FIGURE 127. L. B. Fischer, 1943.
Salter created an honor roll of contemporary literati and émigré culture that continues on the back of the jacket.

FIGURE 128. Holt, 1942.
One of Salter's most beautiful panoramic covers presents the story of three navy fliers adrift in the Pacific for thirty-four days.

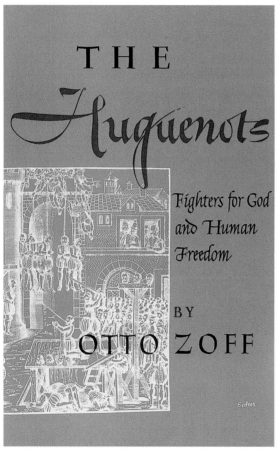

126

127

THE
Raft

ROBERT
TRUMBULL

THE *Raft*

"The story that generations of Americans will
be telling their children to illustrate man's
ability to master any fate"

Holt

ROBERT TRUMBULL

128

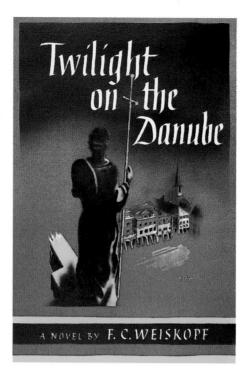

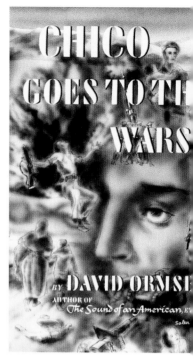

129

130

FIGURE 129. Knopf, 1944.

The suggestive interplay among the title, which broadcasts the drama of the plot; the modified *Fraktur* lettering, which conveys German complicity; and the barren scene of the crime itself—predicts the serious political content.

FIGURE 130. Knopf, 1946.

FIGURE 131. Dutton, 1943.

Open eyes signal psychological insight for Salter. In this depiction of war, artistic simultaneity expresses the protagonist's mind crowded with memories. The soldier falling backwards is drawn from a famous contemporary photograph by Robert Capa, "Death of a Nationalist Soldier."

FIGURE 132. Knopf, 1946.

Strong color contrasts, spare use of detail, and an eye positioned just off center make this face both alluring and sinister. For his inspiration, Salter drew on a 1930 perfume advertisement from a magazine that also featured his own work.

east of
midnight

a novel by
Forrest Rosaire

Salter

FIGURE 133. Random House, 1942.
This sumptuous design is rich in colorful details, which are repeated
on the endpapers inside. The book's immediate popularity led to a
Book of the Month Club edition in the same year, for which Salter
did a simpler cover and binding.

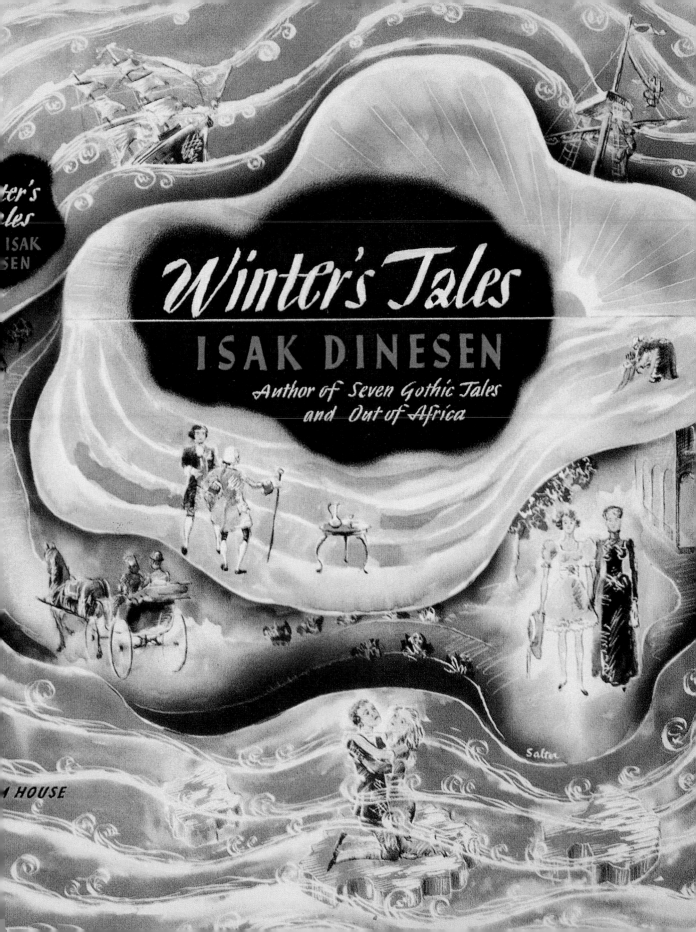

FIGURE 134. David McKay, 1939.

FIGURE 135. Houghton Mifflin, 1943.
This cityscape seems to be viewed from a window on the opposite side of the street. The perspective of the lettered title is integrated pictorially into the scene to suggest a roof-mounted sign.

FIGURE 136. Macmillan, 1945.
Dramatic lettering covers the courtroom scene, obscuring the accused.
The design is reminiscent Salter's 1937 jacket for Kafka's *The Trial.*

FIGURE 137. Random House, 1946.

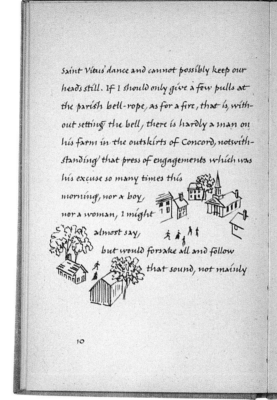

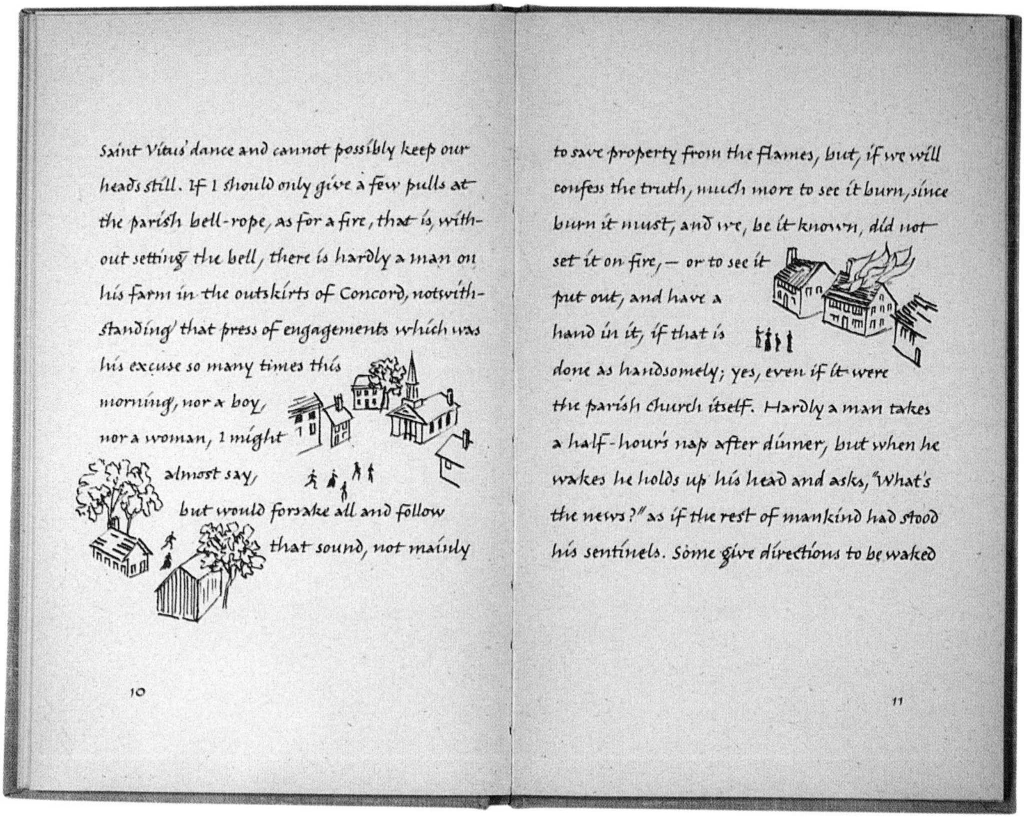

138

FIGURE 138. Archway Press, 1946.
This hand-lettered volume of selections from *Walden* appeared in a
series commissioned from great contemporary calligraphers.

FIGURE 139. Pocket Books, 1942.
In the early 1940s Salter designed four covers for Pocket Books. The
Walt Disney film appeared in the same year as this paperback.

10

BAMBI

Felix Salten

Salter

Pocket **BOOK** *edition* **COMPLETE AND UNABRIDGED**

139

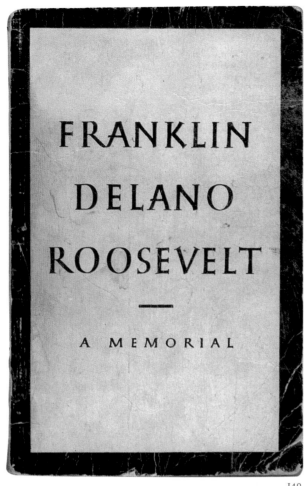

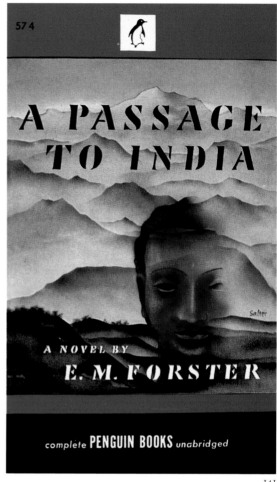

140

141

FIGURE 140. Pocket Books, 1945.

FIGURE 141. Penguin, 1946.
One of six designs Salter produced for Penguin's mass-market
paperbacks in 1946.

FIGURE 142. Knopf, 1947.
For one of his most striking covers, Salter places the shadowy figure of
the novel's eccentric narrator in front of a stylized library, books that will
ultimately be consumed by fire.

The Tower of Babel

Babel

BY

Elias Canetti

TRANSLATED BY *C. V. Wedgwood*

BORZOI BOOKS

A. Knopf

Salter

The combination of author, publisher, and designer made these some of the best-selling literary works at their time. Thomas Mann was pleased with the way Salter's colorful jackets (figures 143–148) reached out to the American market. Since the translation copyrights of these editions have elapsed, Mann's works have been reissued in new—though not always improved—translations and designs.

FIGURE 143. Knopf, 1948.

FIGURE 144. Knopf, 1951.

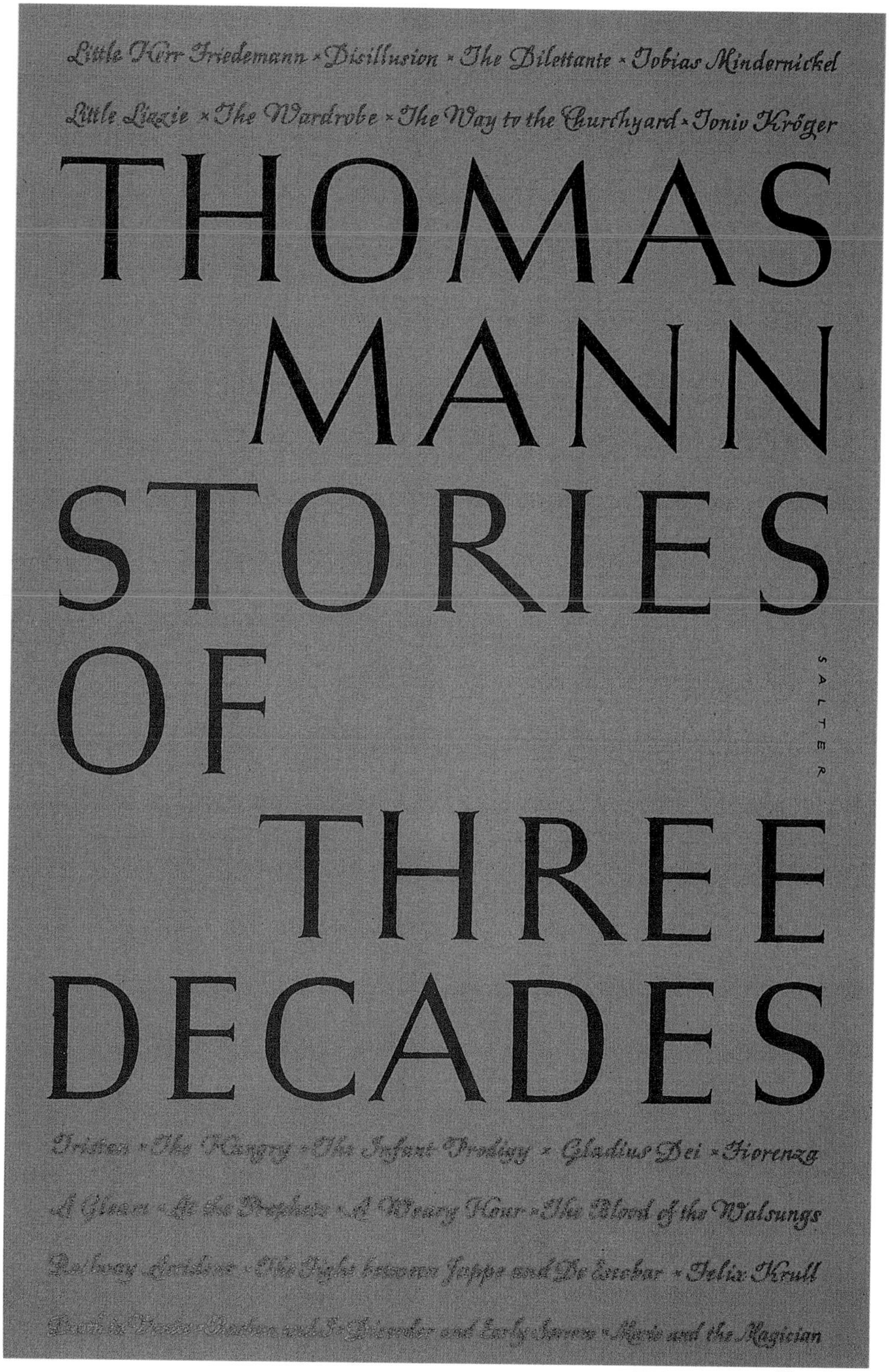

Little Herr Friedemann · Disillusion · The Dilettante · Tobias Mindernickel
Little Lizzie · The Wardrobe · The Way to the Churchyard · Tonio Kröger

THOMAS MANN STORIES OF THREE DECADES

Tristan · The Hungry · The Infant Prodigy · Gladius Dei · Fiorenza
A Gleam · At the Prophet's · A Weary Hour · The Blood of the Walsungs
Railway Accident · The Fight between Jappe and Do Escobar · Felix Krull
Death in Venice · Disorder and Early Sorrow · Mario and the Magician

SALTER

FIGURE 145. Knopf, 1937.

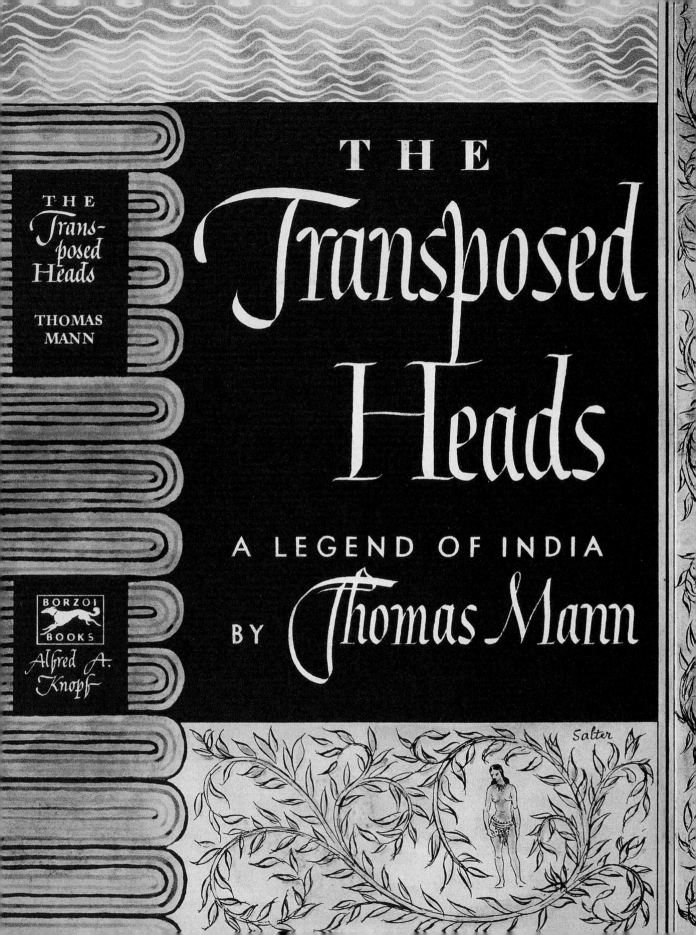

THE
Trans-
posed
Heads

THOMAS
MANN

BORZOI
BOOKS

Alfred A.
Knopf

THE
Transposed
Heads

A LEGEND OF INDIA
BY Thomas Mann

Salter

FIGURE 146. Knopf, 1941.

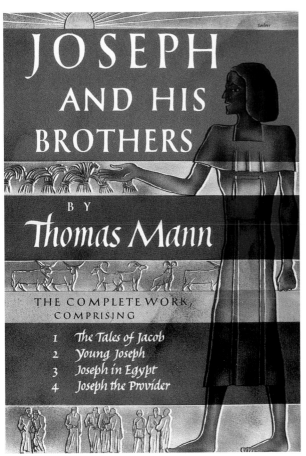

FIGURE 147. Knopf, 1948.

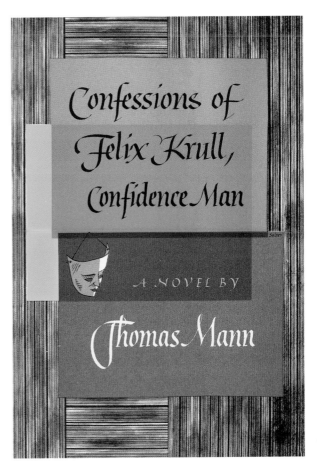

FIGURE 148. Knopf, 1955.

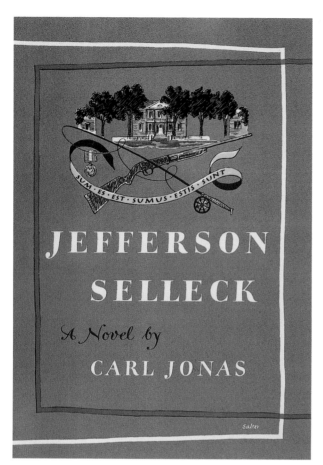

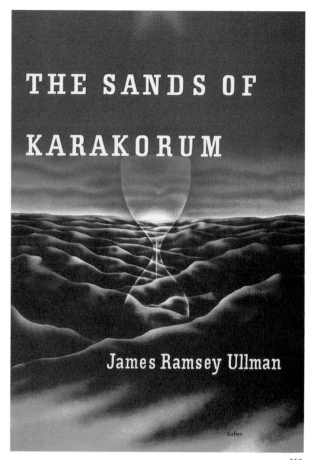

149

150

FIGURE 149. Little, Brown, 1952.
This allusive design was meant to suggest aspects of the main character's life, like
his classical education and his love of the outdoors. One bookseller, stymied by the
visual riddle, complained about Salter's tendency to produce "Guess-What Jackets."
A productive exchange ensued in which Salter emphasized that such designs were
calculated to make people read the flap copy.

FIGURE 150. Lippincott, 1953.
Salter's airbrush technique merges the desert sands with the sands of time.

FIGURE 151. Knopf, 1960.
Salter's abstract design prevailed over the author's own wish to present images of
amputee soldiers against a background of mutilation. The temptation to depict graphically some of the grim content of the novel was great (and encouraged by the editorial
staff), but Salter instead chose a symbolic approach showing battered Venetian blinds
to symbolize a state of despair about cultural dissolution in postwar Germany.

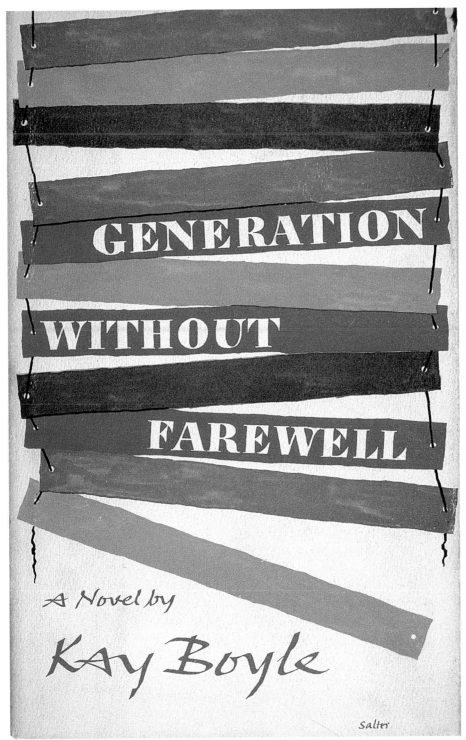

GENERATION WITHOUT FAREWELL

A Novel by

KAy Boyle

Salter

151

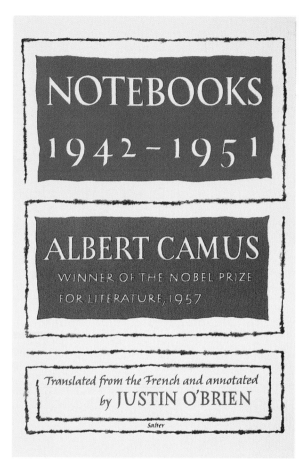

FIGURE 152. Knopf, 1963.

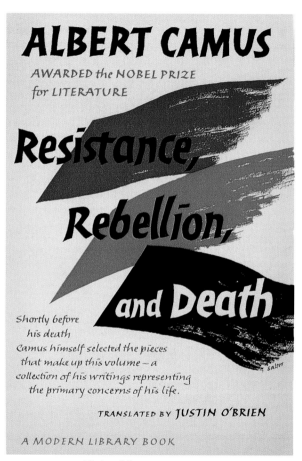

FIGURE 153. Modern Library, 1963.

FIGURE 154. Atheneum, 1963.

FIGURE 155. Knopf, 1959.

FIGURE 156. Knopf, 1950.
Salter's symbolism produced one of his most successful covers for Knopf. Figures outlined in white represent characters remembered or dead; the narrator in the foreground pieces his tale together from fragments that have survived the Warsaw ghetto.

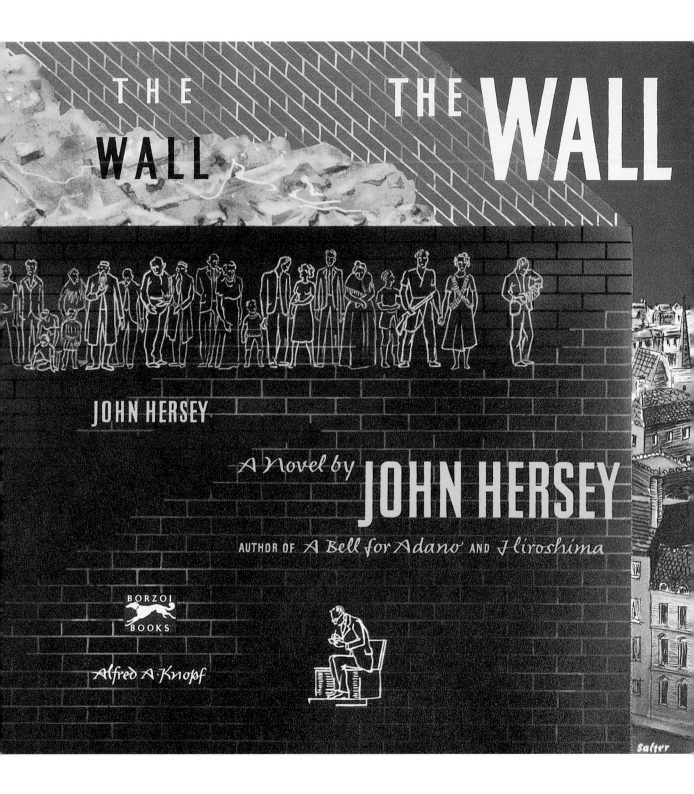

THE WALL

THE WALL

JOHN HERSEY

A Novel by JOHN HERSEY

AUTHOR OF *A Bell for Adano* AND *Hiroshima*

BORZOI BOOKS

Alfred A. Knopf

Salter

THE QUEST

A NOVEL BY

Elisabeth Langgässer

157

158   159   160

FIGURE 157. Knopf, 1960.

The art department at Knopf was as pleased with this jacket as Salter
was. The countless hours he spent on revisions paid off in a design that
symbolically imparts the book's plot: a search for spiritual meaning.

FIGURE 158. Knopf, 1951.

In this clever exercise in color theory, the bands of primary colors cross
each other to produce the secondary.

FIGURE 159. Bobbs-Merrill, 1951.

Salter captures the mood of desolation and grief in this quasi-documentary
novel about the Huk rebellion in the Philippines. Rice is the central
symbol around which the wind of freedom blows.

FIGURE 160. Little, Brown, 1952.

FIGURE 161. Bobbs-Merrill, 1952.
Salter's imagery represents the book's message of the descent into oblivion through drug abuse. The stairway seems to be constructed of folded cigarette papers.

FIGURE 162. Random House, 1952.
The bright, urban, neon lettering in front of the old homestead thematizes the clash of values in this novel.

FIGURE 163. Little, Brown, 1953.

FIGURES 164 AND 165. Knopf, 1961.
Huge, dense novels can present complex design tasks. Here the labyrinthine web that covers the back and spine of the slipcase dwarfs the figure of the narrator—one of Salter's favorite devices for thematizing reading. The binding cloth of the volumes continues the motif.

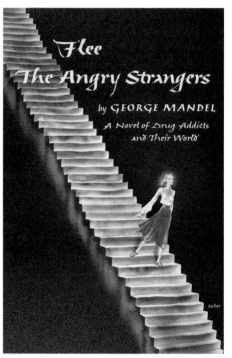

161

162

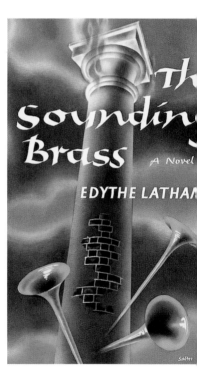

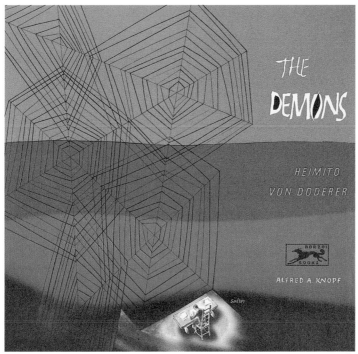

164

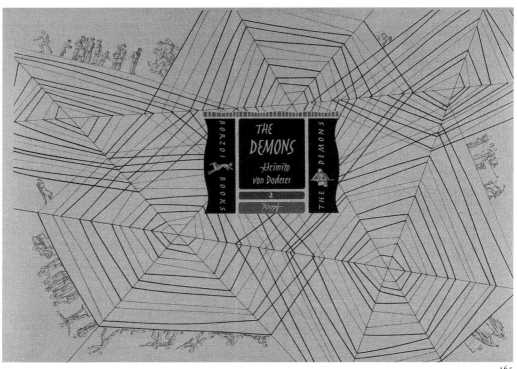

165

Two covers from the same year show Salter's loose style of lettering and intentionally naïve draftsmanship presenting humorous subjects.

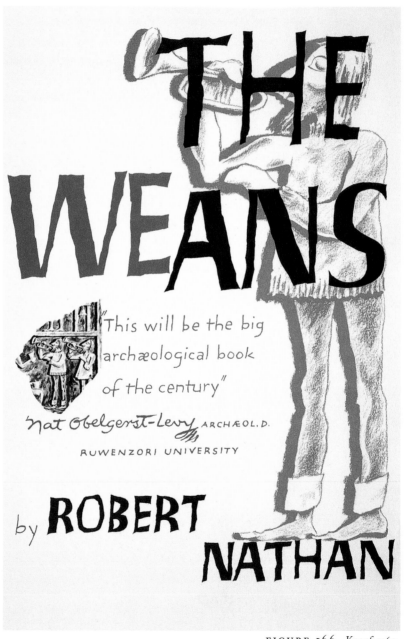

FIGURE 166. Knopf, 1960.

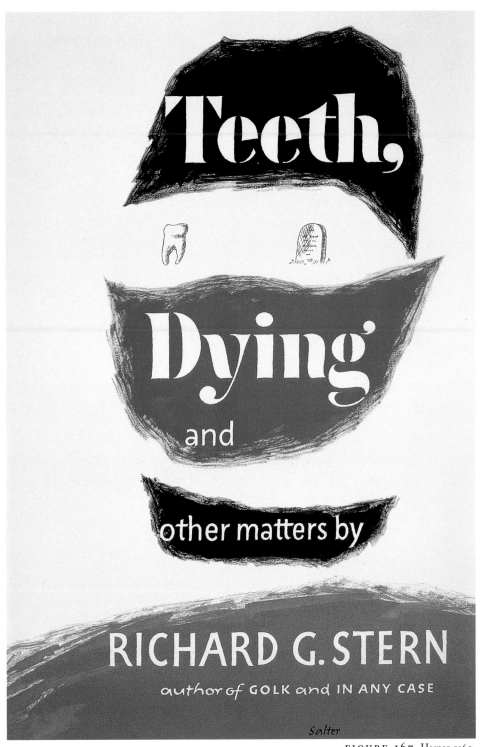

Teeth,

Dying

and

other matters by

RICHARD G. STERN

author of GOLK and IN ANY CASE

Salter

FIGURE 167. Harper, 1960.

MIRACLE
IN
BRITTANY

MILDRED
JORDAN

KNOPF

169

FIGURE 168. Knopf, 1950.
The little Breton town stretches across the front and back of the panoramic design of the book's decorated binding.

FIGURE 169. Bobbs-Merrill, 1951.
Symbolic bands of color convey various levels of the novel, while the bleak street scene suggests the despondency of empty lives in this tale of revenge, alcoholism, and death.

FIGURE 170. Knopf, 1954.
A bleak winter landscape crisscrossed by circuitous paths is the objective correlative for Kafka's existential world.

170

171

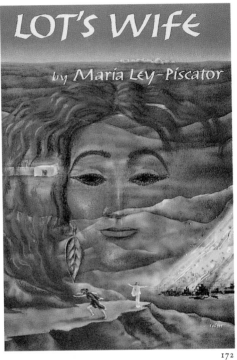

172

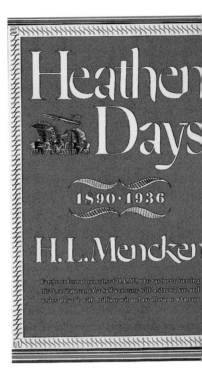

FIGURE 171. Harcourt, Brace, 1954.

FIGURE 172. Bobbs-Merrill, 1954.

FIGURE 173. Knopf, 1955.

174

175

FIGURES 174 AND 175. Knopf, 1956.
Salter designed several books by Robert Nathan for Knopf. The jacket for this
novel about divine intervention shows human drama unfolding, witnessed by the
saints in heaven. The cover takes us metaphysically higher still to the prime
observer. Salter was expert at creating an interplay between jacket and cover,
which then continues on the title page.

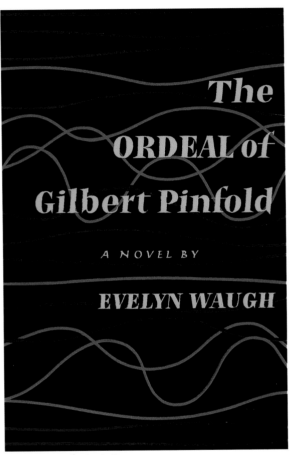

FIGURE 176. Little, Brown, 1957.
These tangled, disjointed strands gain symbolic significance when one reads this tale of a neurological disorder and its treatment.

FIGURE 177. Knopf, 1959.
Salter rarely depicted formulaic open doors or windows on a book jacket unless they hinted at an important element of the text.

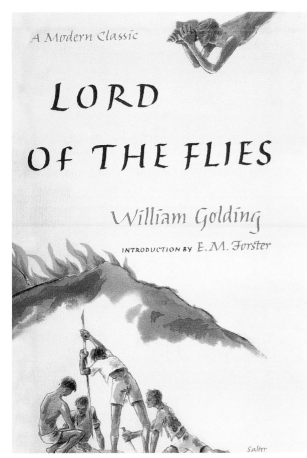

FIGURE 178. Coward-McCann, 1962.
Salter repeats the ominous sharpened stick from this pictorial,
panoramic design on the book's binding.

FIGURE 179. Atheneum, 1960.
These grotesque profiles, which hardly seem to be by the
same hand that designed *Lord of the Flies*, testify to the artist's
versatility.

These mass-market paperbacks show off Salter's functional yet stylish lettering. They also show his predilection for using the cover to communicate details of a book's contents.

FIGURE 180. Viking, 1954.

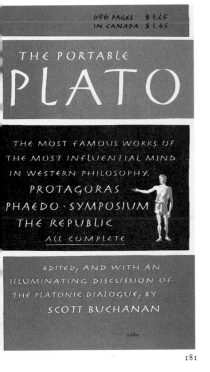

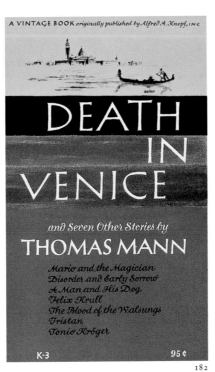

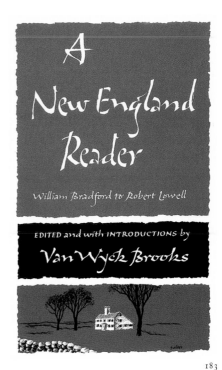

181

182

183

FIGURE 181. Viking, 1966.

FIGURE 182. Vintage, 1954.

FIGURE 183. Atheneum, 1962.

FIGURE 184. Knopf, 1956.

FIGURE 185. Knopf, 1956.

After seeing a draft of this cover design, the author contacted the artist to advise him about the shape of a Chinese junk. Salter corrected the boat to everyone's satisfaction.

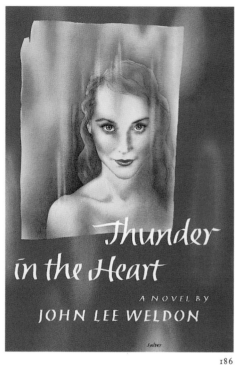

186

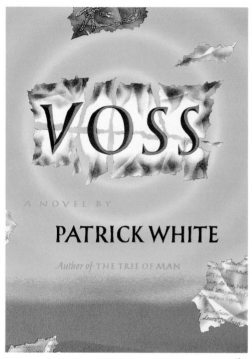

187

FIGURE 186. Random House, 1954.

FIGURE 187. Viking, 1957.
Salter employs fragmentary notes and snippets of writing by which
to suggest the emotional plot of this story of love and adventure in
nineteenth-century Australia.

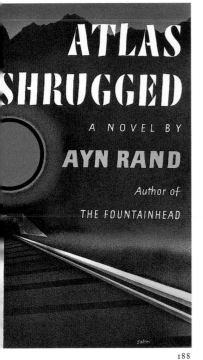

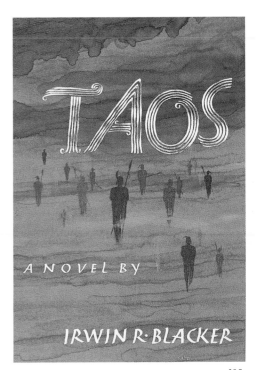

188   189   190

FIGURE 188. Random House, 1957. Salter wrote that he always read a book
for which he designed the cover, but he did not need to read all 1168 pages of
Ayn Rand for this imagery. Instead, he drew his inspiration from an advertising
supplement in a 1930 journal that included an article about him.

FIGURE 189. Random House, 1959.

FIGURE 190. World, 1959.

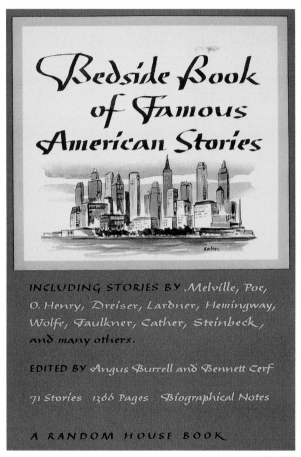

191

FIGURE 191. Random House, 1960.

FIGURE 192. Atheneum, 1965.
Bassani's story tells of a family so attached to property that they cannot flee persecution. Salter's anthropomorphic trees represent psychological roots to a place.

The Garden
of the Finzi-Continis

A Novel by

Giorgio Bassani

Salter

192

161   THE DESIGN LEGACY OF GEORGE SALTER

O Stern und Blume,

Geist und Kleid,

Lieb, Leid

und Zeit

und Ewigkeit!

LV

193

FIGURES 193–195. *Am Wegesrand (By the Wayside),* published
in Germany by Der Goldene Brunnen in 1961, is the most ambitious
collaboration undertaken by Salter and his fellow designer, Fritz Kredel.
Kredel made the twenty-four woodcuts of meadow flowers while
Salter's calligraphy supplied the verses. It is a masterpiece of delicate
images and intimate poetry.

194

195

Salter was the art director for Mercury Publications, for which he designed hundreds of covers for digests in various series.

196

FIGURE 196. Gift card for subscribers, 1950.

FIGURE 197. June 1955.
A praying mantis flew through Salter's open window one summer day and landed on his drawing table. He fed the insect sugar water on a pipe cleaner as he painted it for a couple of different covers in this series.

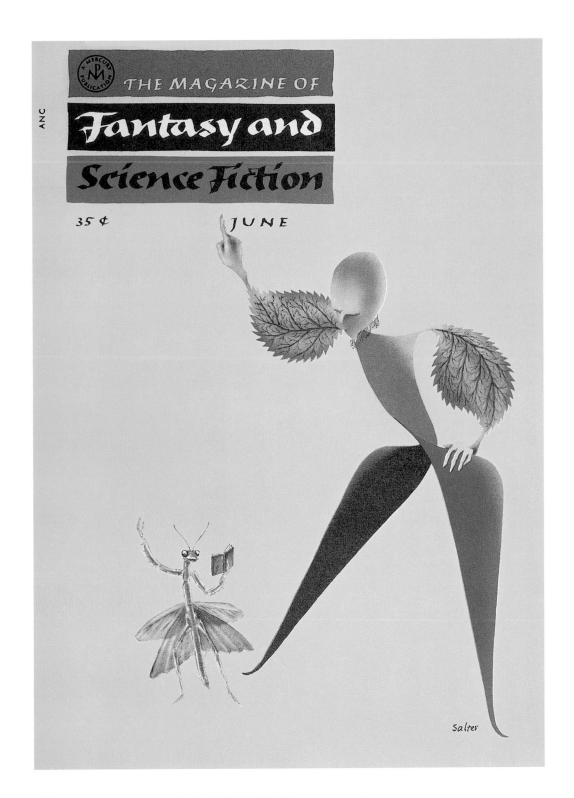

THE MAGAZINE OF
Fantasy and
Science Fiction

35¢   JUNE

Salter

198

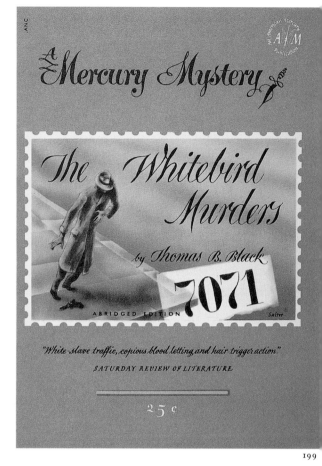

199

FIGURE 198. May 1945.
Omnibook printed abridged versions of best-sellers. This number was planned for the American troops overseas when the end of the war in Europe was imminent. The airbrushed chain in the foreground hints at the constraints on the young queen.

FIGURE 199. (Date unknown).
When Salter took over as art director of Mercury Publications in 1938, he gave the mystery digests a consistent format through a postage stamp window. He usually limited these jobs to the depiction of a corpse or someone in imminent danger of becoming one. In every case, his stylish lettering is eye catching.

FIGURE 200. Fall 1941.
A clever image from the first year of the digest's publication shows the crime confronting its perpetrator in newspaper headlines.

FIGURE 201. May 1952.

FIGURE 202. December 1952.

FIGURE 203. September 1950.

200

201

202

203

204

FIGURE 204. November 1947.

FIGURE 205. January 1943.

FIGURE 206. July 1944.

FIGURE 207. September 1954.
Salter intentionally modeled the face of his victim on the features of
Senator Joseph McCarthy, who at the time was in the news for his
zealous, anti-Communist activity.

FIGURE 208. March 1953.
The background figure of Athena by Praxiteles establishes the allusio
to antiquity.

FIGURE 209. April 1954.
The detailed eye in the background produces a connection to the care
modeled hand in the foreground, linking thought and deed in this
psychologically dramatic scene.

206

207

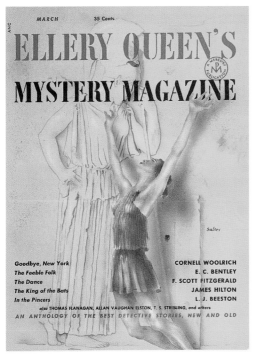

208

209

Salter designed more than just jackets. The following shows his work on logos, posters, fonts, and other miscellaneous items.

THE LITTLE
GREEK ALPHABET BOOK

ΑΒΓΔ

by Ennis Rees

Designed and illustrated by George Salter

FIGURE 210. Prentice Hall, 1968.
This charming children's book was published after Salter's death. He cleverly used crayon to imitate the style of a coloring book, a technique the publisher had to be persuaded to accept.

FIGURE 211. Bookplate for the Book of the Month Club, 1938.

FIGURES 212 AND 213. Two jobs with a holiday theme. The Christmas carol dates from the 1940s. In 1962 S⸱ donated the second work to the United Nations for a popul⸱ UNICEF card.

211

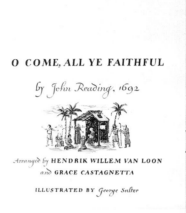

O COME, ALL YE FAITHFUL

by John Reading, 1692

Arranged by **HENDRIK WILLEM VAN LOON**
and **GRACE CASTAGNETTA**

ILLUSTRATED BY *George Salter*

212

213

214

215

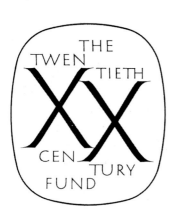

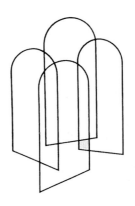

217

218

FIGURE 214. Mercury Publications, 1950.

FIGURE 215. Basic Books, 1953.

FIGURE 216. Columbia University Press, 1937.

FIGURE 217. Twentieth Century Fund, 1960.

FIGURE 218. Lincoln Center for the Performing Arts, 1960.

FIGURE 219. Book Jacket Designers Guild, 1948.

FIGURE 220. One of the few jobs Salter did for the U.S. Government Printing Office during the Depression.

LET'S WORK FOR AMERICA

GOOD
LOSER
CLUB

Salter

FIGURES 221 AND 222. Salter believed that handwriting was the mother of typography. In 1935 he designed a ribbon font called Flex. It is a presentation typeface with three-dimensional qualities inspired by calligraphy.

This is Flex!

A B C D E F G H I J
K L M N O P Q R S
T U V W X Y Z & - $
a b c d e f g h i j k l m n o p q r s t
u v w x y z fi ff ffi ffl " ? . , ! - ; :
1 2 3 4 5 6 7 8 9 0

For proofs in 30 - 48 - 60 Point
Call An. 0409 - Evergreen Press

FIGURE 223. Photo of George Salter by Alfred E. Knopf (March 1965).

Appendix A
Salter's Designs for the German Book Market, 1922–1934

I have been able to draw upon Salter's own hand-written list of commissions, which he began keeping in New York after 1934. Salter kept not only a list of his various jobs, which is almost complete, but also files of the book jackets he designed. When these were sent to him by publishers, he would trim them of their flap copy and file them by publisher. For the most part, these correlate to his dated list. Unfortunately, his personal archive is far from complete. Many designs from the Berlin period are missing. While Salter's list accounts for most of his American designs, I have discovered and corrected inconsistencies and added titles that help reconstruct the list of his pre-exile work.

Translations of terms:
Cover, binding: Einband
Cover design: Einbandgestaltung
Design: Ausstattung
Jacket, book jacket: Schutzumschlag
Series: Reihe
Wrappers: Broschur, broschiert

Abbreviations in text;
Ed. (edition; editor); Ausgabe; Herausgeber
No. (number): Heft
Vol. (volume): Jahrgang; Band.
Trans. (translator): Übersetzer

Note: In the following list, the designation "binding" does not differentiate between a decorated, pictorial cover and a stamped, typographic binding.

Germany

Paul Aretz (Berlin)
Bazhanov, Boris Georgievich. *Stalin: der rote Diktator*. Trans. Paul Murault, 1931. Jacket, binding.

Bibliographisches Institut (Leipzig)
Matthias, Leo. *Griff in den Orient: Eine Reise und etwas mehr*, 1931. Jacket, binding.

Breitkopf und Härtel (Leipzig)
Dahn, Felix. *Ein Kampf um Rom*. Historischer Roman. Ungekürzte Volksausgabe, 1930. Jacket.

Deutsche Buch-Gemeinschaft (Berlin)
Berger, Arthur. *Afrika: Schwarz oder Weiß; Antlitz und Schicksal des dunklen Erdteils*, 1932. Binding.

Deutsche Verlags-Anstalt (Stuttgart, Berlin)
Essad Bey [Leo Noussimbaum]. *Mohammed: Öl und Blut im Orient*, 1929. Jacket, binding.
Kästner, Erich. *Fabian, die Geschichte eines Moralisten*, 1931. Jacket, binding.
Wegner, Armin T. *Fünf Finger über dir: Bekenntnis eines Menschen in dieser Zeit*, 1930. Binding.

Dietrich Reimer; Ernst Vohsen (Berlin)
Eipper, Paul. *Zirkus: Tiere, Menschen, Wanderseligkeit*, 1930. Jacket, binding.
Lukasch, Iwan. *Moskau in Flammen*. Roman. Trans. Oskar von Riesemann, 1931. Jacket, binding.

Dietrich Reimer Verlag (Berlin & Leipzig)
Colin, Paul. *James Ensor*. Junge Kunst 59, 1931. Binding.
Crevel, René, and Georg Biermann. *Renée Sintenis*. Junge Kunst 57, 1930. Binding.
Hartlaub, Gustav Friedrich. *Vincent Van Gogh*, 1930. Jacket, binding.
Justi, Ludwig. *Georg Kolbe*. Junge Kunst 60, 1931. Binding.
Mainzer, Ferdinand. *Siciliana: Aus griechisch-römischer Zeit*, 1930. Jacket, binding.
Simon, Heinrich. *Max Beckmann*. Junge Kunst 56, 1930. Binding.
Thormaehlen, Ludwig. *Erich Heckel*. Junge Kunst 58, 1931. Binding.
Weihnachtskatalog 1930, 1930. Wrappers.

Gebrüder Enoch Verlag (Hamburg)
Belzner, Emil. *Marschieren—nicht träumen; Zerstörte Erinnerungen*. Roman, 1931. Jacket, binding.
Benninghoff, Ludwig. *Gustav Adolf: eine Königssaga*, 1932. Jacket.
Blitz, Karl. *Studienrat Hancke*. Roman, 1930. Jacket.
Cisek, O. W. (Oscar Walter). *Die Tataren*. Erzählungen, 1929. Jacket, binding.
———. *Unbequeme Liebe*. Roman, 1932. Jacket, binding.
Ferber, Edna. *Cimarron*. Roman. Trans. Gertrud von Hollander, 1931. Jacket, binding.
Ferreira de Castro, Josef Maria. *Die Kautschukzapfer: Roman aus dem brasilianischen Urwald* [A selva]. Trans. Arnold Höllriegel, 1933. Binding.
Sander, Ernst [Leo]. *Die Lehrjahre des Herzens*. Roman, 1931. Jacket.

Grethlein & Co. (Leipzig, Zürich)
Bloem, Walter. *Frontsoldaten*. Roman, 1930. Jacket, binding.

J. Engelhorn: J. Engelhorns Nachf. A. Spemann (Stuttgart)
Haensel, Carl. *Das war Münchhausen*. Roman aus Tatsachen, 1933. Jacket, binding.

Kluge, Kurt. *Der Glockengiesser Christoph Mahr*. Roman, 1934. Jacket.
———. *Die silberne Windfahne*. Roman, 1934. Jacket.
Langewiesche, Wolfgang Ernst. *Das amerikanische Abenteuer: deutscher Werkstudent in U.S.A.*, 1933. Jacket, binding.
Thiess, Frank. *Die Verdammten*. Roman, 1930. Jacket, binding.

S. Fischer Verlag (Berlin)
Almanach 1932, 1931. Binding.
Almanach: das 48. Jahr. S. Fischer zum Gedächtnis, 1934.
Almanach für 1935, 1934. Cover design (wrappers).
Armstrong, Harold C. (Courteney). *Der graue Wolf: das Leben des Diktators Mustafa Kemal* [Grey Wolf, Mustafa Kemal: An Intimate Study of a Dictator]. Trans. Peter Wit, 1933. Jacket, binding.
Beer, Max. *Die Reise nach Genf*, 1932. Jacket, binding.
Conrad, Joseph. *Der Geheimagent* [The Secret Agent]. Roman. Trans. Ernst Wolfgang Freissler, 1931. Jacket.
———. *Der goldene Pfeil: Eine Geschichte zwischen zwei Aufzeichnungen* [The Arrow of Gold]. Trans. Elsie McCalman, 1932. Jacket.
———. *Das Herz der Finsternis* [Heart of Darkness]. Erzählung. Trans. Ernst W. Freissler, 1933. Jacket, binding.
———. *Die Rettung* [The Rescue: A Romance of the Shallows]. Trans. Elsie McCalman, 1931. Jacket, binding.
Crevel, René. *Der schwierige Tod* [La Mort difficile]. Roman. Trans. Hans Feist, 1930. Binding, jacket (using drawing of Crevel by C. von Ripper).
Döblin, Alfred. *Berlin Alexanderplatz: Die Geschichte vom Franz Biberkopf*, 1929. Jacket, binding.
———. *Giganten: Ein Abenteuerbuch*. Völlig veränderte Ausgabe von *Berge, Meere und Giganten* (1924), 1932. Jacket, binding.
Dos Passos, John. *Auf den Trümmern* [Nineteen-nineteen]. Roman zweier Kontinente. Trans. Paul Baudisch, 1932. Jacket, binding.
———. *Manhattan Transfer: Der Roman einer Stadt* [Manhattan Transfer]. Trans. Paul Baudisch, 1927. Jacket, binding.
———. *Der 42. Breitengrad* [The 42nd Parallel]. Roman. Trans. Paul Baudisch, 1930. Binding, jacket, title page.
Duhamel, Georges. *Spiegel der Zukunft: Europa oder Amerika* [Scènes de la vie future]. Trans. Käthe Rosenberg, 1931. Jacket, binding.
Flake, Otto. *Montijo, oder die Suche nach der Nation*. Roman, 1931. Jacket.
Fontane, Theodor. *L'Adultera: Cecile*. Zwei Romane, 1928. Jacket.
———. *Effi Briest*, 1928. Jacket.

———. *Irrungen Wirrungen: Frau Jenny Treibel*. Zwei Romane, 1928. Jacket.

———. *Der Stechlin*, 1928. Jacket.

Frank, Leonhard. *Von drei Millionen Drei*, 1932. Jacket design after George Grosz.

Garnett, David. *Die Heuschrecken kommen: Geschichte eines Rekordflugs* [The Grasshoppers Come]. Trans. Herbert Egon Herlitschka, 1933. Jacket, binding.

Grossmann, Stefan. *Ich war begeistert: Eine Lebensgeschichte*, 1930. Binding.

Hauptmann, Gerhart. *Das Meerwunder: Eine unwahrscheinliche Geschichte*, 1934. Cover illustration by Alfred Kubin; lettering by Salter.

———. *Um Volk und Geist: Ansprachen*, 1932. Binding.

Hauser, Heinrich. *Feldwege nach Chicago*, 1931. Jacket, binding.

———. *Die letzten Segelschiffe: Schiff, Mannschaft, Meer und Horizont*, 1930. Jacket, binding.

———. *Ein Mann lernt fliegen*, 1933. Jacket, binding.

———. *Noch nicht: Aufzeichnungen des Christian Heinrich Skeel*, 1932. Jacket, binding.

Hellpach, Willy. *Zwischen Wittenberg und Rom: Eine Pantheodizee zur Revision der Reformation*, 1931. Jacket.

Hesse, Hermann. *Weg nach Innen*. Vier Erzählungen, 1932. Binding and jacket, incorporating a watercolor by Hesse.

Heuser, Kurt. *Abenteuer in Vineta*. Roman, 1933. Jacket, binding.

———. *Buschkrieg*, 1933. Jacket, binding.

———. *Die Reise ins Innere*. Roman, 1931. Jacket, binding.

Holitscher, Arthur. *Wiedersehen mit Amerika: die Verwandlung der U.S.A.*, 1930. Jacket, binding.

Huelsenbeck, Richard. *Der Traum vom großen Glück*. Roman, 1933. Jacket, binding.

Karlweis, Marta. *Schwindel: Geschichte einer Realität*, 1931. Binding.

Keilson, Hans. *Das Leben geht weiter*. Roman, 1933. Jacket, binding.

Kellermann, Bernhard. *Die Stadt Anatol*. Roman, 1932. Jacket.

———. *Der Tunnel*. Roman. Sonderausgabe, 1931. Jacket, binding.

Lernet-Holenia, Alexander. *Ich war Jack Mortimer*. Roman, 1933. Jacket, binding.

———. *Die Standarte*. Roman, 1934. Jacket, binding.

Lewinsohn, Richard, and Franz Pick. *Sinn und Unsinn der Börse*, 1933. Jacket.

Lichnowsky, Mechtilde. *Kindheit*, 1934. Cover illustration by Jack von Reppert-Bismarck; lettering by Salter.

Mann, Thomas. *Königliche Hoheit*. Ungekürzte Sonderausgabe, 1932. Jacket, binding.

Marcu, Valeriu. *Die Geburt der Nationen: Von der Einheit des Glaubens zur Demokratie des Geldes*, 1931. Jacket, binding.

Mehnert, Klaus. *Die Jugend in Sowjet-Russland*, 1932. Jacket, binding.

Mehring, Walter. *Arche Noah S.O.S. Neues trostreiches Liederbuch*, 1931. Binding.

———. *Gedichte, Lieder, Chansons des Walter Mehring*, 1929. Binding by author; lettering by Salter.

Meier-Graefe, Julius. *Der Vater*. Roman, 1932. Jacket, binding.

Nemirowsky, Irene. *David Golder*. Roman. Trans. Magda Kahn, 1930. Jacket, binding.

O'Flaherty, Liam. *Die Bestie erwacht* [Return of the Brute]. Roman. Trans. Heinrich Hauser, 1930. Jacket, binding.

———. *Herr Gilhooley* [Mr. Gilhooley]. Trans. Joseph Sternemann, 1931. Jacket, binding.

———. *Verdammtes Gold* [The House of Gold]. Roman. Trans. Heinrich Hauser, 1931. Jacket, binding.

Priestley, J. B. (John Boynton) *Engelgasse* [Angel Pavement]. Trans. Paul Baudisch, 1931. Jacket.

———. *Englische Reise: Bericht einer Reise durch England im Herbst 1933* [English Journey]. Trans. Efraim Frisch, 1934. Jacket, binding.

Romains, Jules [Louis Farigoule]. *Jemand stirbt* [Mort de quelqin]. Roman. Trans. Nanni Collin, 1932. Jacket, binding.

———. *Kumpane* [Les copains]. Eine heitere Erzählung. Trans. Lissy Rademacher, 1930. Jacket, binding.

Saint-Exupéry, Antoine de. *Nachtflug* [Vol de Nuit]. Roman. Trans. Hans Reisiger, 1932. Jacket.

Schnitzler, Arthur. *Die kleine Komödie: Frühe Novellen*, 1932. Jacket, binding.

———. *Reigen: Zehn Dialoge*, 1931. Jacket.

———. *Traum und Schicksal*. Sieben Novellen. Sonderausgabe, 1931. Jacket, binding.

Sforza, Carlo. *Europäische Diktaturen* [Dittature e dittatori]. Trans. Hans Reisiger, 1932. Jacket.

———. *Die feindlichen Brüder: Inventur der europäischen Probleme* [Les Frères ennemis]. Trans. Hans Reisiger, 1933. Jacket, binding.

———. *Gestalten und Gestalter des heutigen Europa*. Trans. Hans Reisiger, 1931. Jacket, binding.

Shaw, George Bernard. *Junger Wein gärt* [Immaturity]. Roman. Trans. Siegfried Trebitsch, 1930. Jacket, binding.

Smith, Helen Zenna. *Mrs. Biest pfeift: Frauen an der Front* [Not so Quiet: Stepdaughters at War]. Trans. Hans Reisiger, 1930. Jacket, binding.

Steuermann, Carl [Otto Ruehle]. *Der Mensch auf der Flucht*, 1932. Jacket, binding.

Trotzki, Leo. *Geschichte der russischen Revolution*. 2 vols. Vol. I: *Februarrevolution*, 1931. Binding; Vol. II: *Oktoberrevolution*, 1933. Binding. The wrapper of the soft cover edition (vol. II) was a similar typographic design with some colors reversed.

———. *Mein Leben: Versuch einer Autobiographie*. Trans. Alexandra Ramm, 1930. Binding.

Wassermann, Jakob. *Bula Matari: das Leben Stanleys*, 1932. Jacket, binding.

———. *Christian Wahnschaffe*. Roman in zwei Büchern. Neubearbeitete Fassung. 2 vols., 1932. Jacket, binding.

———. *Christoph Columbus: Der Don Quichotte des Ozeans: Ein Porträt*, 1929. Jacket, binding.

———. *Der Fall Maurizius*. Roman, 1928. Jacket.

———. *Das Gänsemännchen*. Roman. Sonderausgabe, 1930. Cover design using a woodcut by Rolf von Hoerschelmann.

G. Grote Verlag (Berlin)

Grote's Almanach 49, 1931. Binding.

Raabe, Wilhelm. *Chronik der Sperlingsgasse*, 1931. Binding, jacket, six color illustrations.

Stinde, Julius. *Die Familie Buchholz: Aus dem Leben der Hauptstadt*, 1930. Binding, jacket, six color illustrations.

———. *Der Familie Buchholz zweiter Teil: Aus dem Leben der Hauptstadt*, 1933. Binding, jacket, six color illustrations.

Horen-Verlag (Leipzig; Berlin-Grunewald)

Brust, Alfred. *Festliche Ehe*, 1930. Jacket.

———. *Jutt und Jula: Geschichte einer jungen Liebe*, 1928. Binding.

Kayßler, Friedrich, *Gesammelte Schriften*. 3 vols., 1929. Binding.

Köppen, Edlef. *Heeresbericht*, 1930. Binding.

Scholz, Wilhelm von. *Unrecht der Liebe*. Roman, 1931. Binding.

———. *Der Weg nach Ilok*. Roman, 1930. Binding.

Insel (Leipzig)

Frank, Leonhard. *Die Räuberbande*. Roman [Insel Bücherei], 1930. Jacket.

Gorki, Maxim. *Erzählungen*. Trans. Arthur Luther, 1931. Jacket.

Huch, Ricarda. *Der große Krieg in Deutschland*. Gekürzte Ausgabe, 1931. Jacket.

Timmermans, Felix. *Pallieter*. Volksausgabe. Trans. Anna Baleton-Hoos, 1931. Jacket.

Zweig, Stefan. *Amok: Novellen einer Leidenschaft*, 1931. Jacket.

Kiepenheuer Verlag (Potsdam; Berlin)

Benn, Gottfried. *Fazit der Perspektiven*, 1930. Jacket, binding.

———. *Gesammelte Gedichte*, 1929. Binding.

———. *Gesammelte Prosa*, 1929. Binding.

Berteaux, Felix, and Hermann Kesten, eds. *Neue französische Erzähler*, 1930. Jacket, binding.

———. *Das weisse Russland: Menschen ohne Heimat*, 1932. Jacket, binding.

Biggers, Earl Derr. *Die Schmerzensspalte* [The Agony Column]. Roman. Trans. Curt Thesing, 1928.

Breitbach, Joseph. *Die Wandlung der Susanne Dasseldorf*. Roman, 1933. Jacket, binding.

Brunner, Constantin [Leo Wertheimer]. *Von den Pflichten der Juden und von den Pflichten des Staates*, 1930. Jacket, binding.

Bücherverzeichnis 1928, 1927. Binding.

Bücherverzeichnis 1931, 1930. Binding.

Cocteau, Jean. *Enfants terribles*. Roman. Trans. Hans Kauders and Efraim Frisch, 1930. Jacket, binding.

Colette [Sidonie-Gabrielle]. *Phil und Vinea* [Le Blé en herbe]. Roman. Trans. Lissy Rademacher, 1928. Jacket, binding.

————. *Sieben Tierdialoge* [Sept dialogues de bêtes]. Trans. Emmy Hirschberg, 1928. Binding.

Essad Bey [Leo Noussimbaum], *Mohammed*. Eine Biographie, 1932. Jacket.

Farrère, Claude [Frédéric Charles Pierre Edouard Bargone]. *Der letzte Gott* [Le dernier dieu]. Roman. Trans. Lissy Rademacher], 1928. Binding.

Feuchtwanger, Lion. *Erfolg: drei Jahre Geschichte einer Provinz*. Roman. 2 vols., 1930. Jacket, binding.

————. *Die hässliche Herzogin Margarete Maultasch*, 1926. Jacket, binding.

Fleisser, Marieluise. *Andorranische Abenteuer*. Ein Reisebuch, 1932. Jacket, binding.

————. *Mehlreisende Frieda Geier: Roman vom Rauchen, Sporteln, Lieben und Verkaufen*, 1931. Jacket, binding.

————. *Ein Pfund Orangen und neun andere Geschichten*, 1929. Jacket, binding.

Freud, Sigmund. *Vorlesungen zur Einführung in die Psychoanalyse*. Volksausgabe, 1933. Jacket, binding.

Frey, Alexander Moritz. *Das abenteuerliche Dasein: Ein biographischer Musterroman*, 1930. Jacket, binding.

————. *Die Pflasterkästen: Ein Feldsanitätsroman*, 1929. Jacket, binding.

Glaeser, Ernst. *Frieden*, 1930. Jacket, binding.

————. *Das Gut im Elsass*. Roman, 1932. Jacket, binding.

————. *Jahrgang 1902*, 1928. Jacket, binding.

Green, Julien. *Leviathan*. Trans. Gina and Hermann Kesten, 1930. Jacket, binding.

————. *Treibgut* [Épaves]. Roman. Trans. Friedrich Burschell, 1932. Jacket, binding.

Haas, Willy. *Gestalten der Zeit*, 1930. Jacket, binding.

————. *Was ist Jugend?*, 1930. Jacket, binding.

Hegemann, Werner. *Der gerettete Christus, oder Iphigenies Flucht vor dem Ritualopfer*, 1928. Jacket, binding.

Hermann, Georg. *Henriette Jacoby*. Roman. Volksausgabe, 1932. Binding.

————. *Jettchen Gebert*. Roman. Volksausgabe, 1930. Binding.

Holitscher, Arthur. *Mein Leben in dieser Zeit (1907–1925)*, 1928. Jacket, binding.

————. *Reisen: Deutschland/Russland/Frankreich/Mittelmeer*, 1928. Jacket, binding.

Kafka, Franz. *Beim Bau der chinesischen Mauer. Ungedruckte Erzählungen aus dem Nachlaß*. Ed. Max Brod and Hans-Joachim Schoeps, 1931. Jacket, binding.

Kaiser, Georg. *Gesammelte Werke in Einzelbänden* (I, II, 1928; III, 1931). Binding.

————. *Hellseherei*. Gesellschaftsspiel in drei Akten, 1929. Binding.

————. *Die Lederknöpfe*. Schauspiel in drei Akten, 1928. Binding and illustrations.

————. *Mississippi*. Schauspiel, 1930. Binding.

————. *Oktobertag*. Schauspiel in drei Akten, 1928. Binding.

————. *Der Silbersee*. Ein Wintermärchen in drei Akten, 1933. Binding.

Kersten, Kurt. *"1848" (Die deutsche Revolution)*, 1933. Jacket, binding.

Kesten, Hermann. *Ein ausschweifender Mensch (Das Leben eines Tölpels)*. Roman, 1929. Jacket, binding.

————. *Glückliche Menschen*. Roman, 1931. Jacket, binding.

————. *Joseph sucht die Freiheit*. Roman, 1928. Jacket, binding.

————. *Die Liebes-Ehe*. Zwei Novellen, 1929. Jacket, binding.

————. *24 neue deutsche Erzähler*, 1929. Jacket, binding.

Koenigsgarten, Hugo F. [later Hugh Frederick Garten]. *Georg Kaiser: Mit einer Bibliographie von Alfred Loewenberg*, 1928. Binding.

Lampel, Peter Martin. *Revolte im Erziehungshaus*. Schauspiel der Gegenwart in drei Akten, 1929. Binding.

Mann, Heinrich. *Geist und Tat. Franzosen 1780–1930*, 1931. Jacket, binding.

————. *Die große Sache*. Roman, 1930. Jacket, binding.

————. *Die Welt der Herzen*. Novellen, 1932. Jacket, binding.

Marcu, Valeriu. *Männer und Mächte der Gegenwart*. Politische Essays, 1930. Jacket, binding.

Marx, Karl. *Das Kapital: Kritik der politischen Ökonomie; Ungekürzte Ausgabe nach der zweiten Auflage von 1872*, 1932. Jacket, binding.

Michaelis, Karin. *Familie Worm*. Roman, 1928. Binding.

————. *Die sieben Schwestern*. Roman, 1928. Jacket.

————. *Sünden, Sorgen und Gefahren (Gunhild heiratet)*. Roman, 1929. Binding.

Ollivant, Alfred. *Old Bob: Der graue Hund von Kenmuir* [Owd Bob; the Grey Dog of Kenmuir (U.S. title, *Bob, Son of Battle*)]. Roman. Trans. Marguerite Thesing, 1928. Binding.

Reimann, Hans. *Quartett zu dritt: alles andere als ein Roman*, 1932. Jacket, binding.

————. *Vergnügliches Handbuch der deutschen Sprache*, 1931. Jacket, binding.

Roth, Joseph. *Hiob, Roman eines einfachen Mannes*, 1930. Jacket, binding.

————. *Radetzkymarsch*. Roman, 1932. Jacket, binding. Two versions, both 1932: first printing is paler color with descriptive text on cover.

————. *Rechts und Links*. Roman, 1929. Jacket, binding.

Seghers, Anna [Netty Radvanyi]. *Auf dem Wege zur amerikanischen Botschaft*. Erzählungen, 1930. Jacket, binding.

————. *Aufstand der Fischer von St. Barbara*. Erzählung, 1928. Binding.

————. *Die Gefährten*. Roman, 1932. Jacket, binding.

Sochaczewer, Hans [José Orabuena]. *Die Untat*. Roman, 1931. Jacket, binding.

Stock, Hans. *Das Erbe des Kapitäns*. Roman, 1932. Cover design, jacket.

Tarassow-Rodionow, Alexander. *Februar*. Roman. Trans. Olga Halpern, 1928. Jacket, binding.

Tcheng, Cheng. *Meine Mutter*. Trans. Paul Cohen-Portheim, 1929. Jacket, binding.

Thiess, Frank. *Frauenraub*. Roman. Two different designs: 1928, jacket, binding; 1933, jacket, binding.

Toller, Ernst. *Feuer aus den Kesseln*. Historisches Schauspiel, 1930. Jacket, binding.

————. *Quer durch: Reisebilder und Reden*, 1930. Jacket, binding.

Trautwein, Susanne. *Die Zauberflöte*. Drei Novellen, 1928. Jacket, binding.

Tügel, Ludwig. *Die Treue*. Erzählung, 1932. Jacket, binding.

Tynjanow, Jurij N. *Wilhelm Küchelbecker: Dichter und Rebell*. Historischer Roman. Trans. Maria Einstein, 1929. Binding.

Vierzig Jahre Kiepenheuer 1910–1950: Ein Almanach, 1951. Contains illustration by Salter.

Villon, François. *Balladen*. Trans. K. L. Ammer, 1930. Jacket, binding.

Vorländer, Karl [J. Hoffmeister]. *Geschichte der Philosophie*. Gekürzte Volksausgabe, 1932. Jacket, binding.

Weininger, Otto. *Geschlecht und Charakter: eine prinzipielle Untersuchung*. Ungekürzte Textausgabe, 1932. Jacket, binding.

Weiskopf, Franz Carl. *Das Slawenlied: Roman aus den letzten Tagen Österreichs und den ersten Jahren der Tschechoslowakei*, 1931. Jacket, binding.

Zweig, Arnold. *Frühe Fährten*. Novellen, 1928. Jacket, binding.

————. *Junge Frau von 1914*. Roman. Erster Band der Grischa-Tetralogie, 1931. Jacket, binding.

————. *Knaben und Männer*. 18 Erzählungen, 1931. Binding.

————. *Mädchen und Frauen*. 14 Erzählungen, 1931. Binding.

————. *Die Novellen um Claudia*. Roman, 1930. Jacket, binding.

————. *Pont und Anna*. Erzählung, 1928. Jacket, binding.

Klinkhardt & Biermann (Berlin)

Cohen-Portheim, Paul. *England: die unbekannte Insel* [England: The Unknown Isle]. Trans. Alan Harris, 1931. Jacket, binding.

————. *Paris*, 1930. Jacket, binding.

Meier-Graefe, Julius. *Die Weisse Strasse*, 1929. Jacket, binding.

Biermann, Georg. *Paula Modersohn*, 1930. Binding.

Huebner, Friedrich Markus. *Zugang zur Welt: Magische Deutungen*, 1929. Binding.

Weihnachtskatalog, 1930. Wrappers.

Knaur (Berlin)

Hamann, Richard. *Geschichte der Kunst: eine vollständige Kunstgeschichte von der altchristlichen Zeit bis zur Gegenwart*, 1932. Jacket.

Herzog, Rudolf. *Die Wiskottens*. Roman, 1932. Binding, end papers.

Friedenthal, Richard, ed. *Knaurs Konversations-Lexikon A–Z*, 1932. Jacket, binding.

Paul Franke Verlag (Berlin)

Dill, Liesbet [Liesbet von Drigalski-Dill]. *Leuchtende Tage*. Roman, 1932. Jacket.

Engel, Georg Julius. *Zauberin Circe*. Roman, 1932. Jacket, binding.

Grabein, Paul. *Die Flammenzeichen rauchen: Roman aus der Zeit der Freiheitskriege*, 1932. Ballonleinen-Ausgabe. Jacket.

Heller, Robert. *Im Banne Goethes: Roman aus Alt-Weimar*, 1932. Jacket, binding.

Ompteda, Georg Freiherr von. *Wie am ersten Tag*. Roman, 1932. Jacket.

Speckmann, Diedrich. *Heidehof Lohe*. Roman, 1932. Jacket.

Wohlbrück, Olga. *Die Frau ohne Mann*, Roman. 1933. Jacket, binding.

Paul List Verlag (Leipzig)

Kayßler, Friedrich. *Hintergrund: Besinnungen und Schauspielernotizen mit zwei neuen Folgen*, 1929. Binding.

Phönix-Verlag Carl Siwinna (Berlin)

André-Cuel, George. *El Gelmuna, der Sandmann*, 1932. Jacket.

Guédy, Pierre, and Moïse Twersky. *Israel in New York*, 1932. Jacket.

R. Piper & Co. (Munich)

Arlen, Michael [Dikran Koujoundijan]. *Zugvögel* [Piracy]. Roman. Trans. E. L. Schiffer, 1932. Jacket, binding.

Fleg, Edmond. *Salomo* [Salomon]. Trans. Alexander Benzion, 1930. Jacket, binding.

Huxley, Aldous. *Das Lächeln der Gioconda und andere englische Erzähler*. Trans. Herbert E. Herlitschka and Willy Seidel, 1931. Jacket, binding.

Istrati, Panait. *Tage der Jugend* [La jeunesse d'Adrian Zograffi]. Trans. Karl Stransky, 1931. Binding.

Kessel, Joseph. *Die Gefangenen* [Les captifs]. Roman. Trans. Paul Alverdes, 1930. Binding.

Maurois, André [Emile Salomon Herzog]. *Die Gespräche des Doktors O'Grady* [Discours du Docteur O'Grady]. Trans. Karl Stransky, 1929. Jacket, binding.

————. *Das Schweigen des Obersten Bramble* [Les silences du colonel Bramble]. Trans. Karl Stransky, 1929. Jacket, binding.

Penzoldt, Ernst. *Die portugalesische Schlacht*, 1930. Jacket, binding.

Suslowa, Polina. *Dostojewskis' ewige Freundin: Tagebuch, Novelle und Briefe an und von Polina Suslowa von Rosa Symchowitsch*. Eds. René Fülöp-Müller and Friedrich Eckstein, 1931. Binding.

Wilde, Percival. *Die gefallenen Engel und andere englische Erzähler*. Merkwürdige Begebenheiten 2. Trans. Willy Seidel and H. E. Herlitschka, 1931. Jacket, binding.

Private Imprints (Privatdrucke)

Haberland, Georg. *Aus meinem Leben*. [Berlin] Privatdruck zum 14. August 1931. Design.

Propyläen Verlag (Berlin)

Körmendi, Franz. *Versuchung in Budapest* [A Budapesti Kaland]. Roman. Trans. Mirza von Schüching, 1933. Jacket, binding.

Reclam: Philipp Reclam, Jun. (Leipzig)

Deutscher Almanach auf das Jahr 1932, 1931. Cover and design.

Deutscher Almanach auf das Jahr 1933, 1932. Cover and design.

Hauser, Heinrich. *Brackwasser*. Roman. Junge Deutsche, 1928. Jacket.

Heuschele, Otto, ed. *Junge Deutsche Lyrik: eine Anthologie*. Junge Deutsche, 1928. Jacket.

Kuhnert, A. Arthur. *Die Männer von St. Kilda*. Roman. Junge Deutsche, 1931. Jacket.

Matzke, Frank. *Jugend bekennt: So sind wir!* Junge Deutsche, 1930. Jacket.

Mendelssohn, Peter. *Paris über mir*. Junge Deutsche, 1931. Jacket.

Reiss: Erich Reiss Verlag (Berlin)

Bromfield, Louis. *Olivia Pentland*. Roman. Trans. J. Sternemann, 1932. Jacket, binding.

————. *Vierundzwanzig Stunden* [Twenty-four Hours]. Roman. Trans. Viktor Wallerstein, 1933. Jacket, binding.

Chardonne, Jacques. *Eva oder das unterbrochene Tagebuch*. [Eva; ou, Le journal interrompu]. Trans. Hans Hennecke and Nanny Collin, 1932. Jacket, binding.

Hughes, Richard. *Ein Sturmwind von Jamaika* [A High Wind in Jamaica]. Roman. Trans. Elsie McCalman, 1931. Jacket, binding.

Kisch, Egon Erwin. *Asien gründlich verändert*, 1932. Jacket, binding.

————. *China geheim*, 1933. Jacket, binding.

————. *Egon Erwin Kisch ("beehrt sich darzubieten"): Paradies Amerika*, 1930. Jacket, binding.

————. *Prager Pitaval*, 1931. Jacket, binding.

————. *"Schreib das auf, Kisch!": das Kriegstagebuch von EEK*, 1930. Jacket, binding.

Levy, Sarah. *Geliebter! O mon goye!* Roman, 1929. Jacket, binding.

————. *Henri und Sarah*. Roman, 1931. Jacket, binding.

Margueritte, Victor. *Die Junggesellin* [La Garconne]. Roman. Trans. Joseph Chapiro, 1932. Jacket, binding.

Pinner, Erna. *Ich reise durch die Welt*, 1931. Jacket.

Roeld, Otto. *Malenski auf der Tour*. Roman, 1930. Jacket, binding.

Seidl, Walter. *Romeo im Fegefeuer*. Roman, 1932. Jacket.

Smirnowa, Nina. *Marfa*. Roman, 1932. Jacket.

Die Schmiede (Berlin)

Altitalienische Liebesnovellen. Klassiker der erotischen Literatur 4, 1926. Binding.

Aretino, Pietro. *Italienischer Hurenspiegel: Ferrante Pallavicino, Der geplünderte Postreuter*. Klassiker der erotischen Literatur 3, 1926. Binding.

Barbusse, Henri. *Kraft* [Force: L'au-delà, and Le crieur]. Novellen. Die Romane des XX. Jahrhunderts. Trans. Paul Cohen-Portheim, 1926. Binding.

Becher, Johannes R. *Maschinenrhythmen*. Gedichte, 1926. Binding.

Benn, Gottfried. *Gesammelte Gedichte*, 1927. Binding.

Bücher aus dem Verlag Die Schmiede, Berlin 1925/26, 1925. Binding.

Carco, Francis [François Carcopino-Tusoli]. *An Straßenecken: Erzählungen* [Au coin des rues: Contes]. Die Romane des XX. Jahrhunderts. Trans. Fred A. Angermayer, 1925. Binding.

Châteaubriant, Alphonse de. *Schwarzes Land* [La Brière]. Die Romane des XX. Jahrhunderts. Trans. Rudolf Schottländer, 1925. Binding.

Chesterton, Gilbert Keith. *Ein Pfeil vom Himmel: Kriminalerzählungen*. Die Romane des XX. Jahrhunderts. Trans. Dora Sophie Kellner, 1927. Binding.

Crèbillon [Prosper Jolyot de Crèbillon; P. J. Sieur de Crais-Billon]. *Tanzai und Neadarne oder Der Schaumlöffel: Eine japanische Geschichte* [L'ecumoire]. Klassiker der erotischen Literatur 5. Trans. Crèbillon, 1926. Binding.

Csokor, Franz Theodor. *Schuß in's Geschäft: Der Fall Otto Eisler.* Aussenseiter der Gesellschaft 10, 1924. Binding.

Das Moskauer Jüdische Akademie Theater. Texts by Ernst Toller, Joseph Roth, Alfons Goldschmidt, 1928. Binding.

Daudistel, Albert. *Das Opfer.* Die Romane des XX. Jahrhunderts, 1925. Binding.

Diderot, Denis. *Die Nonne* [La religieuse]. Klassiker der erotischen Literatur 1. Trans. C. F. Cramer, 1925. Binding.

Döblin, Alfred. *Die beiden Freundinnen und ihr Giftmord.* Aussenseiter der Gesellschaft 1, 1924. Binding.

Federn, Karl. *Ein Justizverbrechen in Italien: Der Prozeß Murri-Bonmartini.* Aussenseiter der Gesellschaft 13, 1925. Binding.

Flake, Otto. *Erzählungen,* 1923. Binding.

Freyhan, Max. *Georg Kaisers Werk,* 1926. Binding.

Guilbeaux, Henri. *Wladimir Iljitsch Lenin: Ein treues Bild seines Wesens* [Le portrait authentique de Vladimir Ilitsch Lénine]. Trans. Rudolf Leonhardt, 1923. Binding.

Goll, Iwan. *Der Eiffelturm.* Gesammelte Dichtungen, 1924. Binding.

———. *Germaine Berton: Die rote Jungfrau.* Aussenseiter der Gesellschaft 5, 1925. Binding.

Haas, Willy. *Das Spiel mit dem Feuer.* Prosaschriften, 1923. Binding.

Hasenclever, Walter. *Mord: ein Stück in zwei Teilen,* 1926. Binding.

Holitscher, Arthur. *Ravachol und die Pariser Anarchisten.* Aussenseiter der Gesellschaft 8, 1925. Binding.

Ihering, Herbert. *Die vereinsamte Theaterkritik,* 1928. Binding.

Jacobi, Friedrich Heinrich. *Die Schriften Friedrich Heinrich Jacobi's.* In Auswahl und mit einer Einleitung von Leo Matthias, 1926. Binding.

Janowitz, Hans. *Jazz.* Roman. Die Romane des XX. Jahrhunderts, 1927. Binding.

Kafka, Franz. *Ein Hungerkünstler.* Vier Geschichten. Die Romane des XX. Jahrhunderts, 1924. Binding.

———. *Der Prozess.* Roman. Die Romane des XX. Jahrhunderts, 1925. Binding.

Kafka, Hans [later John Kafka]. *Das Grenzenlose.* Fünfundzwanzig Geschichten. Die Romane des XX. Jahrhunderts, 1927. Binding.

Kaiser, Georg. *Kolportage: Komödie in einem Vorspiel und drei Akten nach zwanzig Jahren,* 1924. Binding.

Kasack, Hermann. *Die Heimsuchung.* Erzählung. Kleine Roland Bücher 21, 1922. Binding.

Kersten, Kurt. *Der Moskauer Prozeß gegen die Sozialrevolutionäre 1922: Revolution und Konterrevolution.* Aussenseiter der Gesellschaft 12, 1925. Binding.

Kisch, Egon Erwin. *Der Fall des Generalstabchefs Redl.* Aussenseiter der Gesellschaft 2, 1924. Binding.

———. *Kriminalistisches Reisebuch.* Berichte aus der Wirklichkeit 1, 1927. Binding.

La Rochefoucauld. *Gedanken zur Liebe* [Maximes]. Trans. Klabund, 1923. Binding.

Lania, Leo [Lazar Herman]. *Der Hitler-Ludendorff-Prozeß.* Aussenseiter der Gesellschaft 9, 1925. Binding.

———. *Indeta: Die Fabrik der Nachrichten.* Berichte aus der Wirklichkeit 2, 1927. Binding.

Leonhard, Rudolf. *Die Ewigkeit dieser Zeit: eine Rhapsodie gegen Europa,* 1924. Binding.

———. *Das nackte Leben.* Sonette, 1925. Binding.

———. *Segel am Horizont: (Towarischtsch) Schauspiel in vier Akten,* 1925. Binding.

———. *Tragödie von heute: fünf Akte,* 1927. Binding.

Lessing, Theodor. *Haarmann: die Geschichte eines Werwolfs.* Aussenseiter der Gesellschaft 6, 1925. Binding.

Lewin, Ludwig. *Die Jagd nach dem Erlebnis: ein Buch über Georg Kaiser,* 1926. Binding.

MacOrlan, Pierre. *Alkoholschmuggler.* Berichte aus der Wirklichkeit 3, 1927. Binding.

Mann, Heinrich. *Diktatur der Vernunft,* 1923. Binding.

Matthias, Leo. *Ausflug nach Mexiko,* 1926. Binding.

Mehring, Walter. *Algier oder Die 13 Oasenwunder,* 1927. Binding, using designs by Walter Mehring.

Möbius, Martin Richard. *Verwünschtes Gold.* Roman. Die Romane des XX. Jahrhunderts, 1927. Binding. Two designs published: edition A in red; edition B in yellow.

Moskauer Jüdische Akademische Theater, Das. 1928. Binding.

Otten, Karl. *Der Fall Strauss.* Aussenseiter der Gesellschaft 7, 1925. Binding.

Panter, Peter [Kurt Tucholsky]. *Ein Pyrenäenbuch,* 1927. Jacket, binding. Rowohlt took over this design in 1930.

Petronius [Petronius Arbiter], *Begebenheiten des Enkolp* [Satyrikon]. Klassiker der erotischen Literatur 2. Trans. Wilhelm Heinse, 1925. Binding.

Proust, Marcel. *Auf den Spuren der verlorenen Zeit: Der Weg zu Swann* [A la recherche du temps perdu]. 2 vols. Die Romane des XX. Jahrhunderts. Trans. Rudolf Schottländer, 1926. Binding.

———. *Im Schatten der jungen Mädchen: Auf den Spuren der verlorenen Zeit* [A la recherche du temps perdu]. Zweiter Roman. Die Romane des XX. Jahrhunderts. Trans. Walter Benjamin and Franz Hessel, 1927. Binding.

Radiguet, Raymond. *Das Fest* [Le bal du comte d'Oryel]. Roman. Die Romane des XX. Jahrhunderts. Trans. Hans Jacob, 1925. Jacket, binding.

———. *Den Teufel im Leib* [Le diable au corps]. Roman. Die Romane des XX. Jahrhunderts. Trans. Hans Jacob, 1925. Jacket, binding.

Roth, Joseph. *Hotel Savoy.* Roman. Die Romane des XX. Jahrhunderts, 1924. Binding.

———. *Juden auf Wanderschaft.* Berichte aus der Wirklichkeit 4, 1927. Binding.

Schramek, Thomas. *Freiherr von Egloffstein.* Aussenseiter der Gesellschaft 11, 1925. Binding.

Siemsen, Hans. *Verbotene Liebe: Briefe eines Unbekannten.* Berichte aus der Wirklichkeit 5. Ed. Eduard Trautner, 1927. Binding.

Strassnoff, Ignatz. *Ich, der Hochstapler Ignatz Strassnoff,* 1926. Binding.

Swedenborg, Emanuel. *Himmel, Hölle, Geisterwelt (Eine Auswahl aus dem Lateinischen)* [De coleo et ejus mirabilibus]. Trans. Walter Hasenclever, 1925. Binding.

Trautner, Eduard. *Gott, Gegenwart und Kokain.* Berichte aus der Wirklichkeit 6, 1927. Binding.

———. *Der Mord am Polizeiagenten Blau.* Aussenseiter der Gesellschaft 3, 1924. Binding.

Turel, Adrien. *Christi Weltleidenschaft,* 1923. Binding.

Ungar, Hermann. *Die Ermordung des Hauptmanns Hanika: Tragödie einer Ehe.* Aussenseiter der Gesellschaft 14, 1925. Binding.

Weiss, Ernst. *Daniel.* Erzählung, 1924. Binding.

———. *Der Fall Vukobrankovics.* Aussenseiter der Gesellschaft 4, 1924. Binding.

Seemann: E. A. Seemann Verlag (Leipzig)

Nichols, Beverly. *U.S.A.: Glossen um das Sternenbanner* [The Star-Spangled Manner]. Trans. Elisabeth Schmidt-Pauli, 1930. Jacket, binding.

Silex, Karl. *John Bull zu Hause: der Engländer im täglichen Leben; wie er wohnt, sich amüsiert, sich anzieht, was er lernt, wird, treibt, verdient, ausgibt, season, sport, society; mit acht Tafeln,* 1930. Jacket, binding.

Tal: E. P. Tal & Co. (Leipzig, Wien)

Glaspell, Susan. *Narzissa* [Brooke Evans]. Roman. Trans. Georg Schwarz, 1929. Jacket, binding.

Hinzelmann, Hans H. *Achtung! Der Otto Puppe kommt!* Roman, 1929. Jacket, binding.

McEvoy, J. P. [Joseph Patrick]. *Revue-Girl* [Show Girl]. Roman. Trans. Arthur Rundt, 1929. Jacket, binding.

Wendler, Otto Bernhard. *Soldaten Marieen.* Roman, 1929. Jacket, binding.

Transmare Verlag (Berlin)
Alain-Fournier [Henry Fournier]. *Der große Kamerad* [Le grand Meaulnes]. Roman. Trans. A. Seiffhart, 1930. Jacket, binding.
Graves, Robert. *Strich drunter* [Good-bye to All That]. Trans. Gottfried Reinhold Treviranus, 1930. Jacket, binding.
Russell, Elizabeth [Marie Annette Gräfin von Arnim]. *Hochzeit, Flucht und Ehestand der schönen Salvatia* [Introduction to Sally]. Roman. Trans. Alwin Bergolt, 1930. Jacket, binding.

Universitas (Munich)
Bilbo, Jack [Hugo Baruch]. *Chicago-Schanghai: Gangster in besonderer Verwendung*, 1932. Jacket.
————. *Ein Mensch wird Verbrecher: die Aufzeichnungen des Leibgardisten von Al Capone* [Carrying a Gun for Al Capone: The Intimate Experiences of a Gangster in the Bodyguard of Al Capone], 1932. Jacket.
Mendelssohn, Peter. *Schmerzliches Arkadien*. Roman, 1932. Jacket.
Graf, Oskar Maria. *Einer gegen Alle*. Roman, 1932. Jacket.
London, Jack. *König Alkohol* [John Barleycorn]. Trans. Erwin Magnus, 1926. Jacket.
————. *Meuterei auf der Elsinore* [The Mutiny of the Elsinore]. Trans. Erwin Magnus, 1932. Jacket, binding.
————. *Das Wort der Männer* [The Faith of Men]. Trans. Erwin Magnus, 1926. Jacket.
Michaelis, Karin. *Justine*. Roman, 1933. Jacket.
Romanow, Panteleimon. *Drei Paar Seidenstrümpfe*. Trans. Markus Joffé, 1932. Jacket.
Vegesack, Siegfried von. *Das fressende Haus*. Roman, 1932. Jacket.

Ullstein (Berlin)
Johann, A. E., *Amerika: Untergang am Überfluss*, 1932. Jacket, binding.

Verlagsgesellschaft des Allgemeinen Deutschen Gewerkschaftsbundes (Berlin)
Marx, Karl. *Das Kapital: Kritik der politischen Ökonomie*. Erstes Buch. Ungekürzte Ausgabe nach der zweiten Auflage von 1872, 1932. Binding.

Walter Verlag (Olten)
Döblin, Alfred. *Berlin Alexanderplatz: Die Geschichte vom Franz Biberkopf*, 1955. Jacket. Reissue of the 1929 S. Fischer design.

C. Weller & Co. Verlag (Leipzig, Wien)
Plivier, Theodor. *Zwölf Mann und ein Kapitän*. Novellen, 1930. Jacket, binding.

Paul Zsolnay Verlag (Berlin, Wien, Leipzig)
Werfel, Franz. *Barbara: oder, die Frömmigkeit*. Ungekürzte Sonderausgabe, 1933. Jacket.

The Netherlands

Querido Verlag (Amsterdam)
Mann, Klaus, ed. *Die Sammlung: Literarische Monatsschrift* 1:4 (December 1933). Cover design.

Appendix B
Salter's Designs for the American Book Market, 1934–1967

The entries are arranged alphabetically by publisher, author, and title. Four designs that were published after 1945 in Germany, Mexico, and Brazil are included. Private commissions are listed under Private Publications. Series titles are included only in selected cases. When the list of Salter's designs for the series is relatively short, the individual titles are listed. Not listed are the miscellaneous designs Salter did for broadsides, publishers' prospectuses, cards, menus, letterheads, and private bookplates.

George Salter produced hundreds of covers for the inexpensive paperback books in digest format published by Lawrence Spivak's firm, Mercury Publications. This company published many different series: *The American Mercury* (which was originally owned by Alfred A. Knopf, Inc.), *Mercury Books, Mercury Library, Mercury Mysteries, Jonathan Press Mysteries, Bestseller Mysteries, Bestseller Library, Ellery Queen, Fantasy and Science Fiction Magazine*. The bibliographical complexity and unavailability of these series publications have made it impossible to verify a complete list of individual titles.

A. A. Wyn (New York)
Phelan, James Leo. *Moon in the River*, 1946. Jacket.
Rowe, Fynette. *The Chapin Sisters*, 1945. Jacket.

Alliance (New York)
Gontard, Gert von. *In Defense of Love: A Protest Against "Soul Surgery,"* 1940. Jacket.
Heiden, Konrad. *The New Inquisition*, 1939. Jacket.
Litten, Irmgard. *Beyond Tears*, 1940. Jacket.
Ludwig, Emil. *Quartet*. Trans. Ernest Boyd, 1939. Jacket, binding.
Muhlen, Norbert. *Schacht: Hitler's Magician, Life and Loans of Dr. Hjalmar Schacht*. Trans. Ernest Walter, 1939. Jacket.
Rosskam, Edwin. *San Francisco: West Coast Metropolis*. Face of America, 1939. Jacket.
————. *Washington, Nerve Center*. Face of America, 1939. Jacket.
Valtin, Jan. *Bend in the River*, 1942. Jacket.
————. *Out of the Night*, 1941. Jacket, binding.
————. *Out of the Night*, 1941. Second jacket, binding. Slightly changed for the Book of the Month Club edition.

Wells, H. G. *All Aboard for Ararat*, 1941. Jacket, design.

Ampersand Press (New York)
Price, Mary Grant, and Vincent Price. *A Treasury of Great Recipes: Famous Specialties of the World's Foremost Restaurants Adapted for American Kitchens*. Illustrated by Fritz Kredel; design by Arthur Hawkins, 1965. Endpaper lettering.

Appleton-Century, Appleton-Century Crofts (New York)
Marks, Richard Lee. *March of the Hero*, 1952. Jacket.
Remarque, Erich Maria. *Arch of Triumph*. Trans. Walter Sorell and Denver Lindley, 1945. Jacket, binding.
————. *Spark of Life*. Trans. James Stern, 1952. Jacket, binding.
Wickes, Frances G. *Receive the Gale*, 1946. Jacket.
Winsor, Kathleen. *The Lovers*, 1952. Jacket.
————. *Star Money*, 1950. Jacket.

Archway Press (New York)
Thoreau, Henry David. *What I Lived For: From Walden*. The Scribe, 1946. Entire text hand lettered.

Atheneum (New York)
Bassani, Giorgio. *The Garden of the Finzi-Continis*. Trans. Isabel Quigly, 1965. Jacket.
Brooks, Van Wyck, ed. *A New England Reader*, 1962. Jacket.
Fülöp-Miller, René. *The Silver Bacchanal*. Trans. Richard and Clara Winston, 1960. Jacket.
Klein-Haparash, J. *He Who Flees the Lion*. Trans. Richard and Clara Winston, 1963. Jacket.
Lynx, J. J. *The Prince of Thieves: A Biography of George Manolesco*, 1963. Jacket.
Morton, Frederic. *The Rothschilds*, 1962. Jacket.
————. *The Schatten Affair*, 1965. Jacket.
Pearson, Kenneth, and Patricia Connor. *The Dorak Affair*, 1968. Jacket.
Rosten, Leo. *A Most Private Intrigue*, 1967. Jacket.
Schwarz-Bart, André. *The Last of the Just*. Trans. Stephen Becker, 1961. Jacket. Salter's design also used on 1965 paperback edition.

Basic Books (New York)
Caplan, Gerald, ed. *Emotional Problems of Early Childhood*, 1955. Jacket.
Jones, Ernest. *Sigmund Freud: Four Centenary Addresses*, 1956. Jacket, design.
Leighton, Alexander H., John A. Clausen, and Robert N. Wilson, eds. *Explorations in Social Psychiatry*, 1957. Jacket.
Lewis, Oscar. *Five Families: Mexican Case Studies in the Culture of Poverty*, 1959. Design. Salter's design also used on the 1975 reprint.

Seeley, John R., R. Alexander Sim, and E. W. Loosley. *Crestwood Heights: A Study in the Culture of Suburban Life*, 1956. Jacket.

Stanton, Alfred H., and Morris S. Schwartz. *The Mental Hospital: A Study of Institutional Participation in Psychiatric Illness and Treatment*, 1954. Jacket.

Trembley, Abraham. *On the Hydra*. The Collector's Series in Science, ed. Derek Price, 1962. Design, slipcase.

Wiener, Philip P. *Roots of Scientific Thought: A Cultural Perspective*, 1957. Jacket.

Berkley (New York)

Borek, Ernest. *The Atoms Within Us*. Berkley Medallion SE 11, 1961. Cover.

Chang, Eileen [Ailing Zhang]. *The Naked Earth*. A Ladder Edition, 1962. Cover.

Davis, Russel G., and Brent K. Ashabrenner. *Point Four Assignment*, 1962. Cover.

Gould, Jean. *Young Mariner Melville*. Berkley Medallion SE 12, 1962. Cover.

Hawthorne, Nathaniel. *The Scarlet Letter*, 1962. Cover.

Hughes, Langston. *Fight for Freedom: The Story of the NAACP*, 1962. Cover.

LaFarge, Oliver. *Behind the Mountains*, 1962. Cover.

Shippen, Katherine Binney. *Miracle in Motion: The Story of America's Industry*. Berkley Medallion SE 13, 1962. Cover.

Stevenson, O. J. (Orlando John). *The Talking Wire: The Story of Alexander Graham Bell*. Illustrated by Lawrence Dresser, 1962. Cover.

Viscardi, Jr., Henry. *Give Us the Tools*, 1963. Cover.

Walker, Richard Louis. *The Continuing Struggle: Communist China and the Free World*, 1962. Cover.

Wallace, Irving. *The Square Pegs: Some Americans Who Dared to be Different*. Berkley Medallion X646, 1961. Cover.

Bobbs-Merrill (Indianapolis & New York)

Alexander, Sidney. *The Celluloid Asylum*, 1951. Jacket.

Appel, Benjamin. *Fortress in the Rice*, 1951. Jacket.

Berman, Richard Arnold, and Elizabeth R. Hapgood. *Home from the Sea: Robert Louis Stevenson in Samoa*, 1939. Jacket.

Fülöp-Miller, René. *The Night of Time*, 1955. Jacket.

Heinrich, Willi. *The Cross of Iron*. Trans. Richard and Clara Winston, 1956. Jacket.

Ley-Piscator, Maria. *Lot's Wife*, 1954. Jacket.

Mandel, George. *Flee the Angry Strangers*, 1952. Jacket.

Schenk, Earl. *Come Unto These Yellow Sands*, 1940. Jacket.

Styron, William. *Lie Down in Darkness*, 1951. Jacket. In 1979 Random House reprinted a pale variation in cream color, minus Salter's lettering.

Young, Jefferson. *A Good Man*, 1953. Jacket.

Braziller (New York)

Aiken, Conrad. *Thee*. Illustrated by Leonard Baskin, 1967. Lettering.

Goulet, Robert. *The Violent Season*, 1962. Jacket.

Charles E. Merrill Co. (New York & Chicago)

Hahn, Mary Louise, and Charles Edward Amory Winslow. *Let's Grow*. Illustrated by Phyllis I. Britcher, 1938. Cover.

———. *Let's Stay Well*. Illustrated by Phyllis I. Britcher, 1938. Cover.

Chilton and Co. (Philadelphia)

Shubin, Seymour. *Wellville, U.S.A.*, 1961. Jacket.

Columbia University Press (New York)

Emerson, Ralph Waldo. *Letters of Ralph Waldo Emerson*, 1939. Binding and advertising prospectus.

Van Kleffens, Eelco Nicolaas. *Juggernaut Over Holland: The Dutch Foreign Minister's Personal Story of the Invasion of the Netherlands*, 1940. Jacket.

Paulsen, Friedrich. *Friedrich Paulsen: An Autobiography*. Trans. Theodor Lorenz, 1938. Jacket.

Read, Conyers. *The Constitution Reconsidered*, 1938. Jacket.

Tindall, William York. *D. H. Lawrence and Susan His Cow*, 1939. Jacket.

The Composing Room (New York)

Mendel, Hortense, and Robert L. Leslie, eds. *Young Faces: An Illustrated Album of Type Faces for Children's Books*, 1952. Calligraphy, cover, and title page.

Covici, Friede (New York)

Steinbeck, John. *Of Mice and Men*, 1937. Jacket, binding. The trial binding design was produced in small quantity as sample and subsequently abandoned for Robert Josephy's design. Jacket is unsigned.

Coward-McCann (New York)

Golding, William. *Lord of the Flies*, 1962. Jacket.

La Farge, Christopher. *Each to the Other: A Novel in Verse*, 1939. Robert Josephy's design uses Salter's Flex typeface on jacket and title page.

Windham, Donald. *Two People*, 1965. Jacket.

Crowell (New York)

Maiden, Cecil. *Jonathan Found*, 1957. Jacket.

Wood, Morrison. *The Devil is a Lonely Man*, 1946. Jacket.

Cumbre, Editorial Cumbre (Mexico City)

Mi Libro Encantado. 12 vols., 1958. Binding.

Enciclopedia ilustrada Cumbre, 2nd ed. 14 vols., 1956. Binding.

D. C. Heath & Co. (Boston)

Norvell, George Whitefield, and Carol Hovious, eds. *Conquest*. Illustrated by Kurt Wiese, 1946. Binding.

Dial Press (New York)

Bloch, Robert. *The Scarf*, 1947. Jacket.

Lyons, Herbert. *The Rest They Need*, 1950. Jacket.

Richards, S. L. M. (Sarah Louise Mende). *Shadow Without Light*, 1947. Jacket.

Stuart, William. *Night Cry*, 1948. Jacket.

Van Paassen, Pierre. *That Day Alone*, 1941. Jacket.

———. *Jerusalem Calling!* 1950. Jacket.

Doubleday; Doubleday, Doran (Garden City, New Jersey, & New York)

Greene, Graham. *This Gun For Hire*, 1936. Jacket.

Hindus, Maurice. *Sons and Fathers*, 1940. Jacket.

Inglis-Jones, Elisabeth. *Pay Thy Pleasure*, 1940. Jacket.

Johnston, Eric Allen. *America Unlimited*. An American Mercury Book, 1944. Jacket.

Keene, Donald. *Living Japan*, 1959. Jacket, design.

Slaughter, Frank G. *Spencer Brade, M. D.*, 1942. Jacket.

Duell, Sloan, and Pearce (New York)

Frank, Waldo. *South American Journey*, 1943. Design, endpapers.

Hichens, Jacobine. *The Marriage of Elizabeth Whitacker*, 1953. Jacket.

Dutton (New York)

Ormsbee, David. *Chico Goes to the Wars: A Chronicle...1933–1943*, 1943. Jacket. Salter's design also used on 1943 Book Club Edition.

———. *The Sound of an American*, 1942. Jacket.

Vidal, Gore. *A Search for the King*, 1950. Jacket.

Edita (Lausanne, Switzerland)

Peyre, Henri. *Splendors of Christendom*. Text by Dmitri Kessel, 1964. Lettering, title page.

Farrar & Rhinehart (New York)

Bombal, Maria Luisa. *House of Mist*, 1947. Jacket.

Golding, Louis. *The Camberwell Beauty*, 1935. Jacket.

Hutchinson, R. C. *Shining Scabbard*, 1936. Jacket.

Rhine, J. B. *New Frontiers of the Mind: The Story of the Duke Experiments*, 1937. Jacket.

Frederick Fell (New York)

Fabricant, Noah D., and Heinz Werner, eds. *A Treasury of Doctor Stories by the World's Great Authors*, 1946. Jacket.

Nichols, Fan. *Possess Me Not*, 1946. Jacket.

Owen, Frank, ed. *Murder for the Millions: A Harvest of Horror and Homicide*, 1946. Jacket.

Frederick Stokes (New York)
Lawrence, Josephine. *If I Have Four Apples*, 1935. Jacket.

Frederick Ungar (New York)
Raabe, Wilhelm, *Die Chronik der Sperlingsgasse*. Reprint of Grote publication (Berlin, 1931), minus Salter's illustrations and jacket, n.d. (after 1940). Lettering on title page and binding.

Funk and Wagnalls (New York)
Fernald, James, ed. *Funk and Wagnall's Desk Standard Dictionary: Ready Reference Edition*. Rev. Frank H. Vizetelly, 1935. Jacket, binding.

George Braziller (New York)
Huguenin, Jean-René. *The Other Side of the Summer*. Trans. Richard Howard, 1961. Jacket, binding.

Der Goldene Brunnen, (Frankfurt am Main, Germany)
Kredel, Fritz, and George Salter. *Am Wegesrand: Blüten, Blätter, frisch und welk, Wurzeln, Rinden und Lebewesen, die es Am Wegesrand, diesseits und jenseits des Altantischen Ozeans fand, sind hier....* Illustrations by Fritz Kredel, 1961. Calligraphy.

Grosset & Dunlap (New York)
Busch, Niven. *They Dream of Home*, 1944. Jacket.
Wood, Clement. *A Popular History of the World*, 1935. Jacket.

Harcourt, Brace (New York)
Clarke, Arthur Charles. *The City and the Stars*, 1956. Jacket.
Remarque, Erich Maria. *Heaven Has No Favorites*. Trans. Richard and Clara Winston, 1961. Jacket.
———. *The Night in Lisbon*. Trans. Ralph Manheim, 1964. Jacket.
———. *A Time to Love and a Time to Die*. Trans. Denver Lindley, 1954. Jacket.

Harper and Brothers; Harper & Row (New York)
Frankau, Pamela [Eliot Naylor]. *The Bridge*, 1957. Jacket.
Gunther, John. *Inside Asia*, 1939. Cover.
———. *Inside Europe*. Rev. ed., 1939. Cover, advertising brochure for Book of the Month Club.
———. *Inside Latin America*, 1941. Binding, endpaper maps.
Hertzler, Arthur E. *The Horse and Buggy Doctor*, 1938. Jacket.
Hesse, Hermann. *Demian*. Trans. Michael Roloff and Michael Lebeck, 1965. Jacket.
———. *Narziss and Goldmund*. Trans. Ursule Molinore, 1965. Jacket.

Johnson, Annabel, and Edgar Johnson. *The Bearcat*, 1960. Jacket.
———. *The Black Symbol*, 1959. Jacket.
———. *The Rescued Heart*, 1961. Jacket.
———. *Torrie*, 1960. Jacket.
Johnson, Josephine W. *Wildwood*, 1946. Jacket.
Neumann, Erich. *The Origins and History of Consciousness: Part I*. Harper Torchbooks, The Bollingen Library TB 2008, 1962. Cover.
———. *The Origins and History of Consciousness: Part II*. Harper Torchbooks, The Bollingen Library TB 2008, 1962. Cover.
Prokosch, Frederic. *Age of Thunder*, 1945. Jacket, endpapers.
———. *The Conspirators*, 1943. Jacket, endpapers.
———. *Night of the Poor*, 1939. Jacket, endpapers.
———. *The Seven who Fled*, 1937. Jacket, endpapers.
———. *Skies of Europe*, 1941. Jacket, endpapers.
Schwezoff, Igor. *Russian Somersault*, 1935. Jacket.
Silone, Ignazio. *Bread and Wine*. Trans. Gwenda David and Eric Mosbacher, 1937. Jacket.
Stern, Richard D. *Teeth, Dying & Other Matters*, 1960. Jacket.
Streit, Clarence Krishman. *Union Now with Britain*, 1941. Jacket, endpaper maps.

Henry Holt (New York)
Burgess, Perry. *Who Walk Alone: The Life of a Leper*, 1940. Jacket.
Trumbull, Robert. *The Raft*, 1942. Jacket.

Hillman-Curl (New York)
Van Paassen, Pierre. *Days of Our Years*, 1939. Jacket.

Holiday House (New York)
Selden, Samuel, ed. *Shakespeare: A Player's Handbook of Short Scenes*, 1960. Jacket.

Holt, Rinehart and Winston (New York)
Montaurier, Jean. *A Passage Through Fire*. Trans. Irene Uribe, 1965. Jacket.

Homecrafts (New York)
Rhodes, Peter C. *Beautify Your Home Grounds: A Complete Guide to Small Plot Landscaping and Ground Improvement*, 1952. Design.

Houghton Mifflin (Boston, Massachusetts)
Ames, Evelyn. *Daughter of the House*, 1962. Jacket.
Auchincloss, Louis. *Portrait in Brownstone*, 1962. Jacket.
Braine, John. *Life at the Top*, 1962. Jacket.
Balchen, Bernt *War Below Zero: The Battle for Greenland*, 1944. Jacket.
Balchin, Nigel. *The Small Back Room*, 1945. Jacket.
Dohrman, Richard. *For Innocents Only*, 1960. Jacket.
Dos Passos, John. *Manhattan Transfer*, 1943. Jacket.

Douglas, Ellen. *Black Cloud, White Cloud: Two Novellas and Two Stories*, 1963. Jacket.
———. *A Family's Affairs*, 1962. Jacket.
Greenslet, Ferris. *The Lowells and their Seven Worlds*, 1946. Jacket.
———. *Under the Bridge: An Autobiography*, 1943. Jacket, decorations.
Hatano, Isoko, and Ribo Hatano. *Mother and Son: The Wartime Correspondence of Isoko and Ichiro Hatano*. Trans. Margaret Shenfield, 1962. Jacket.
Tabori, George. *Beneath the Stone*, 1945. Jacket.
Todd, Helen. *The Roots of the Tree*, 1944. Jacket.

Huntington Press (New York)
Inglis, William. *George F. Johnson and his Industrial Democracy*, 1935. Design.

Intertype (Brooklyn, New York)
Intertype Corporation. *How to Select Type Faces and How to Make Better Use of Machine Faces*, 1949. Cover.

John Day (New York)
Standard, Stella. *Whole Grain Cookery: A Gourmet Guide to Glowing Health*, 1951. Design.

Julian Messner (New York)
Herisko, Ilona. *Brucknerstrasse: A Novel of Nazi Germany, 1944*, 1964. Jacket.

Knight (New York)
Cronyn, George W. *Mermaid Tavern: Kit Marlowe's Story*, 1937. Jacket.

Knopf, Alfred A. Knopf (New York)
Amado, Jorge. *Shepherds of the Night*. Trans. Harriet de Onis, 1967. Jacket.
Ambler, Eric. *The Light of Day*, 1963. Jacket.
Angarsky, Andrew. *Eighty-Seven Days*, 1963. Design.
Anthony, Katherine Susan. *The Lambs: A Story of Pre-Victorian England*, 1945. Jacket.
Arnold, Eliott. *The Time of the Gringo*, 1953. Jacket.
Barry, Henry M. *I'll Be Seeing You*, 1952. Jacket.
Beck, Warren. *Into Thin Air*, 1951. Jacket.
Berto, Giuseppe. *Incubus*. Trans. William Weaver, 1966. Jacket, design.
Born, Edith de. *Fielding Castle*, 1959. Jacket, binding, typography.
———. *The House in Vienna*, 1960. Jacket, design.
———. *State of Possession*, 1963. Design.
Bowen, Elizabeth. *The Death of the Heart*, 1939. Jacket, design.
———. *A World of Love*, 1954. Jacket, design.
Boyle, Kay. *Generation Without Farewell*, 1960. Jacket, design.
Breitbach, Joseph. *Report on Bruno*, 1964. Jacket.
Brown, Harry. *A Quiet Place to Work*, 1968. Jacket. Finished by Philip Grushkin and published after Salter's death.

Brown, Hilton. *Glory's Children*, 1936. Jacket.

Bullett, Gerald William. *The Snare of the Fowler*, 1936. Jacket.

Campbell, Harriet Russell. *The String Glove Mystery*, 1936. Design.

Camus, Albert. *Notebooks 1935–1942*. Trans. and preface by Philip Thody, 1963. Jacket, design.

———. *Notebooks 1942–1951*. Trans. and preface by Justin O'Brien, 1965. Jacket, design.

Canetti, Elias. *The Tower of Babel*. Trans. C. V. Wedgwood, 1947. Jacket.

Castillo, Michel de. *Child of Our Time*. Trans. Peter Green, 1958. Jacket, design.

Charles, Gerda. *The Crossing Point*, 1961. Jacket, design.

———. *A Logical Girl*, 1967. Jacket, binding.

———. *A Slanting Light*, 1963. Jacket.

Chekhov, Anton. *The Image of Chekhov: Forty Stories in the Order in Which They Were Written*. Trans. Robert Payne, 1963. Jacket, design.

Cost, March [Peggy Morrison]. *The Dark Star*, 1939. Jacket.

Coxe, George Harmon. *Camera Clue*, 1937. Jacket.

———. *Murder With Pictures*, 1935. Jacket.

Cram, Mildred. *Kingdom of Innocents*, 1940. Jacket, design.

———. *The Promise*, 1949. Jacket, design.

Currier, Isabel. *The Young and the Immortal*, 1941. Jacket.

Deeping, Warwick. *No Hero—This*, 1936. Jacket.

Descalzo, José Luiz Martin. *God's Frontier*. Trans. Harriet de Onis, 1959. Jacket, typography, binding.

Diehl, Charles. *Byzantine Empresses*. Trans. Harold Bell and T. de Kerpely, 1963. Jacket, design.

Doderer, Heimito von. *The Demons*. Trans. Richard and Clara Winston. 2 vols., 1961. Design, jacket, slipcase.

———. *Every Man a Murderer*, 1964. Jacket, design.

Donath, Stanley F. *The Lord is a Man of War*, 1944. Jacket.

Donoso José. *Coronation*. Trans. Jocaste Goodwin, 1965. Jacket, design.

———. *This Sunday*. Trans. Lorraine Freeman, 1967. Jacket.

Dürrenmatt, Friedrich. *Once a Greek....* Trans. Richard and Clara Winston, 1965. Jacket.

———. *The Pledge*. Trans. Richard and Clara Winston, 1959. Jacket.

Ehrenburg, Ilya. *The Fall of Paris*. Trans. Gerard Shelley, 1943. Jacket.

Engstrand, Stuart David. *The Invaders*, 1937. Jacket.

Evans, John. *Shadows Flying*, 1936. Jacket, design.

Farrell, Michael. *Thy Tears Might Cease*, 1964. Jacket, design.

Freyre Gilberto. *Mother and Son: A Brazilian Tale*. Trans. Barbara Shelby, 1967. Jacket, typography, binding.

Gallico, Paul. *The Abandoned*, 1950. Jacket, binding, typography.

———. *The Lonely*, 1949. Jacket, binding, typography.

———. *The Snow Goose*, 1941. Jacket, design.

Gayn, Mark. *Journey from the East: An Autobiography*, 1944. Jacket.

Gibbons, Robert F. *The Patchwork Time*, 1948. Jacket.

Godden, Jon. *In the Sun*, 1965. Jacket, design.

———. *Mrs. Panopoulis*, 1959. Jacket.

———. *The Seven Islands*, 1956. Jacket, binding, typography.

———. *A Winter's Tale*, 1961. Jacket.

Godden, Jon, and Rumer Godden. *Under the Indian Sun*, 1966. Jacket, design.

Goetzmann, William H. *Exploration and Empire: The Explorer and the Scientist in the Winning of the American West*, 1966. Jacket, design. Design of later editions based on this version.

Grau, Shirley Ann. *The Hard Blue Sky*, 1958. Jacket, design.

———. *The House on Coliseum Street*, 1961. Jacket, design.

———. *The Keepers of the House*, 1964. Jacket, design.

Gregor-Dellin, Martin. *The Lamp Post*. Trans. Richard and Clara Winston, 1964. Jacket, design.

Guerard, Albert J. (Joseph) *Maquisard: A Christmas Tale*, 1945. Jacket.

Haalke, Magnhild. *Alli's Son*. Trans. Arthur G. Chater, 1937. Jacket.

Hammerskjöld, Dag. *Markings*. Trans. Leif Sjoberg and W. H. Auden, 1966. Jacket, design, slipcase.

Harris, Mark. *Bang the Drum Slowly*, 1956. Jacket.

Hazzard, Shirley. *Cliffs of Fall and Other Stories*, 1963. Jacket, design.

———. *The Evening of the Holiday*, 1966. Jacket.

———. *People in Glass Houses*, 1967. Jacket.

Hecht, Ben. *Miracle in the Rain*, 1943. Jacket, design.

Hersey, John. *A Bell for Adano*, 1944. Jacket.

———. *A Single Pebble*, 1956. Jacket, typography, binding.

———. *Under the Eye of the Storm*, 1967. Jacket, binding

———. *The Wall*, 1950. Jacket.

Hinkson, Pamela. *The Golden Rose*, 1944. Jacket.

Hubner, Robert Norman. *The Fabulous People*, 1942. Jacket.

Jensen, Johannes V. *The Long Journey*. Trans. Arthur G. Chater, 1945. Jacket.

Jordan, Mildred. *Apple in the Attic*, 1942. Jacket, design.

———. *Miracle in Brittany*, 1950. Jacket, typography, binding.

Kafka, Franz. *The Castle*. Definitive ed. Trans. Willa and Edwin Muir, 1954. Jacket, typography, binding.

———. *The Trial*. Trans. Willa and Edwin Muir, 1937. Jacket, design, illustrations.

———. *The Trial*. Definitive ed. Trans. Willa and Edwin Muir; revised and with additional materials translated by E. M. Butler, 1957. Jacket, design, illustrations.

Karp, David. *All Honorable Men*, 1956. Jacket.

Kästner, Erich. *The Missing Miniature, or The Adventures of a Sensitive Butcher*. Trans. Cyrus Brooks, 1937. Jacket.

Katz, Milton. *The Things That Are Caesar's*, 1966. Jacket, design.

Koningsberger, Hans. *The Affair*, 1958. Jacket, design.

Kytle, Elizabeth. *Willie Mae*, 1958. Jacket, design.

Langgässer, Elisabeth. *The Quest*. Trans. Jane Bannard Greene, 1960. Jacket, design.

Lauer, Stefanie. *Home is the Place*, 1957. Jacket, design.

Lawrence, Frieda. *The Memoirs and Correspondence*. Ed. E. W. Tedlock, 1964. Jacket, design.

Lofts, Norah. *Blossom Like the Rose*, 1939. Binding.

———. *Colin Lowrie*, 1939. Design.

———. *Here was a Man: A Romantic History of Sir Walter Raleigh, His Voyages, His Discoveries, and His Queen*, 1936. Jacket, design.

———. *I Met a Gypsy*, 1935. Jacket, design.

———. *Requiem for Idols*, 1938. Jacket, design.

Loomis, Edward. *Heroic Love*, 1960. Jacket.

Loomis, Frederic. *The Bond Between Us: The Third Component*, 1942. Jacket.

———. *Consultation Room*, 1939. Jacket.

Malania, Fae. *A Quantity of a Hazel Nut*, 1968. Jacket.

Mankiewicz, Don M. *See How They Run*, 1951. Jacket.

Mann, Thomas. *The Confessions of Felix Krull, Confidence Man*. Trans. H. T. Lowe-Porter, 1955. Jacket.

———. *Death in Venice*. Trans. Kenneth Burke, 1965. Jacket, binding, design, slipcase.

———. *Doctor Faustus: The Life of the German Composer Adrian Leverkühn as Told by a Friend*. Trans. H. T. Lowe-Porter, 1948. Jacket.

———. *The Holy Sinner*. Trans. Helen T. Lowe-Porter, 1951. Jacket.

———. *Joseph and his Brothers*. Trans. H. T. Lowe-Porter, 1948. Jacket.

———. *A Sketch of My Life*. Trans. H. T. Lowe-Porter, 1960. Jacket, design.

———. *Stories of Three Decades*. Trans. H. T. Lowe-Porter, 1936. Jacket.

———. *The Story of a Novel: The Genesis of Doctor Faustus*. Trans. Richard and Clara Winston, 1961. Jacket, design.

———. *The Thomas Mann Reader*. Trans. H. T. Lowe-Porter, 1950. Jacket.

———. *The Transposed Heads: A Legend of India.* Trans. H. T. Lowe-Porter, 1941. Jacket, binding, typography.

Martenet, May Davies. *Taw Jameson,* 1953. Jacket.

McArthur, Edwin. *Flagstad: A Personal Memoir,* 1965. Jacket, design.

McCoy, Horace. *I Should Have Stayed Home,* 1938. Jacket.

Mencken, H. L. *Heathen Days,* 1955. Jacket.

———. *Newspaper Days,* 1941. Jacket drawing.

Monserrat, Nicholas. *Castle Garac,* 1955. Jacket.

Morante, Elsa. *Arturo's Island.* Trans. Isabel Quigley, 1959. Design.

Murrow, Edward R. *In Search of Light: The Broadcasts of Edward R. Murrow,* 1967. Jacket, design.

Napier, Elma. *Duet in Discord,* 1937. Jacket.

Nathan, Robert. *The Journey of Tapiola,* 1938. Jacket, design, illustrations.

———. *The Rancho of the Little Loves,* 1956. Jacket, typography, binding, illustrations.

———. *The River Journey,* 1949. Jacket.

———. *The Train in the Meadow,* 1953. Jacket.

———. *The Weans,* 1960. Jacket, typography, binding, illustrations.

O'Connor, Jack. *Boom Town: A Novel of the Southwestern Silver Boom,* 1938. Jacket.

Pick, Robert. *The Escape of Socrates,* 1954. Jacket.

Pinchon, Edgcumb. *Until I Find: A Novel of Boyhood,* 1936. Jacket.

Poe, Edgar Allan. *The Complete Poems and Stories.* 2 vols. The Borzoi Poe. Illustrated by E. McKnight Kauffer, 1946. Lettering on jacket and slipcase label.

Reiner, Anna [Anna Gmeyner]. *The Coward Heart.* Trans. Trevor and Phyllis Blewitt, 1941. Jacket, design.

———. *Five Destinies.* Trans. Philip Owens, 1939. Design.

Richter, Conrad. *The Waters of Kronos,* 1960. Jacket, design.

Robbins, Harold [Francis Kane]. *The Dream Merchants,* 1949. Jacket.

Rollins, Jr., Alfred Brooks. *Roosevelt and Howe,* 1962. Jacket.

Romains, Jules. *The Depths and the Heights,* 1937. Jacket.

Rosaire, Forrest. *East of Midnight,* 1946. Jacket.

Rourke, Thomas. *Haven for the Gallant,* 1935. Design.

Rusk, Rogers D. *Atoms, Men, and Stars,* 1937. Jacket.

Saltmarsh, Max. *The Clouded Moon,* 1938. Jacket.

Samuel, Maurice. *The Devil That Failed,* 1952. Jacket.

Sandoz, Mari. *Crazy Horse, the Strange Man of the Oglalas: A Biography,* 1942. Jacket, design.

Schachtel, Hyman Judah. *The Shadowed Valley: A Solace for the Bereaved,* 1962. Jacket, design.

Schisgall, Oscar. *Swastika,* 1939. Jacket.

Schuschnigg, Kurt. *My Austria.* Trans. John Segrue, 1938. Jacket, cover.

The Shining Tree and Other Christmas Stories. 1940. Jacket.

Shirer, William. *Berlin Diary,* 1941. Jacket, binding.

Silberstang, Edwin. *Nightmare of the Dark,* 1967. Jacket, design.

Singer, I. J. (Israel Joshua). *The Brothers Ashkenazi.* Trans. Maurice Samuel, 1938. Jacket.

———. *East of Eden.* Trans. Maurice Samuel, 1939. Jacket.

Singer, Isaac Bashevis. *The Family Moskat,* 1950. Jacket, binding, design.

Spark, Muriel. *The Girls of Slender Means,* 1963. Jacket, design.

———. *The Mandelbaum Gate,* 1965. Jacket, design.

Spengler, Oswald. *The Decline of the West.* Abr. ed. Trans. Charles Francis Atkinson, 1962. Jacket, typography, binding. Salter's design also used on 1965 Modern Library edition.

Stern, G. B. (Gladys Bronwyn). *The Matriarch Chronicles,* 1936. Jacket.

Straight, Michael Whitney. *Carrington,* 1960. Jacket, design.

———. *A Very Small Remnant,* 1963. Jacket.

Strong, L. A. G. (Leonard Alfred George). *The Seven Arms,* 1935. Jacket.

Stuart, Francis. *Julie,* 1938. Jacket

Szeps, Berta. *My Life and History.* Trans. John Sommerfield, 1939. Jacket.

Thirlwall, John C. *In Another Language: A Record of the Thirty-year Relationship Between Thomas Mann and His English Translator, Helen Tracy Lowe-Porter,* 1966. Jacket, design.

Tolstoy, Alexei. *Road to Calvary.* Trans. Edith Bone, 1946. Jacket.

Tute, Warren. *The Golden Greek,* 1961. Jacket, design.

Ukers, William Harrison. *The Romance of Tea: An Outline History of Tea and Tea Drinking through Sixteen Hundred Years,* 1936. Jacket.

Undset, Sigrid. *Four Stories.* Trans. Naomi Walford, 1959. Jacket.

———. *Madame Dorothea.* Trans. Arthur D. Chater, 1940. Jacket.

———. *The Winding Road (The Wild Orchid and The Burning Bush),* 1936. Jacket.

Vailland, Roger. *Fête.* Trans. Peter Wiles, 1961. Design.

———. *The Law.* Trans. Peter Wiles, 1958. Design.

Wahlöö, Per. *The Thirty-First Floor.* Trans. Joan Tate, 1967. Jacket.

Watkin, Lawrence Edward. *Geese in the Forum,* 1940. Jacket.

———. *On Borrowed Time,* 1937. Jacket, title page, binding. Robert Josephy used Salter's display font Flex in his design.

Weber, Carl Jefferson. *Hardy of Wessex: His Life and Literary Career,* 1940. Jacket.

Weiskopf, F. C. (Franz Carl). *The Firing Squad.* Trans. James A. Galston, 1944. Jacket.

———. *Twilight on the Danube.* Trans. Olga Marx, 1946. Jacket.

L. B. Fischer (New York)

Bercovici, Konrad. *Citizens in Uniform,* 1942. Jacket.

Brooks, Howard Lee. *Prisoners of Hope: Report on a Mission,* 1942. Jacket.

Elbogen, Paul, ed. *Dearest Mother: Letters of Famous Sons to their Mothers,* 1942. Jacket.

Huie, William Bradford. *Mud on the Stars,* 1942. Jacket.

Huie, William Bradford, with Colonel Hugh J. Knerr. *The Fight for Air Power,* 1942. Jacket.

Leonov, Leonid. *Road to the Ocean.* Trans. Norbert Guterman, 1944. Jacket.

Mann, Klaus, and Hermann Kesten, eds. *Heart of Europe: An Anthology of Creative Writing in Europe, 1920–1940,* 1943. Jacket.

Newman, Joseph. *Goodbye Japan,* 1942. Jacket.

Pauli, Herta Ernestine. *Alfred Nobel: Dynamite King, Architect of Peace,* 1942. Jacket.

Pope, Arthur Upham. *Maxim Litvinoff,* 1943. Jacket.

Schwarzschild, Leopold. *World in Trance: From Versailles to Pearl Harbor.* Trans. Norbert Guterman, 1942. Jacket.

Tate, Allen, and John Peale Bishop, eds. *American Harvest: Twenty Years of Creative Writing in the United States,* 1942. Jacket.

Totheroh, Dan. *Deep Valley,* 1942. Jacket.

Werfel, Franz. *Verdi: The Man in His Letters.* Trans. Edward Downes 1942. Jacket.

Zoff, Otto. *The Huguenots: Fighters for God and Human Freedom.* Trans. Ernst Basch and Jo Mayo, 1942. Jacket.

Limited Editions Club (New York)

Du Maurier, George. *Peter Ibbetson.* Limited Editions Club 350. Illustrated by the author, 1963. Design, slipcase.

Gautier, Théophile. *Mademoiselle de Maupin.* Limited Editions Club 154. Illustrated by André Dugo, 1944. Design.

Heine, Heinrich. *Poems of Henrich Heine.* Limited Editions Club 273. Trans. Louis Untermeyer. Illustrated by Fritz Kredel, 1957. Design, slipcase.

Leach, MacEdward, ed. *The Book of Ballads.* Limited Editions Club 394. Illustrated by Fritz Kredel, 1967. Design.

Raspe, Rudolph Erich, and John Carswell. *The Singular Adventures of Baron Münchhausen.* Limited Editions Club 221. Illustrated by Fritz Kredel, 1952. Design.

Twain, Mark. *The Innocents Abroad, or The New Pilgrims' Progress.* Illustrated by Fritz Kredel, 1962. Design.

Virgil (Publius Virgilius Maro). *The Eclogues.* Limited Editions Club 310. Trans. C. S. Calverley. Illustrated by Vertès, 1960. Design, slipcase.

Zola, Emile. *Nana*. Trans. F. J. Vizetelly, 1948. Design.

Lippincott (Philadelphia & New York)
Gogarty, Oliver St. John. *Mad Grandeur*, 1941. Jacket.
Kutak, Rosemary. *Darkness of Slumber*. Mainline Mysteries, 1944. Jacket.
Kyd, Thomas. *Blood is a Beggar*, 1945. Jacket.
O'Hara, Mary. *My Friend Flicka*, 1944. Design.
———. *Thunderhead*. Illustrated by John Stueart Curry, 1941. Design.
Ullmann, James Ramsey. *The Sands of Karakorum*, 1953. Jacket.

Little, Brown (Boston, Massachusetts)
Albrand, Martha. *Endure No Longer*, 1944. Jacket.
Clark, Christopher. *The Unleashed Will*, 1947. Jacket.
Cronin, A. J. (Archibald Joseph). *Beyond This Place*, 1953. Jacket.
———. *Spanish Gardener*, 1950. Jacket.
———. *A Thing of Beauty*, 1956. Jacket.
Edmonds, Walter D. *Drums Along the Mohawk*, 1936. Jacket.
Frankau, Pamela [Eliot Naylor]. *The Offshore Light*, 1953. Jacket.
Gibbs, Arthur Hamilton. *Obedience to the Moon*, 1956. Jacket.
Hopkinson, Tom. *Mist in the Tagus*, 1947. Jacket.
Javellana, Stevan. *Without Seeing the Dawn*, 1947. Jacket.
Jonas, Carl. *Jefferson Selleck*, 1952. Jacket.
———. *Riley McCullough*, 1954. Jacket.
Latham, Edythe. *The Sounding Brass*, 1953. Jacket.
Macaulay, Rose. *The World My Wilderness*, 1950. Jacket.
MacInnes, Helen. *While Still We Live*, 1944. Jacket.
MacLennan, Hugh. *Each Man's Son*, 1951. Jacket.
Maltz, Albert. *The Underground Stream*, 1940. Jacket.
Marquand, John P. *B. F.'s Daughter*, 1946. Jacket.
———. *Melville Goodwin, USA*, 1951. Jacket.
———. *North of Grand Central. Three Novels of New England: The Late George Apley, Wickford Point, H. M. Pulham, Esquire*, 1956. Jacket.
———. *Point of No Return*, 1947. Jacket.
———. *Sincerely, Willis Wayde*, 1955. Jacket.
———. *So Little Time*, 1943. Jacket.
———. *Thirty Years*, 1954. Jacket.
Marsh, Ngaio. *Night at the Vulcan*, 1951. Jacket.
Mergendahl, Charles. *His Days are as Grass*, 1946. Jacket.
Oppenheim, E. Phillips. *The Oppenheim Secret Service Omnibus*. Vol. 1, 1946, Jacket.
Polonsky, Abraham. *The World Above*, 1951. Jacket.
Prokosch, Frederic. *A Tale for Midnight*, 1955. Jacket.
Raddall, Thomas H. *The Nymph and the Lamp*, 1950. Jacket.

Sherman, Richard. *The Bright Promise*, 1947. Jacket.
Sklar, George. *The Two Worlds of Johnny Truro*, 1947. Jacket.
Stead, Christina. *The People with the Dogs*, 1952. Jacket.
Vance, Ethel [Grace Zaring]. *Escape*, 1939. Binding
Vidal, Gore. *The Judgment of Paris*, 1952. Jacket.
Waugh, Evelyn. *The Ordeal of Gilbert Pinfold*, 1957. Jacket.
Wilson, Mitchell. *My Brother, My Enemy*, 1952. Jacket.

Longmans, Green (New York & Toronto)
Massie, Chris. *Falcon Road*, 1936. Jacket.
Meade, Julian R. *Adam's Profession and its Conquest by Eve*, 1936. Jacket, illustrations.
Phillips, N. D. *The Home Guide to Modern Nutrition*. Pamphlet, 1942. Cover.

Macmillan (New York)
Askham, Francis. *A Foolish Wind*, 1947. Jacket.
Eells, Richard. *The Corporation and the Arts. Studies in the Modern Corporation*, 1967. Jacket, design.
Hawthorne, Julian. *Memoirs of Julian Hawthorne*, 1938. Jacket, design.
MacManus, Seamus. *The Rocky Road to Dublin*, 1938. Jacket.
Neumann, Alfred. *Six of Them*. Trans. Anatol Murad, 1945. Jacket.
Royde-Smith, Naomi Gladys. *For Us in the Dark*, 1937. Jacket.
Stern, G. B. (Gladys Bronwyn). *Oleander River*, 1937. Jacket, binding.

McDowell, Obolensky (New York)
Hauser, Marianne. *The Choir Invisible*, 1958. Jacket.

McGraw-Hill (New York)
Adams, Elwood A., and Edward Everett Walker. *Living in the City*, 1949. Design, binding.
Margolies, Joseph A., and Christopher Morley, eds. *Strange & Fantastic Stories: Fifty Tales of Terror, Horror and Fantasy*, 1946. Jacket.
Samuelson, Paul A., *Economics: An Introductory Analysis*, 1948. Binding, first edition only.
Waugh, Albert Edmund. *Principles of Economics*, 1947. Binding.

Merito, Editora Merito (São Paolo, Brasil)
Enciclopedia brasiliera mérito, 2nd ed. 20 vols., 1957. Binding.

Morrow (New York)
Wicker, Thomas. *Kennedy Without Tears*, 1964. Design.

New York Times (New York)
Morley, Christopher. *Ex Libris: A Small Anthology, Printed and Bound (and Sold) at the First National Book Fair Sponsored by the New York Times and the National Association of Book Publishers*, 1936. Jacket.

Oxford University Press (New York)
Bartlett, Vernon. *Intermission in Europe: The Life of a Journalist and Broadcaster*, 1938. Jacket.
Douglas, Norman. *Old Calabria*. The World's Classics 467, 1938. Jacket.
Garcia-Lorca, Federico. *Lament for the Death of a Bullfighter*. Trans. A. L. Lloyd, 1938. Jacket.
Gubsky [Gubskii], Nikolai. *Angry Dust: An Autobiography*, 1937. Jacket.
Gumpert, Martin. *Dunant: The Story of the Red Cross*, 1938. Jacket.
Haggin, Bernhard H. *The Book of the Symphony*, 1937. Jacket. Same design used by edition published by Methuen (London).
Jones, Jack. *Unfinished Journey*, 1937. Jacket.
Luling, Elizabeth, with Sylvia Thompson and George Salter. *Do Not Disturb: The Adventures of M'm and Teddy*, 1937. Jacket, illustrations.
Mallarmé, Stéphane. *Poems of Mallarmé*. Trans. Roger Fry, 1937. Jacket.
Noel-Baker, Philip. *The Private Manufacture of Armaments*, 1937. Jacket.
Whitman, Willson. *Bread and Circuses: A Study of Federal Theatre*, 1937. Jacket.

Pantheon (New York)
Cortázar, Julio. *Hopscotch*. Trans. Gregory Rabassa, 1966. Jacket, design.
Lindbergh, Anne Morrow. *The Gift from the Sea*. Special edition. Illustrated by George W. Thompson, 1955. Binding, slipcase.
Zoshchenko, Mikhail. *Nervous People and Other Satires*. Trans. Maria Gordon and Hugh McLean, 1963. Jacket.

Penguin Books (New York)
Forster, E. M. (Edward Morgan). *A Passage to India*, 1946. Cover.
Hasek, Jaroslav. *The Good Soldier Schweik*, 1946. Cover lettering.
Lawrence, D. H. (David Herbert). *The Lovely Lady*, 1946. Cover.
Shaw, George Bernard. *Major Barbara: A Screen Version*, 1946. Cover.
———. *Pygmalion: A Romance in Five Acts*, 1946. Cover.
———. *Saint Joan: A Chronicle Play in Six Scenes and an Epilogue*, 1946. Cover.
Silone, Ignazio. *Bread and Wine*. Trans. Gwenda David and Eric Mosbacher, 1946. Cover.
Withers, Carl, ed. *Penguin Book of Sonnets*, 1943. Cover.

Woolf, Virginia. *Orlando: A Biography*, 1946. Cover.

Pitman (New York)
Schneiderman, Harry, and Itzhak Carmin, ed. *Who's Who in World Jewry*, 1955. Design.

Pergamon (New York)
Columbia School of Business, Columbia University. *Columbia Journal of World Business*, 1965. Cover design, typography.
Thewlis, James, and R. C. Glass, et. al. *Encyclopaedic Dictionary of Physics*, 1966. Jacket.

Pocket Books (New York)
Geddes, Donald Porter, ed. *Franklin Delano Roosevelt: A Memorial*, 1945. Cover.
Hinds, Arthur, ed. *The Complete Sayings of Jesus*, 1945. Cover.
Salten, Felix. *Bambi*. Trans. Whittaker Chambers, 1942. Cover.
Sharp, Margery. *The Nutmeg Tree*, 1942. Cover.

Prentice-Hall (Englewood Cliffs, New Jersey)
Cochran, Hamilton. *These are the Virgin Islands*, 1947. Jacket.
Rees, Ennis. *The Little Greek Alphabet Book*, 1968. Jacket, design, illustrations.

Private Publications
Buckminster, Harold C. *To Help Other Men: A Selection from the Sermons of Harold C. Buckminster*. Pinehurst, N.C.: Edmonde W. Buckminster, 1960. Jacket, design.
Heublein & Brothers, Inc., *The House of Heublein: An American Institution*. Illustrated by Fritz Kredel. Hartford, Conn.: G. F. Heublein & Brothers, 1962. Design, lettering.
Karagheusian, Inc. *Carpeting by Karagheusian in the American Scene of Today*. N.Y.: A. & M. Karagheusian, Inc. 1941. Cover.

Putnam (New York)
Asch, Sholem. *The Nazarene*. Trans. Maurice Samuel, 1939. Jacket.
Churchill, Winston. *Blood, Sweat and Tears*, 1941. Binding

Pyramid Books (New York)
Nathan, Robert. *So Love Returns*, 1962. Cover

R. M. McBride (New York)
Buck, Frank, and Ferrin Fraser. *All in a Lifetime*, 1941. Jacket.

Random House, including Modern Library (New York)
Barker, Shirley. *Swear By Apollo*, 1958. Design.
Barrett, Leighton. *Though Young*, 1938. Jacket.
Becker, Belle, and Robert N. Linscott. *Bedside Book of Famous French Stories*, 1945. Jacket.
Bemelmans, Ludwig. *My War with the United States*. Modern Library. Illustrated by L. Bemelmans, 1941. Design.
Bliven, Bruce. *The American Revolution, 1760–1783*. Landmark Books 83, 1958. Jacket, maps.
Boccaccio, Giovanni. *The Decameron*. Modern Library 71. Trans. Frances Winwar, 1955. Jacket.
Brunngraber, Rudolf. *Radium*. Trans. Eden and Cedar Paul, 1937. Jacket.
Buckmaster, Henrietta [Henrietta Henkle]. *All the Living: A Novel of One Year in the Life of William Shakespeare*, 1962. Jacket, design.
Burrell, Angus, and Bennett Cerf, eds. *An Anthology of Famous American Stories*. Modern Library Giant 77, 1946. Jacket.
———. *Bedside Book of Famous American Stories*. Modern Library Giant 77, 1953. Jacket.
Callaghan, Morley. *They Shall Inherit the Earth*, 1935. Jacket.
Calvino, Italo. *The Baron in the Trees*. Trans. Archibald Colquhoun, 1959. Jacket, design.
Camus, Albert. *Notebooks 1935–1942*. Modern Library 349. Trans. and preface by Philip Thody, 1963. Jacket.
———. *Resistance, Rebellion, and Death*. Modern Library 339. Trans. Justin O'Brien, 1963. Jacket.
Capote, Truman. *The Thanksgiving Visitor*, 1967. Binding, typography, slipcase.
———. *A Christmas Memory*, 1967. Binding, typography, slipcase.
Carroll, Lewis [Charles L. Dodson]. *Alice's Adventures in Wonderland and Through the Looking-glass*. Illustrations colored by Fritz Kredel. 2 vols., 1946. Design, slipcase.
Carroll, Lewis. *Complete Works of Lewis Carroll*. Modern Library Giant 28, 1954. Jacket.
Cerf, Bennett, and Henry Curran Moriarty, eds. *An Anthology of Famous British Stories*. Modern Library Giant 54, 1952. Jacket.
de Cervantes Saavedra, Miguel. *The First Part of the Life and Achievements of the Renowned Don Quixote de la Mancha*. Trans. Peter Motteux. Illustrated by Hans Alexander Mueller, 1941. Design, slipcase.
———. *The First Part of the Life and Achievements of the Renowned Don Quixote de la Mancha*. Trans. Peter Motteux. Illustrated by Salvador Dalí, 1946. Design and jacket lettering on clear plastic over decorated cover.
Chang, Diana C. *The Frontiers of Love*, 1946. Jacket.
Chase, Allan. *The Five Arrows*, 1944. Jacket.

Clark, Walter van Tilburg. *The City of Trembling Leaves*, 1945. Jacket, design.
Dickens, Charles. *The Posthumous Papers of the Pickwick Club*. Illustrated by Donald McKay, 1943. Design, slipcase.
Dinesen, Isak [Karen Blixen]. *Shadow on the Grass*, 1960. Design.
———. *Winter's Tales*, 1942. Jacket, endpapers.
———. *Winter's Tales*. Book of the Month Club Edition, 1942. Jacket, binding.
Dostoevski, Fyodor. *Brothers Karamazov*. Modern Library 151. Trans. Constance Garnett, 1943. Design.
Eyster, Warren. *The Goblins of Eros*, 1957. Jacket.
Faulkner, William. *Absalom, Absalom!*, 1936. Jacket.
———. *The Hamlet*, 1940 Jacket.
Fowler, Gene. *Illusion in Java*, 1939. Jacket.
Garrett, Zena. *The House in the Mulberry Tree*, 1959. Jacket.
Godfrey, John Trevor. *The Look of Eagles*, 1958. Design.
Hammerstein, Oscar. *Oklahoma!*, 1943. Binding.
Hamner, Earl Henry. *Fifty Roads to Town*, 1953. Jacket.
Healy, Raymond, and J. Francis McComas. *Famous Science-Fiction Stories: Adventures in Time and Space*. Modern Library Giant 31, 1957. Jacket.
Healy, Raymond J., and J. Francis McComas, eds. *Adventures in Time and Space: An Anthology of Modern Science-Fiction Stories*, 1946. Jacket, design, binding.
Hillyer, Robert. *My Heart for Hostage*, 1942. Jacket.
Josephs, Ray. *Argentine Diary: The Inside Story of the Coming of Fascism*, 1944. Design, title page lettering, endpapers.
Kafka, Franz. *The Trial*. Definitive ed. Modern Library 318. Trans. Willa and Edwin Muir. Revised and with additional materials translated by E. M. Butler, 1956. Illustrations from 1937 Knopf ed.
Krasna, Norma. *Dear Ruth: A Comedy*, 1945. Binding.
Longstreet, Stephen. *The Land I Live*, 1943. Jacket.
Marshall, Lenore. *The Hill is Level*, 1959. Design.
Millar, Margaret. *The Iron Gates*, 1945. Jacket.
Odlum, Floyd B. *Selected Speeches 1930–1960*, 1960. Jacket, design.
Pagano, Jo. *Golden Wedding*, 1943. Jacket.
Paul, Elliot. *The Life and Death of a Spanish Town*, 1937. Jacket.
Pratt, Rex K. *You Tell My Son*, 1958. Design.
Raichlis, Eugene. *They Came to Kill: The Story of Eight Nazi Saboteurs in America*, 1961. Design, map.
Rand, Ayn. *Atlas Shrugged*, 1957. Jacket.
Randau, Carl, and Leane Zugsmith. *The Visitor*, 1944. Jacket.
Rodgers, Richard, and Oscar Hammerstein. *Oklahoma*, 1944. Binding.

Santayana, George. *The Sense of Beauty*. Modern Library 292, 1955. Jacket.

Scherman, Harry. *One-Legged Nation*, 1938. Reprinted from *The Saturday Evening Post*. Illustrations.

Sheean, Vincent. *Bird of the Wilderness*, 1941. Jacket.

Snow, Edgar. *The People on Our Side*, 1944. Illustrations by Fritz Kredel. Lettering on jacket, endpaper maps.

Spengler, Oswald. *The Decline of the West*. Abr. ed. Modern Library Giant 92. Trans. Charles Francis Atkinson, 1965. Jacket, typography, binding. Salter's design for 1962 Knopf ed., altered here without permission and his signature omitted.

Statler, Oliver. *Japanese Inn*, 1961. Design.

Styron, William. *Lie Down in Darkness*, 1979. Jacket based on Salter's 1951 design for the novel published by Bobbs-Merrill.

Stendhal [Marie-Henri Beyle]. *The Red and the Black*. Modern Library 157. Trans. C. K. Scott-Moncrieff, 1953. Jacket.

Tolstoy, Leo. *Anna Karenina*. 2 vols. Trans. Constance Garnett. Introduction by Thomas Mann. Illustrated by Philip Reisman, 1939. Design.
——. *Selected Essays*. Modern Library 347. Trans. Aylmer Maude, 1964. Jacket.
——. *Short Stories*. Vol. I. Modern Library 346, 1964. Jacket.
——. *Short Stories*. Vol. II. Modern Library 361, 1964. Jacket.

Treece, Henry. *Red Queen, White Queen*, 1958. Design.

Tregaskis, Richard. *Invasion Diary*, 1944. Maps.
——. *Stronger Than Fear*, 1945. Jacket.

Van der Lugt, Arie. *The Crazy Doctor*. Trans. Alfred van Duym, 1954. Jacket.

Van Druten, John. *The Voice of the Turtle: A Comedy in Three Acts*, 1944. Jacket.

Ward, Mary Jane. *The Snake Pit*, 1946. Jacket, title page lettering.

Warren, Robert Penn. *Brother to Dragons: A Tale in Verse and Voices*, 1953. Design.

Weldon, John Lee. *Thunder in the Heart*, 1954. Jacket.

West, Anthony. *The Trend is Up*, 1960. Design.

Whitcomb, Catherine. *In the Fine Summer Weather*, 1938. Jacket, binding.

Wilhelm, Gale. *Torchlight to Valhalla*, 1938. Jacket, design.

Wise, Herbert Alvin, and Phyllis M. Fraser, eds. *Great Tales of Terror and the Supernatural*, 1944. Jacket, typography.

Wolff, Maritta. *Back of Town*, 1952. Jacket.
——. *The Big Nickelodeon*, 1956. Jacket.
——. *Night Shift*, 1942. Jacket.

Readers Library (Chicago)

Chidsey, Donald Barr. *Weeping is for Women*. Readers Library 1, 1940. Cover.

Cozzens, James Gould. *The Last Adam*. Readers Library 3, 1940. Cover.

Hardy, J. L. (Jocelyn Lee). *Everything is Thunder*. Readers Library, 1940. Cover.

Steinbeck, John. *Cup of Gold: A Lusty Buccaneer Novel*. Readers Library 4, 1940. Cover.

Reilly-Lee (Chicago)

Bogan, Louise, and William Jay Smith. *The Golden Journey: Poems for Young People*. Illustrated by Fritz Kredel, 1965. Design.

Roy Publishers (New York)

Kossak, Zofia. *Blessed are the Meek: A Novel about St. Francis of Assisi*. Trans. Rulka Langer, 1944. Jacket, title page.

Kossak, Zofia. *The Leper King*. Trans. Floyd S. Placzek, 1945. Jacket.

Odic, Charles Jean. *Stepchildren of France*. Trans. Henry Noble Hall, 1945. Jacket.

Sales Research Institute (New York)

Epstein, Leon D. *Where Do You Go From No: Selling Simplified*, 1951. Jacket, design.

Scribners (New York)

Aldanov, Mark. *The Fifth Seal*. Trans. Nicholas Wreden, 1943. Jacket, binding.

Simon & Schuster (New York)

Adler, Elmer, ed. *Breaking into Print: Being a Compilation of Papers Wherein each Select Group of Authors Tells the Difficulties of Authorship & How Such Trials are Met*, 1937. Jacket.

Auslander, Joseph. *The Unconquerables: Salutes to the Undying Spirit of the Nazi-occupied Countries*, 1943. Jacket.

Bell, Adrian. *The Balcony*, 1936 Jacket.

Brand, Millen. *The Outward Room*, 1937. Jacket.

Breuer, Bessie. *Memory of Love*, 1935. Jacket.

Buck, Frank, and Ferrin Fraser. *Fang and Claw*, 1935. Jacket.

Cleator, P. E. (Philip Ellaby). *Rockets Through Space: The Dawn of Interplanetary Travel*, 1936. Jacket.

Craven, Thomas. *Men of Art*, 1936. Jacket.

Dimnet, Ernest. *My New World*, 1937. Jacket.
——. *My Old World*, 1935. Jacket.

Durant, Will. *The Story of Civilization: Our Oriental Heritage*, 1935. Jacket.

Fallada, Hans. *An Old Heart Goes A-Journeying*. Trans. Eric Sutton, 1936. Jacket.

Faulkner, Virginia. *The Barbarians*, 1935. Jacket.

Godowsky, Leopold, ed. *Operatic Masterpieces: Carmen, by Georges Bizet*, 1936. Cover.
——. *Operatic Masterpieces: Faust, by François Gounod*, 1936. Cover.
——. *Operatic Masterpieces: Il Trovatore, by Giuseppe Verdi*, 1936. Cover.
——. *Operatic Masterpieces: Tannhäuser, by Richard Wagner*, 1936. Cover.

Johnson, Josephine. *Winter Orchard and other Stories*, 1935. Jacket.

MacFarlane, Katherine Jean. *Divide the Desolation: A Novel Based on the Life of Emily Jane Brontë*, 1936. Jacket.

Modell, Merriam [Evelyn Piper]. *The Sound of Years*, 1946. Jacket.

Ofaire, Cilette. *The San Luca*. Trans. Beren Van Slyke, 1935. Jacket.

Peattie, Donald Culross. *Green Laurels: The Lives and Achievements of the Great Naturalists*, 1936. Jacket, title page lettering.

Pitkin, Walter B. *Take it Easy: The Art of Relaxation*, 1935. Jacket, spine label.

Powys, John Cowper. *The Art of Happiness*, 1935. Jacket.

Slesinger, Tess. *Time: the Present: A Book of Short Stories*, 1935. Jacket.

Speyer, Wilhelm. *The Court of Fair Maidens*. Trans. Trevor and Phyllis Blewitt, 1936. Jacket.

Stravinsky, Igor. *An Autobiography*, 1936. Jacket.

Smith and Haas; Harrison Smith and Robert Haas (New York)

Coleman, McAlister, and Stephen Rauschenbush. *Red Neck*, 1936. Jacket.

Doolaard, A. Den[Cornelius Johannes George (Bob) Spoelstra]. *Express to the East*. Trans. David C. de Jong, 1935. Jacket.

Time-Life Books (Alexandria, Virginia)

Guthrie, Jr., Alfred Bertram. *The Big Sky*, 1964. Cover.

Smith, Gene. *When the Cheering Stopped: The Last Years of Woodrow Wilson*, 1966. Cover.

The Typophiles (New York)

Bennett, Paul A., and Christopher Morley. *Left to Their Own Devices*, 1937. Jacket and two designs ("devices") by Salter, p. 168, 170.

Knopf, Alfred, and Paul A. Bennett. *Portrait of a Publisher 1915–1965*. Typophiles Chapbook 43. 2 vols., 1965. Design.

Vanguard (New York)

Dickinson, Roy. *The Ultimate Frog: An Unforgettable Story of a Strange Quest*, 1939. Jacket, binding, illustrations.

Jagendorf, M. A. (Moritz Adolph). *Tyll Ulenspiegel's Merry Pranks*. Illustrated by Fritz Eichenberg, 1938. Jacket.

McClintock, Theodore. *The Underwater Zoo*, 1938. Design.

Nexø, Martin Andersen. *Under the Open Sky: My Early Years*. Trans. J. B. C. Watkins, 1936. Jacket.

Shadid, Michael Abraham. *A Doctor for the People: The Autobiography of the Founder of America's First Co-operative Hospital*, 1939. Jacket.

Young, Art. *The Best of Art Young*, 1936. Jacket, design.

Viking (New York)

Auden, W. H. (Wystan Hugh), ed. *The Portable Greek Reader*, 1954. Cover.

Beagle, Peter S. *A Fine and Private Place*, 1960. Jacket.

Broch, Hermann. *The Unknown Quantity*. Trans. Willa and Edwin Muir, 1935. Jacket.

Buchanan, Scott, ed. *The Portable Plato: "Protagoras", "Symposium", "Phaedo", and "The Republic."* Trans. Benjamin Jowett, 1966. Cover.

Dornfeld, Iris. *Jeeney Ray*, 1962. Jacket.

Edman, Irwin. *Philosopher's Holiday*, 1938. Jacket.

Franko, Sam. *Chords and Discords: Memoirs and Musings of an American Musician*, 1938. Jacket.

Godden, Rumer. *A Breath of Air*, 1951. Jacket.

———. *China Court: The Hours of a Country House*, 1961. Jacket, design.

———. *An Episode of Sparrows*, 1955. Jacket.

Greene, Graham. *Brighton Rock: An Entertainment*, 1938. Jacket.

Jennison, Keith Warren. *The Boys and Their Mother*, 1956. Jacket.

Jones, Madison. *A Buried Land*, 1963. Jacket.

Milano, Paolo, ed. *The Portable Dante*. Trans. Laurence Binyon, et al., 1947. Cover.

Prokosch, Frederic. *Nine Days to Mukalla*, 1953. Jacket.

Wells, H. G. *The Croquet Player*, 1937. Jacket.

White, Patrick. *Riders in the Chariot*, 1961. Jacket.

———. *The Tree of Man*, 1955. Jacket.

———. *Voss*, 1957. Jacket.

Zuckmayer, Carl. *The Moons Ride Over*. Trans. Moray Firth [pseud.], 1937. Jacket.

Zweig, Arnold. *Education Before Verdun*. Trans. Eric Sutton, 1936. Jacket.

Zweig, Stefan. *Beware of Pity*. Trans. Phyllis and Trevor Blewitt, 1939. Jacket.

———. *Mary, Queen of Scotland and the Isles*. Trans. Eden and Cedar Paul, 1935. Jacket, binding.

Vintage (New York)

Auden, W. H. (Wystan Hugh). *The Enchafed Flood, or The Romantic Iconography of the Sea*. V-398, 1967. Cover.

Cash, W. J. (Wilbur Joseph). *The Mind of the South*. K-98, 1960. Cover.

Fedin, Konstantin. *Early Joys*. V-709. Trans. Mrs. G. Kazanina, 1960. Cover.

Fenno, Richard F. *The President's Cabinet: An Analysis in the Period from Wilson to Eisenhower*. V-501, 1962. Cover.

Forster, E. M. (Edward Morgan). *A Room With a View*. V-187, 1961. Cover.

Mann, Thomas. *Death in Venice and Seven Other Stories*. V-K3. Trans. H. T. Lowe-Porter, 1954. Cover.

Mencken, H. L. (Henry Louis). *Treatise on the Gods*. V-232, 1963. Cover.

Synge, John Millington. *The Aran Islands and Other Writings*. V-53, 1962. Cover.

William Morrow (New York)

Blackmar, Mary K., and Bruce Gould. *Conversations on the Edge of Eternity*, 1965. Design.

William E. Rudge's Sons (New York)

Anderson, Lee. *Prevailing Winds: A Poem in Four Parts in the Shape of a Symphony*, 1941. Design.

World Publishing Co. (Cleveland & New York)

Bellamy, Edward. *Looking Backward 2000–1887*, 1946. Design, illustrations, slipcase. Limited edition of 950 copies.

Blacker, Irwin R. *Taos*, 1959. Jacket.

Cottrell, Leonard. *Digs and Diggers: A Book of World Archeology*, 1964. Jacket.

Dodge, Mary Mapes. *Hans Brinker, or The Silver Skates*. Illustrated by Hilda Van Stockum, 1946. Lettering.

Hagen, Victor W. von. *The Ancient Sun Kingdoms of the Americas*, 1961. Jacket.

Kennedy, Jay Richard. *Short Term*, 1959. Jacket, title page lettering.

Sitwell, Sacheverell. *The Bridge of the Brocade Sash: Travels and Observations in Japan*, 1959. Jacket.

Ullmann, James Ramsey. *The Day on Fire: A Novel Suggested by the Life of Arthur Rimbaud*, 1958. Jacket, binding.

Zara, Louis. *Dark Rider: A Novel Based on the Life of Stephen Crane*, 1961. Jacket.

Ziff-Davis (Chicago & New York)

Todorov, Kosta. *Balkan Firebrand: The Autobiography of a Rebel Soldier and Statesman*, 1943. Jacket.

Designs for series

[Abrams] Harry N. Abrams (in association with Pocket Books) (New York)

Salter did the cover lettering for The Pocket Library of Great Art in 1953:

Faison, S. Lane. *Edouard Manet* (A13).

Fox, Milton S. *Pierre Auguste Renoir* (A11).

Goldwater, Robert John. *Vincent Van Gogh* (A6).

Greenberg, Clement. *Matisse* (A10).

Hartt, Frederick. *Sandro Botticelli* (A9).

Held, Julius Samuel. *Peter Paul Rubens* (A17).

Hunter, Sam. *Henri de Toulouse-Lautrec* (A3).

Koehler, Wilhelm. *Rembrandt Harmenszoon van Rijn* (A8).

Lieberman, William Slattery. *Pablo Picasso: Blue and Rose Periods* (A20).

Lipchitz, Jacques. *Amedeo Modigliani* (A16).

Maritain, Jacques. *Georges Rouault* (A14).

Matthews, John F. *El Greco* (A2).

Rewald, John. *Paul Gauguin* (A15).

———. *Camille Pisarro* (A18).

Rich, Daniel Catton. *Paul Degas* (A1).

Rousseau, Theodor. *Paul Cezanne* (A4).

Salinger, Margaretta M. *Michelangelo Buonarroti: The Last Judgment* (A23).

———. *Diego Velázquez* (A19).

Wechsler, Herman Joel. *French Impressionists and their Circle* (A7).

Werner, Alfred. *Maurice Utrillo* (A12).

———. *Raoul Dufy* (A5).

[Abrams] Harry N. Abrams (New York)

Salter designed, lettered, and produced the series logo for The Library of Great Painters, Portfolio Editions.

[Black] Walter J. Black (New York) for The Classics Club Library.

Salter designed the series binding (1941–1942).

[Black] Walter J. Black for the Detective Book Club (New York)

Salter's own work log lists 46 separate jackets done for this series between 1942 and 1945.

David McKay (Philadelphia)

Salter designed the jacket for the Living Thoughts Library. Titles include:

Clausewitz, Carl von. *The Living Thoughts of Clausewitz*. Ed. Joseph Ingham Greene, 1943.

Confucius. *The Living Thoughts of Confucius*. Ed. Alfred Döblin, 1940.

Darwin, Charles. *The Living Thoughts of Darwin*. Ed. Julian Huxley, 1939.

Emerson, Ralph Waldo. *The Living Thoughts of Emerson*. Ed. Edgar Lee Masters, 1940.

Freud, Sigmund. *The Living Thoughts of Freud*. Ed. Robert Waelder, 1941

Jefferson, Thomas. *The Living Thoughts of Jefferson*. Ed. John Dewey, 1940.

Kant, Immanuel. *The Living Thoughts of Kant*. Ed. Julien Benda, 1940.

Machiavelli, Niccolo. *The Living Thoughts of Machiavelli*. Ed. Count Carlo Sforza, 1940.

Marx, Karl. *The Living Thoughts of Marx*. Ed. Leon Trotzky, 1939.

Mazzini, Giuseppe. *The Living Thoughts of Mazzini*. Ed. Ignazio Silone, 1939.

Montaigne, Michel de. *The Living Thoughts of Montaigne*. Ed. André Gide, 1939.

Nietzsche, Friedrich. *The Living Thoughts of Nietzsche.* Ed. Heinrich Mann, 1939.
Paine, Thomas. *The Living Thoughts of Tom Paine.* Ed. John Dos Passos, 1940.
Pascal, Blaise. *The Living Thoughts of Pascal.* Ed. François Mauriac, 1940.
Paul. *The Living Thoughts of Saint Paul.* Ed. Jacques Maritain, 1941.
Rousseau, Jean Jacques. *The Living Thoughts of Rousseau.* Ed. Romain Rolland, 1939.
Schopenhauer, Arthur. *The Living Thoughts of Schopenhauer.* Ed. Thomas Mann, 1939.
Spinoza, Benedictus de. *The Living Thoughts of Spinoza.* Ed. Arnold Zweig, 1939.
Thoreau, Henry David. *The Living Thoughts of Thoreau.* Ed. Theodore Dreiser, 1939.
Tolstoi, Leo. *The Living Thoughts of Tolstoi.* Ed. Stefan Zweig, 1939.
Voltaire. *The Living Thoughts of Voltaire.* Ed. André Maurois, 1939.

Foreign Policy Association (New York)
Salter lettered a different jacket for each title in the series Headline Books.

Bisson, T. A., and Rhyllis Alexander Goslin. *Clash in the Pacific.* Headline Books 5, 1936.
Buell, Raymond Leslie, and Rhyllis Alexander Goslin. *War Drums and Peace Plans.* Headline Books 6, 1936.
Goslin, Rhyllis Alexander. *Church and State.* Headline Books 10, 1937.
———. *Cooperatives.* Headline Books 8, 1937.
———. *War Tomorrow. Will We Keep Out?* Headline Books 1, 1935.
Goslin, Rhyllis Alexander, ed. *Changing Governments Amid New Social Problems: A Survey of the Present Governments in France, Italy, Germany, Russia, and Denmark.* Headline Books 11, 1937.
———. *Dictatorship.* Headline Books 3, 1936.
———. *Made in U.S.A.* Headline Books 2, 1935.
Goslin, Rhyllis Alexander, and William T. Stone. *America Contradicts Herself: The Story of Our Foreign Policy.* Headline Books, 1936.
Stone, William T. *Peace in Party Platforms.* Headline Books 4, 1936.
Stone, William T., and Clark M. Eichelberger. *Peaceful Change: The Alternative to War.* Headline Books 12, 1937.
Stone, William T., and Rhyllis Alexander Goslin. *Billions for Defense.* Headline Books 9, 1937.

League of Nations (printed by Columbia University Press)
Seven spiral-bound pamphlets were published for distribution in the League of Nations Pavilion at the 1939 New York World's Fair. In 1940 these were collected and published as a single volume under the title *Windows on the World: American Views on Attempts to Organize International Life.*

As a series, the individual volumes were:
Abbott, Grace. *Social Welfare Co-operation: The League's Advisory Committee on Social Questions.*
Boudreau, Frank G. *Ancient Diseases–Modern Defences: The Work of the Health Organization of the League of Nations.*
Grady, Henry F. *Attempts at a Freer Trade: The Economic and Financial Work of the League of Nations.*
Hudson, Manley O. *A Tribunal of Nations: The Permanent Court of International Justice, 1920–1939.*
May, Herbert L. *Fighting Dangerous Drugs: The Work of the League's Anti-opium Agencies.*
Shotwell, James T. *Where Minds Meet: The Intellectual Co-operation Organization of the League of Nations.*
Wright, Quincy. *In Search of Peace: The Political Aims and Activities of the League of Nations.*

National Home Library (Washington, D.C.)
Salter's designs for lettering and different pictorial jackets appeared in 1935.

Defoe, Daniel. *Robinson Crusoe.*
Dickens, Charles. *A Tale of Two Cities.*
Dodge, Mary Mapes. *Hans Brinker, or The Silver Skates.*
Ellis, Havelock. *The New Spirit.*
Emerson, Ralph Waldo *The Conduct of Life.*
Flaubert, Gustave. *Salammbô.*
France, Anatole. *The Queen Pedauque.*
Kipling, Rudyard. *Selected Tales.*
Paine, Thomas. *Selections from the Writings of Thomas Paine.*
Scott, Walter. *Ivanhoe.*
Shakespeare, William. *The Tragedy of Hamlet, Prince of Denmark.*
Tolstoy, Leo. *Selected Tales.*
Winslow, Floyd Truman, and Herbert Bruce Brougham. *Money and its Power.*

Time-Life Records (New York)
Salter did the lettering for the record covers in the series "The Story of Great Music" (1966–1967). These 11 volumes comprised 44 analog discs.
1. The Romantic Era.
2. Age of Elegance.
3. The Opulent era.
4. Age of Revolution.
5. The Baroque Era.
6. The Music of Today.
7. The Early Twentieth Century.
8. Prelude to Modern Music.
9. Slavic Traditions.
10. The Spanish Style.
11. From the Renaissance.

Magazines (partial list)
American Institute of Graphic Arts, 1935.
Atlas: The Magazine of the World Press, 1959. Title, logo, layout.
Bell Telephone Magazine, Spring, 1954.
Book-of-the-Month Club News, 1945–1948. Layout and different title lettering for each issue.
Columbia Journal of World Business, 1965. Cover lettering and layout.
Eve Magazine, 1945. Masthead and layout.
Mercury Publications, including *The American Mercury* (layout and masthead). For the following Mercury Publications in digest format, Salter designed the cover art and title: *Mercury Books, Mercury Mysteries, Jonathan Press Mysteries, Ellery Queen, Bestseller Mysteries, Fantasy and Science Fiction Magazine.*
Omnibook Magazine, May–Nov. 1945.
Production Manager (PM), Sept 1935; May 1936.

Devices, Trademarks, Logos for Series and Institutions
Alliance Books
Book Jacket Designers Guild
Book-of-the-Month-Club News
Book-of-the-Month-Club, Bookplate
Borzoi Books (selection)
Columbia University Press (Crown logo)
Commonwealth Fund
Haiti Exposition International
L. B. Fischer
Lincoln Center for the Performing Arts
Manual of Bookmaking
Master Drawings Association
Mercury Magazine
Operatic Masterpieces Series (Simon & Schuster)
The Living Thoughts Library
The Twentieth Century Fund
U.S. Government printing office sticker: "Good Loser Club, Let's Work for America"
UNICEF, Christmas card (1966)
Vassar College Art Gallery
Who's Who in World Jewry
World Publishing Company

Notes

Introduction, pages 11–12

1 George Salter, "Designing Book Jackets," *The Fifth Advertising and Publishing Production Yearbook 1939. The Reference Manual of the Graphic Arts* (New York: Colton Press, 1939), 48a–48h. Salter's seven categories are paraphrased here.

George Salter's Berlin Years, pages 12–24

1 See Georg Kurt Schauer, "Georg Salter und die jüngste Phase des Schutzumschlags," *Börsenblatt für den deutschen Buchhandel* (Frankfurter Ausgabe) 100 (December 16, 1957): 1525–32; Eberhard Hölscher, "Georg Salter," *Sonderdruk aus dem Archiv für Buchgewerbe und Gebrauchsgraphick* 67:9 (Reihe: Deutsche Buchkünstler und Gebrauchsgraphiker der Gegenwart, 1930), 36 pp. (unpaginated); *The Reminiscences of Agnes O'Shea Salter*, 1979. [Carbon copy of typescript of interview conducted by Paul Shaw, *The Reminiscences of Agnes O'Shea Salter*, January 27, 1979, George Salter Papers, Mortimer Rare Book Room, Neilson Library (Smith College).] Errors are continually perpetuated in the brief attempts to present Salter's life and career as, for example, most recently in *Buchgestaltung im Exil 1933–1950. Eine Ausstellung des Deutschen Exilarchivs 1933–45 der Deutschen Bibliothek* (Wiesbaden: Harrassowitz, 2003).

2 Stefan Salter, chapter 1, in *From Cover to Cover* (Englewood Cliffs, N.J.: Prentice-Hall, 1969). It may be significant that Stefan Salter published this book two years after the death of his older brother. Stefan mentions George only once by name, when referring to their youth in Berlin. He does not refer to the help George reputedly gave him in New York, to George's own achievements in the field of book design, or to their occasional collaboration on design projects.

3 Norbert Salter also had ambitions as an agent for German writers seeking representation in the United States. Among Salter's papers is a brief correspondence between his father and the brothers Heinrich and Thomas Mann. In 1925 and 1926 Norbert Salter agreed to negotiate with Hollywood studios on their behalf for the film rights to certain novels. Heinrich Mann was particularly eager to pursue film writing, but Norbert Salter discussed a variety of titles and terms with both brothers. Although the plans bore no fruit, the correspondence documents the Manns' early interest in this lucrative new entertainment industry.

4 Janet Salter Rosenberg, conversation with author, March 30, 2001. Furthermore, Salter urged his students always to sign their work; Salter's own signature was prominent on his published jacket designs. (Anita Karl, conversation with author, March 14, 2001.)

5 The most reliable source for Salter's years in Germany is Eberhard Hölscher, "Georg Salter"

(1930), paraphrased here.

6 Georg Kurt Schauer, "Georg Salter und die jüngste Phase des Schutzumschlags," 1525.

7 For a concise summary of the German publishing trade in this period to which this brief summary is indebted, see "Die Zeit der Inflationskrise" in Ernst Piper and Bettina Raab, eds., *90 Jahre Piper: die Geschichte des Verlags von der Gündung bis heute* (Munich: Piper, 1994).

8 Janet Salter Rosenberg, conversation with author, March 30, 2001.

9 See Hans Peter Willberg, "Zur Situation der Buch- und Schriftkunst in den Zwanziger Jahren," in *Das Buch in den Zwanziger Jahren: Vorträge des Zweiten Jahrestreffens des Wolfenbüttler Arbeitskreises des Buchwesens* (Hamburg: E. Hauswedell, 1977).

10 See Steven Heller and Louise Fili, *German Modern: Graphic Design from Wilhelm to Weimar* (San Francisco: Chronicle Books, 1998), 6.

11 This information is taken from the most complete history of the publishing house; other accounts omit mention of Georg Salter as one of the managing partners. The two other partners were Heinz Wendriner and Fritz Wurm. See Frank Hermann and Heinke Schmitz, *Der Verlag Die Schmiede 1921–1929: eine kommentierte Bibliographie* (Morsum, Sylt: Cicero Presse, 1996).

12 Georg Salter played a less active role in the business end of the publishing house than he did in its art department.

13 Eberhard Hölscher, "Georg Salter," (1930), 5.

14 Salter created thirteen out of the nineteen titles for the series of contemporary novels, Die Romane des XX. Jahrhunderts.

15 Rudolf Förster, "Deutschland im Spiegel seiner Verleger: Die Schmiede A.-G.," *Die neue Bücherschau* 6:4 (1927): 174.

16 See Cornelia Caroline Funke, "Im Verleger verkörpert sich das Gesicht seiner Zeit." *Unternehmungsführung und Programmgestaltung im Gustav Kiepenheuer Verlag 1909 bis 1944* (Wiesbaden: Harrassowitz, 1999), 123 ff.

17 These are preserved in box 5, George Salter Papers, Mortimer Rare Book Room, Neilson Library (Smith College).

18 See also Hölscher, "Georg Salter."

19 Friedrich Pfäfflin, *100 Jahre S. Fischer Verlag, 1886–1986: Buchumschläge; über Bücher und ihre äussere Gestalt* (Frankfurt am Main: S. Fischer, 1986), 17.

20 Friedrich Pfäfflin and Ingrid Kussmaul, *S. Fischer Verlag: von der Gründung bis zur Rückkehr aus dem Exil*, Marbacher Katalog 40, ed. Bernhard Zeller, (Marbach am Neckar: Deutsche Schillergesellschaft, 1983), 373.

21 F. H. Ehmcke, *Broschur und Schutzumschlag am deutschen Buch der neuen Zeit* (Mainz: Gutenberg Gesellschaft, 1951), 9.

22 See *Photographie auf dem deutschen Buchumschlag*, exhib. cat. (Mainz: Gutenberg Museum, 1982),

6–17. The catalog includes illustrations of jackets by Allgeier, Heartfield, and Salter.

23 The first two covers in the Junge Kunst series from 1930 are attributed to Salter by name, whereas the following volumes of the same design from 1930 and 1931 omit an attribution.

24 A tale follows *Chronik der Sperlingsgasse* into its refugee existence. When the exile publisher Frederick Ungar brought out an edition of Raabe's novel in New York in the 1940s, the title page echoed the 1931 Grote edition stating, "Mit sechs Bildern von Georg Salter" ["With six illustrations by Georg Salter"]. These, however, did not appear in the text. The only remnant of Salter in this undated bibliographical oddity, which otherwise used the plates of the original edition, is the *Fraktur* lettering on the title page, which is also stamped in gold on the black cover. Salter probably never knew of the existence of this book.

25 Hölscher, "Georg Salter," 20.

26 Kurt Löb's *Exil-Gestalten: deutsche Buchgestalter in den Niederlanden 1932–1950* (Amsterdam: Gonda Quint, 1995) presents a good overview of German book design in this period.

27 See Heller and Fili, *German Modern*, 16.

28 See Sebastian Carter, *Twentieth Century Type Designs* (New York: Taplinger, 1987), 59.

29 See, for example, the appraisals by Eberhard Hölscher and Kurt Georg Schauer, who both lauded Salter.

From Berlin to New York: The 1930s and 1940s, pages 25–37

1 See *Vita activa. Georg Trump. Bilder, Schriften, und Schriftbilder* (Munich and Hamburg: Typographische Gesellschaft [Auslieferung] Dr. Hauswedell, 1967).

2 See Kurt Löb, *Exil-Gestalten: Deutsche Buchgestalter in den Niederlanden 1932–1950* (Amsterdam: Gonda Quint, 1995), 219; Fritz Landshoff, *Amsterdam, Keizersgracht 333, Querido Verlag: Erinnerungen eines Verlegers* (Berlin and Weimar: Aufbau Verlag, 1991), 90.

3 Georg Salter, letter to Dr. Eberhard Jungfer (Notary), June 6, 1963, George Salter Papers, Mortimer Rare Book Room, Nielson Library (Smith College).

4 After he was safely out of Germany, a letter arrived at his Baden-Baden address from the president of the *Reichskammer der bildenden Künste* (Reich Chamber of Fine Arts). Ironically, it was notification that denied him eligibility for membership in the official organization (based on "lack of qualifications") and forbade his use of the designation *Gebrauchsgraphiker* (commercial artist). The letter quotes the statute of the *Reichskulturkammergesetz* of November 1933. It is signed Dr. Gaber, and carries the official document reference number: Aktenzeichen V. 502/8707. Private collection of Janet Salter Rosenberg, Dobbs Ferry, New York.

5   Rudolph Ruzicka had come to America in 1894; Ernst Reichl, Lucien Bernhard, and Hellmut Lehmann-Haupt were also émigrés but not refugees. For a thorough treatment of refugee book designers on the American scene, see Ronald Salter, "Deutsche Emigranten in der amerikanischen Buchkunst," *Marginalien, Leitschrift für Buchlumst und Bibliophilia* 147:3 (1997): 6–24. For design in the Netherlands, see Löb, *Exil-Gestalten*. The most comprehensive treatment is the exhibition calatog "Buchgestaltung im Exil 1933–1950: Eine Ausstellung des Deutschen Exilarchivs 1933–45 der Deutschen Bibliothek" in *Gesellschaft für das Buch* 9 (Wiesbaden: Harrassowitz, 2003).

6   Georg Salter, letter to Dr. Eberhard Jungfer (Notary), June 30, 1963; Carbon copy of typescript of interview conducted by Paul Shaw, *The Reminiscences of Agnes O'Shea Salter*, January 27, 1979. George Salter Papers, Mortimer Rare Book Room, Neilson Library (Smith College). Salter himself once wrote: "ten English words [and] ten marks, which the German government had allowed me to export." Georg Salter. *A Third of a Century of Graphic Work*, ex. cat. (New York: The Composing Room, Inc., 1961), 2.

7   This information was kindly provided by Ms. J. Siegel, June 20, 2000. Personal communication with the author. See also Donald Peter Geddes, "Hellmut Lehmann-Haupt—Humanist," *Print* 2:2 (Summer 1941): 73–76.

8   *The Reminiscences of Agnes O'Shea Salter*, 17.

9   John Tebbel, *A History of Book Publishing in the United States* (New York: R. R. Bowker, 1972–1981), 3:372.

10 Paul Standard, *Ten Years of Book Making Progress at H. Wolff* (New York: H. Wolff, 1938).

11 See Helmut Pfanner, *Exile in New York: German and Austrian Writers after 1933* (Detroit: Wayne State University Press, 1983), n.p.

12 In Greenwich Village Salter was a good friend and neighbor of Margaret and H. A. Rey (originally Reyersbach), the authors of the *Curious George* books. He also provided advice and technical help on color to the young Theodore Geisel (Dr. Seuss) in his early children's book *And to Think that I Saw it on Mulberry Street* (New York: Vanguard, 1937). Geisel thanked Salter for his help in the dedication copy of the book that he signed and gave to him. Private collection of Janet Salter Rosenberg, Dobbs Ferry, New York.

13 Standard, *Ten Years of Book Making Progress*. n.p.

14 An unidiomatic expression that he never shed, despite being corrected, was the expression, "Does it rain?" Janet Salter Rosenberg, conversation with author, June 17, 2003.

15 *PM (Production Manager)* "A New Star." (No author; book cover) 2:9 (May 1936).

16 Robert L. Leslie, "Georg Salter—An Appreciation," *PM (Production Manager)* 2:1 (September 1935): 16, 24.

17 Salter also taught a class called Lettering and Art work in Book Design and Book Jackets in the winter and spring of 1935 in the Columbia University School of Library Service. (Siegel, communication with the author, June 20, 2000.) Both Salter and Reichl donated original drawings and dummies of their work to the Columbia Book Arts collection.

18 Janet Salter Rosenberg, interview with author, March 30, 2001; and Charles Skaggs interview with author, August 22, 2002. Skaggs describes Salter as "a giant in the field of calligraphy." The two men knew each other from their joint membership in the Book Jacket Designers Guild and work at Knopf.

19 *Pace* John Tebbel, who states that Salter did one uniform design for the series; see *A History of Book Publishing in the United States*, 3:500.

20 Chandler Grannis, "Designers of Book Jackets: I—Georg Salter," *Publishers Weekly,* March 1952, 1098.

21 The work is both a fine tribute to Salter and good reference source on comparative book arts.

22 Adrian H. Goldstone and John R. Payne, *John Steinbeck: A Bibliographical Catalogue of the Adrian H. Goldstone Collection* (Austin, Texas: Humanities Research Center, University of Texas at Austin, 1974), 33–35.

23 I am indebted to Mr. Paul F. Gehl, custodian of the John M. Wing Foundation of the History of Printing, The Newberry Library, Chicago, Illinois, for his expert help in explaining Salter's role in the publication history of *Of Mice and Men.* The Newberry Library owns a copy of this variant edition that came from Salter's own library.

24 These include Thomas Mann, Stefan Zweig, Arnold Zweig, Leopold Schwarzschild, Robert Pick, Konrad Heiden, Carl Zuckmayer, Bertha Zuckerkandl, Otto Zoff, Hermann Broch, Wilhelm Speyer, Emil Ludwig, Felix Salten, Maria Ley-Piscator, Alfred Neumann, Kurt Schuschnigg (the Austrian chancellor who tried to oppose Hitler in 1938), Franz Werfel, F. C. Weiskopf, Erich Maria Remarque, Elias Canetti, Hertha Pauli, Klaus Mann, Erich Neumann, and an anthology edited by Klaus Mann and Hermann Kesten. Salter also designed American covers for writers such as Hans Fallada and Erich Kästner, who did not leave Germany.

25 One ambitious job that Salter planned for the Book of the Month Club reveals information about his pay scale during this period. Harry N. Abrams, president of the BOMC, was a friend of Salter who commissioned him to produce the firm's letterhead and the calligraphic title for the *Book of the Month Club News.* In the spring of 1938, Abrams wrote to Salter to confirm a new edition of a two-volume set of *The Complete Shakespeare,* a work that was to bear the imprint of Random House (for its retail sales) and be sent to subscribers as a book-club dividend. After Salter submitted drawings and dummies for the books, he

received a contract letter offering $3,000 for approximately fifty two-color drawings and the same number of black-and-white illustrations. Abrams suggested a payment schedule of $100 per week until the full amount was paid. For reasons unknown, the Shakespeare edition was never published and the design dummies were returned to Salter when the project failed to materialize. On his Personnel Record at the Cooper Union in November 1938, he listed the job as in progress. Harry A. Abrams, letter to Georg Salter, May 25, 1938, box 16, George Salter Papers, Mortimer Rare Book Room, Neilson Library (Smith College).

26 Salter's official Certificate of Naturalization includes a physical description: height five feet, seven inches; weight 168 lbs. Both the signature below his photograph and his official signature on the document show a still tentative "e" appended to his German first name in a different color ink.

27 Janet Salter Rosenberg, conversation with author, March 30, 2001.

28 Agnes O'Shea graduated from Smith College, Northampton, Massachusetts, in 1927; Janet Salter Rosenberg was in the class of 1954. The establishment of an archive of George Salter's materials at Smith thus reflects this family connection to the college. In her career as an editor, Salter Rosenberg worked for several publishing houses including Random House, Berkley, Pyramid Books, World Publishers, and Columbia University Press.

29 In 1941 an art critic observed that there were at present about four particularly recognizable artists in the book jacket field: Boris Artyzbasheff, Georg Salter (Adler and Lubalin being his followers), Arthur Hawkins, and E. McKnight Kauffer. H. Felix Kraus, "Some Outstanding American Book Jackets of 1941," *Art and Industry* 32 (1942): 181.

30 See Fritz H. Landshoff, *Amsterdam, Keizergracht 333, Querido Verlag. Erinnerungen eines Verlegers* (Berlin and Weimar: Aufbau Verlag, 1991), 129–130. Landshoff recounts that he and his (later) wife lived in Greenwich Village and that she worked as an assistant to Georg Salter. This is unlikely; perhaps Landshoff meant Stefan Salter.

31 Tebbel, *A History of Book Publishing in the United States*, 4:10–13. Salter produced a slightly different version of this cover for the Book of the Month Club edition of *Out of the Night.*

32 The following section on L. B. Fischer follows Friedrich Pfäfflin and Ingrid Kussmaul, *S. Fischer Verlag: von der Gründung bis zur Rückkehr aus dem Exil.* Marbacher Katalog 40. Ed. Bernhard Zeller (Marbach am Neckar: Deutsche Schillergesellschaft, 1983).

33 Pfäfflin and Kussmaul, *S. Fischer Verlag,* 556.

34 The designer Brigitte Bermann Fischer (wife of Gottfried), who replaced Salter, produced several handsome jackets for the firm.

35 Janet Salter Rosenberg, conversation with author, June 17, 2003. Woods became a prolific designer of jackets, mostly in the lettered rather than illustrated style, and her early work shows a striking debt to Salter, her mentor and uncle by marriage.

36 In addition to Salter, Jeanyee Wong, Reynard Biemiller, and Philip Grushkin contributed volumes to the project; ones by W. A. Dwiggins and Arnold Bank were also planned. Jeanyee Wong, personal communication, March 13, 2001. See Tebbel, *A History of Book Publishing*, 4:416. Despite the high quality of craftsmanship in this series, the concept of marketing mass-produced books that imitated hand-lettered editions did not appeal widely enough to prove profitable. Reichl was forced to sell the attractive series.

37 Charles E. Skaggs, "American Calligraphy Revisited, 1945–1965," *Fine Print: A Review for the Arts of the Book* 10:4 (October 1984): 163.

38 See Alan Powers, *Front Cover: Great Book Jackets and Binding* (London: Mitchell Beazley, 2001), 90–91, 118–119.

39 See Piet Schreuders, *Paperbacks, U.S.A.: A Graphic History, 1939–1959,* trans. Josh Pachter (San Diego, Calif.: Blue Dolphin Enterprises, 1981), 22–25.

40 George Salter Papers, Mortimer Rare Book Room, Neilson Library (Smith College).

41 Georg Salter, "Book Jacket Designs 1940–1947," *Print* 6:1 (1948): 23.

42 Alvin Eisenman, conversation with author, June 22, 2002.

43 See Schreuders, *Paperbacks*, 107–109.

44 *First Annual Exhibition Book Jacket Designers Guild 1948* (New York: The Guild, 1948) 1.

45 *Sixth Annual Exhibition Book Jacket Designers Guild 1953* (New York: The Guild, 1953), 1–2.

46 Schreuders, *Paperbacks*, 109.

Designs of the 1950s and 1960s, pages 37–48

1 Joseph Blumenthal, *Typographic Years: A Printer's Journey through Half a Century, 1925–1975* (New York: F. C. Beil, 1982), 142.

2 John Tebbel, *A History of Book Publishing in the United States* (New York: R. R. Bowker Co., 1972–1981), 4:42.

3 Alan Powers makes this point in his comprehensive history of British book jackets, *Front Cover: Great Book Jackets and Cover Design* (London: Mitchell Beazley, 2001), 41.

4 See Introduction, page 12.

5 See John Reed, "What is This Book About? The Vogue of the Guess-What Jacket," *Publishers Weekly* (2 February 1952): 686–688 *passim*.

6 See Chandler Grannis, "Designers of Book Jackets: I—Georg Salter," *Publishers Weekly* (1 March 1952): 1096–1102.

7 Ibid.

8 See Carl Van Vechten, "Meet Mr. Knopf," in *Portrait of a Publisher 1915–1965*, 2 vols. (New York: The Typophiles, 1965), 2:119ff.

9 Tebbel, *A History of Book Publishing in the United States*, 4:46. He could also have mentioned, among others, Rudolph Ruzicka, Paul Rand, and Sam Bass.

10 George Salter, "There Is a Borzoi Style," in *Portrait of a Publisher 1915–1965* (New York: The Typophiles, 1965): 2:280–283.

11 Alfred Knopf Jr., Letter to Mrs. Agnes Salter, November 2, 1967, box 5, George Salter Papers, Mortimer Rare Book Room, Neilson Library (Smith College).

12 These comments summarize statements in the correspondence between Salter and editors at Knopf. The records of Alfred A. Knopf, Inc., May 1960, box 720, folder 3, Harry Ransom Humanities Research Center (University of Texas at Austin). In recognition of Salter's effort he received four copies of the finished book, which was twice as many as most designers were normally given. Sidney Jacobs, a friend and the art editor at Knopf, was full of praise for the design but complained about the inevitability of high production costs.

13 Records of Alfred A. Knopf, Inc., May 1960, box 293, folder 8, Harry Ransom Humanities Research Center (University of Texas at Austin).

14 See Introduction, page 11.

15 Gordon B. Neavill, "The Modern Library Series: Format and Design, 1917–1977," *Printing History* 1:1 (1979): 26–37.

16 George Salter, letter to Sidney Jacobs, November 20, 1965, Wing Collection, Newberry Library, Chicago, Illinois.

17 Creative photography was an early design feature of twentieth-century German books, but it came comparatively late to the American book jacket. In the 1940s one writer complained about the lack of progressive techniques, saying, "Photo and photomontage are nearly not in existence as yet." H. Felix Kraus, "Some Outstanding American Book Jackets of 1941," *Art and Industry* 32 (1942): 180.

18 George Salter, "50 Books of 1965," *Book Production Industry* 42, no. 5 (May 1966): 48–52.

19 Martin Huttner and Jerry Kelly, eds., *A Century for the Century: Fine Printed Books 1900–1999* (New York: Grolier Club, 1999). See entries 20 and 63.

20 This summary follows the authoritative work on this aspect of American publishing: Piet Schreuders, *Paperbacks, U.S.A.: A Graphic History, 1939–1959,* trans. Josh Pachter (San Diego, Calif.: Blue Dolphin Enterprises, 1981), 16ff. See also Jonathan White, "The Mystery and Detective Paperback," *AB Bookman's Weekly*, April 16, 1984, 2891–2899.

21 Janet Salter Rosenberg, conversation with author, June 17, 2003.

22 Schreuders, *Paperbacks*, 130.

23 Janet Salter Rosenberg, conversation with author, March 30, 2001.

24 Paul A. Bennett, "A Visit with George Salter—Designer, Calligrapher, Illustrator, and Teacher," *Publishers Weekly* 186–10 (7 September 1964): 83.

25 See Hans Peter Willberg, "Zur Situation der Buch-und Schriftkunst in den zwanziger Jahren," in *Das Buch in den zwanziger Jahren: Vorträge des zweiten Jahrestreffens des Wolfenbütteler Arbeitskreises für Geschichte des Buchwesens 16. bis 18. Mai 1977.* Ed. Paul Raabe and Barbara Strutz (Hamburg: E. Hauswedell, 1978), 47–62.

26 For a good discussion of Salter and typography in the Berlin years, see the essay by Peter Nils Dorén, "Zwischen Klassik und Moderne. Zur Typographie von Georg Salter in seinen Berliner Jahren" ["Between Classicism and Modernity. On the Typography of Georg Salter in his Berlin Years"], in Jürgen Holstein, *Georg Salter: Bucheinbände und Schutzumschläge aus Berliner Zeit, 1922–1934* [Georg Salter: Book Bindings and Dust Jackets from the Berlin Period, 1922–1934] (Berlin: Jürgen Holstein, 2003), 133–146.

27 See Ronald Eason and Sarah Rookledge, *Rookledge's International Directory of Type Designers* (New York: Sarabande Press, 1994), 183. The typeface is advertised in *Fourth Annual Advertising and Production Yearbook: The Reference Manual for the Graphic Arts* (New York: Colton Press, 1937), 298–299.

28 "Salter's Flex Type," *PM*, 3:4 (December 1936): 40.

29 Janet Salter Rosenberg, interview with author, March 30, 2001.

30 "Book Jackets and the 1935 Book Jacket Show," *Publishers Weekly* 72:22 (1 June 1935): 2154.

31 The jackets by Edgard Cirlin come to mind. His version of Antoine de Saint-Exupéry's *Night Flight* (Penguin Books, 1945) echoes Salter's design for that title (S. Fischer, 1932). Cirlin's design is illustrated in Alan Powers, *Front Cover: Great Book Jackets and Cover Design* (London: Mitchell Beazley, 2001). Cirlin's cover for Frederick Prokosch, *The Idols of the Cave* (Doubleday, 1946), is also uncannily like the work of Salter.

32 Kurt Georg Schauer, *Deutsche Buchkunst 1890 bis 1960* (Hamburg: Maximilian Gesellschaft, 1963) 1:253–54. I have drawn on Schauer's summary here.

33 For further discussion of this general phenomenon, see Thomas S. Hansen, "Berlin Culture in Exile, 1935–1945," *Views of Berlin*, ed. Gerhard Kirchhoff (Boston, Basel, Berlin: Birkhäuser, 1988), 98–111.

34 Charles Skaggs, interview with author, August 22, 2002. Skaggs, who knew Salter through Knopf and the Book Jacket Designers Guild, stresses that Salter deserves credit for perfecting and keeping his own design style throughout his career.

35 Jost Hochuli, *Designing Books: Practice and Theory* (London: Hyphen, 1996), 89.

36 The shared headstone was designed by Miriam Woods after the grave marker George Salter had designed for his own mother. Janet Salter Rosenberg, conversation with the author, August 20, 2002.

Bibliography

This list is very selective. The complete citations in the notes augment these titles. For a comprehensive bibliography of book design, see Jürgen Holstein (below).

Baker, Eric. "The Art of the Borzoi." *Graphis* 50 (September/October 1994): 92–103.

Beck, Knut. *100 Jahre S. Fischer Verlag 1886–1986: Eine Bibliographie.* Frankfurt am Main: S. Fischer, 1986.

Bennett, Paul A. "Distinguished American Book Designers and Printers." *The Penrose Annual* 15 (1961): 20–42.

Blumenthal, Joseph. *The Printed Book in America.* Boston: David. R. Godine, 1977.

Bonn, Thomas L. *Under Cover: An Illustrated History of American Mass Market Paperbacks.* New York: Penguin Books, 1982.

Buchumschläge 1900–1950: Aus der Sammlung Kurt Tillmann. Ed. Bernhard Zeller, Munich: Kösel Verlag, 1971.

Ehmcke, F. H. *Broschur und Schutzumschlag am deutschen Buch der neuen Zeit.* Mainz: Gutenberg Gesellschaft, 1951.

Enoch, Kurt. "Memoirs of Kurt Enoch: Written for His Family." New York: 1984. Privately printed.

Förster, Rudolf, "Deutschland im Spiegel seiner Verleger: Die Schmiede A.–G." *Die Neue Bücherschau* (Berlin) 6:4 (1927): 173–174.

Funke, Cornelia Caroline. "Im Verleger verkörpert sich das Gesicht seiner Zeit." *Unternehmungsführung und Programmgestaltung im Gustav Kiepenheuer Verlag 1909 bis 1944.* Wiesbaden: Harrassowitz, 1999.

Gabrie, Rudolf. "Der Schutzumschlag des Buches/The Book-Wrapper." *Gebrauchsgraphik/International Advertising Art* 5:7 (July 1928): 44–51.

Glaser, Milton. *Graphic Design.* Woodstock, N.Y.: Overlook, 1973.

Halbey, Hans Adolf. *Der Erich Reiss Verlag 1908–1936: Versuch eines Porträts.* Frankfurt am Main: Buchhändler-Vereinigung, 1981.

Hermann, Frank, and Heinke Schmitz. *Der Verlag Die Schmiede 1921–1929: eine kommentierte Bibliographie.* Morsum, Sylt: Cicero Presse, 1996.

Jaeger, Roland. "Kurt Enoch (1895–1982) und der Gebrüder Enoch Verlag (1913–1936)." *Aus dem Antiquariat* 5 (2000): A288–A300.

Kelly, Jerry, and Alice Koeth. *Artist and Alphabet: Twentieth Century Calligraphy and Letter Art in America.* Boston: David R. Godine, 2000.

Kraus, H. Felix. "Some Outstanding American Book-jackets of 1941." *Art and Industry* 32 (1942): 177–181.

Landshoff, Fritz H. *Amsterdam, Keizergracht 333, Querido Verlag: Erinnerungen eines Verlegers.* Berlin and Weimar: Aufbau Verlag, 1991.

Lehmann-Haupt, Hellmut. *The Book in America: A History of the Making and Selling of Books in the Unites States.* 2nd American ed. New York: R. R. Bowker, 1952. First published in Leipzig as: *Das amerikanische Buchwesen* (Leipzig: K. W. Hiersemann, 1937).

Löb, Kurt. *Exil-Gestalten: deutsche Buchgestalter in den Niederlanden 1932–1950.* Amsterdam: Gonda Quint, 1995.

Loubier, Hans. *Die neue deutsche Buchkunst.* Stuttgart: Felix Krais Verlag, 1921.

Pfäfflin, Friedrich. *100 Jahre S. Fischer Verlag, 1886–1986: Buchumschläge; über Bücher und ihre äußere Gestalt.* Frankfurt am Main: S. Fischer, 1986.

Pfäfflin, Friedrich, and Ingrid Kussmaul. *S. Fischer Verlag: von der Gründung bis zur Rückkehr aus dem Exil.* Marbacher Katalog 40. Ed. Bernhard Zeller. Marbach am Neckar: Deutsche Schillergesellschaft, 1983.

Photographie auf dem deutschen Buchumschlag. Ausstellungskatalog. Mainz: Gutenberg-Museum, August 1982.

Portrait of a Publisher 1915–1965. 2 vols. New York: The Typophiles, 1965.

Powers, Alan. *Front Cover: Great Book Jackets and Binding.* London: Mitchell Beazley, 2001.

Reed, John. "What is This Book About? The Vogue of the Guess-What Jacket." *Publishers Weekly* 161:5 (February 2, 1952): 686–688.

Salter, Ronald. "Deutsche Emigranten in der amerikanischen Buchkunst." *Marginalien: Zeitschrift für Buchkunst und Bibliophilie* 147:3 (1997): 6–24.

———. *Fritz Kredel: Das buchkünstlerische Werk in Deutschland und Amerika.* Rudolstadt: Burgart-Presse, 2003.

Schauer, Georg Kurt. "The Art of the Book in Germany in the Nineteenth and Twentieth Centuries." In *Book Typography, 1815–1965, in Europe and the United States of America,* by Kenneth Day, 97–136. Chicago: University of Chicago Press, 1966.

———. "Die Buchgestaltung des S. Fischer Verlags in seinen ersten sechs Jahrzehnten." In *Almanach des S. Fischer Verlags 75: Jahr,* 44–56. Frankfurt am Main: Fischer, 1961.

———. *Deutsche Buchkunst 1890 bis 1960.* 2 vols. Hamburg: Maximilian Gesellschaft, 1963.

———. *Kleine Geschichte des deutschen Buchumschlages im 20. Jahrhundert.* Königstein im Taunus: K. R. Langwiesche Nachfolger, 1962.

———. *Wege der Buchgestaltung: Erfahungen und Ratschläge.* Stuttgart: C. E. Poeschel, 1953.

———. *Von den Herbergen des Geistes: Eine Anthologie aus Versuchen.* Ed. Kurt Londonberg. Krefeld: Scherpe Verlag, 1976.

Schrift in unserer Zeit: Eine Ausstellung der Internationalen Typographischen Vereinigung. Mainz: Internationalen Typographischen Vereinigung, with Schauer, 1966. Piece by Salter included among the 120 exhibits.

Standard, Paul. "Calligraphy Brings Us Liberation from Rigidity of Printing Types." *Direct Advertising* 34:1 (July 1948): 11–18.

———. "Calligraphy in Recent U.S. Book Production." *The Penrose Annual* 42 (1940): 1–5.

———. *Calligraphy's Flowering, Decay and Restoration.* Chicago: Society of Typographic Arts, 1947. Contains a design for an initial by Salter on p. 13; a logo for L. B. Fischer on p. 17; an illustration of a cover for a novel by Thomas Mann on p. 25; the endpaper map for *People on Our Side* on p. 26; and a device from *Prevailing Winds* on p. 32.

———. *Ten Years of Book Making Progress at H. Wolff.* New York: H. Wolff, 1938.

Works by George Salter
including works containing his designs.

[Bennett, Paul A.]. *P. A. B.: His Book; Produced by the Friends of Paul A. Bennett and Presented on the Evening of Thursday December 3, 1953.* New York: The Typophiles, 1953. Contains verses lettered by Salter.

Child, Heather. *Calligraphy Today: A Survey of Tradition and Trends.* New York: Watson-Gutpill, 1964. Contains examples by Salter.

Hardeg, Walter, and Charles Rosner, eds. *Graphis Annual: International Advertising Art.* New York: Pellegrini and Cudahy, 1952/53. Page 164 shows small reproduction of Salter cover for *Fantasy and Science Fiction.*

Hölscher, Eberhard. *Der Briefbogen in der Welt.* [s.l. Germany]: J. W. Zanders, 1963. Leaf 62 is letterhead of The Book Jacket Designers Guild, by Salter.

[Kredel, Fritz]. *The Typophiles Welcome Fritz Kredel.* New York: The Typophiles, 1938. This collection of finely printed leaves contains texts lettered by Salter.

Lee, Marshall, ed. *Kafka: The Trial of Six Designers.* Lock Haven, PA: Hammermill Paper Co., 1968. Salter's design for Kafka's novel is presented with those of five other designers.

Peter Piper's Practical Principles of Plain & Perfect Pronunciation: A Typographical Extravaganza. Brooklyn, N.Y.: Mergenthaler Linotype Co., 1936. Designs by Salter for the letters x, y, and z.

Salter, George. "50 Books of 1965." *Book Production Industry* 42:5 (May 1966): 48–52.

———. "The Book Jacket." *Third Annual Exhibition, Book Jacket Designers Guild 1950.* New York: A-D Gallery, 1950.

———. "Book Jacket Designs 1940–1947." *Print: A Quarterly Journal of the Graphic Arts* 6:1 (1948): 13–23.

———. "Book Jackets and the 1935 Book Jacket Show." *Publishers Weekly* 77:22 (June 1, 1935): 2152–2154.

———. "Designing Book Jackets." *The Fifth Advertising and Publishing Production Yearbook 1939: The Reference Manual of the Graphic Arts* (New York: Colton Press, 1939): 48a–48h.

———. "Ernst Schneidler." *Sixth Annual Exhibition: Book Jacket Designers Guild 1953.* New York: A-D Gallery, 1953.

———. "Fancy Penmanship, 1854." Review of *Ornamental Penmanship,* by George J. Becker. *A-D* 8:2 (December 1941–January 1942): 56–57.

———. "Illustrators View Illustrations: Symposium." *Print: A Quarterly Journal of the Graphic Arts* 3:3 (1943): 33–46. Contribution by Salter, pp. 39–40.

———. "Letter, Word, and Line." *Cooper Union Art School* 4 (n.d.): 1–2, 19–20 (unpaginated).

———. "Letter, Word, and Page." *The Bulletin of the Society for Italic Handwriting* 5:16 (Fall 1958): 10–11.

———. "Strathmore is a Habit with Me!" Advertisement, Prominent Artist Users of Strathmore: no. 95 of a series. Testimonial for Strathmore paper illustrated with photograph of Salter at his drawing board. *American Artist* (April 1951).

———. "There *is* a Borzoi Style." In *Portrait of a Publisher 1915–1965,* II: 280–283.

Salter, George, and Paul Standard. "Calligraphy in Current Advertising and Publishing." *Print: A Quarterly Journal of the Graphic Arts* 3:4 (Fall 1945): 41–52. Illustration by Salter, p. 49.

———. "Cooper Union Calligraphy." *Print: A Quarterly Journal of the Graphic Arts* 9:3 (1957): 25–47. Presentation of works by students of Salter and Standard.

———. *Lettering and Calligraphy in Current Advertising and Publishing.* New York: A-D Gallery, May 11–June 29, 1945.

The Typophiles. *Bouquet for B. R.: A Birthday Garland Gathered by the Typophiles.* Typophiles Chapbook 24. New York: The Typophiles, 1950. Calligraphic tributes to Bruce Rogers by several designers, including Salter.

———. *Calligraphics: Hands & Forms, Rendered by Twenty-five American Scribes for the Typophiles.* Ed. Paul A. Bennett. Typophiles Chapbook 28. New York: The Typophiles, 1955. Contains contribution by Salter.

———. *John Archer, Sagittarius: His Book.* Typophiles Chapbook 25. New York: The Typophiles, 1951. Collection of tributes to Archer upon his retirement from friends and colleagues, including Salter, p. 80.

———. *Forty Devices from (and by) Many Typophiles.* Selected by O. Alfred Dickman and printed as special keepsake by Robert L. Leslie (The Composing Room). New York: The Typophiles, n.d. Includes Salter's design for letter T.

———. *Left to Their Own Devices: With a Salute to Typophiles Desipient by Christopher Morley.* New York: The Typophiles, 1937. Collection of 156 devices based on the letter T (same as that in *Forty Devices* above) contributed by 113 artists, including Salter, who also designed the book jacket.

Works about George Salter

Badaracco, Claire Hoertz. "George Salter's Book Jacket Designs: 1925–1940." *Design Issues* 17:3 (Summer 2001): 40–48.

Bennett, Paul A. "A Visit with George Salter: Designer, Calligrapher, Illustrator, and Teacher." *Publishers Weekly* 186:10 (September 7, 1964): 82–87.

Bockwitz, H. "Neue Arbeiten von Georg Salter." *Archiv für Buchgewerbe und Gebrauchsgraphik* 69:4 (1932): 186–91.

The Cable, 1953–54: The Student Annual of the Cooper Union. New York: The Cooper Union, 1954. Photograph of Georg Salter, p. 54.

The Cable, 1958: The Student Yearbook of the Cooper Union. New York: The Cooper Union, 1958. Photograph of Georg Salter, p. 48.

Fourth Annual Advertising and Production Yearbook: The Reference Manual for the Graphic Arts. New York: Colton Press, 1937. Contains advertisement for Salter's typeface, Flex, 298–299.

Frenzel, Hermann K. "Georg Salter." *Gebrauchsgraphik: International Advertising Art* 9:8 (1932): 2–9.

Grannis, Chandler. "Designers of Book Jackets: I: George Salter." *Publishers Weekly* (March 1, 1952): 1096–1102.

George Salter: A Third of a Century of Graphic Work. Exhibition Catalogue. Gallery 303, New York. New York: The Composing Room, Inc., December 1961.

Gilbert, Dorothy B., ed. *Who's Who in American Art.* New York: R. Bowker, 1953. Contains biographical entries for George and Stefan Salter.

Gondor, Emery I. *You are...: A Puzzle Book for Children 8 to 80.* New York: Modern Age Books, 1937. The animal figures in puzzle 23 are named Georg and Stefan in lighthearted homage to the Salter brothers.

Hansen, Thomas S. *George Salter (1897–1967): An Exhibition of Book Jackets and Designs.* Boston: The Club of Odd Volumes, March 2001.

Catalogue of ca. 125 items. The first 25 copies numbered; five colored illustrations tipped in.

Hölscher, Eberhard. "Georg Salter." *Sonderdruck aus dem Archiv für Buchgewerbe und Gebrauchsgraphik* 67:9. Reihe: Deutsche Buchkünstler und Gebrauchsgraphiker der Gegenwart, 1930, 36 pp. (unpaginated).

Holstein, Jürgen. *Georg Salter: Bucheinbände und Schutzumschläge aus Berliner Zeit, 1922–1934/Georg Salter: Book Bindings and Dust Jackets from the Berlin Period, 1922–1934.* Berlin: Jürgen Holstein, 2003.

Jacobs, Sidney R. "Georg Salter: A Profile." *Publishers' Weekly* 85:22 (June 3, 1939): 2053–2056.

Leslie, Robert. "Georg Salter: An Appreciation." *PM (Production Manager)* 2:1 (September 1935): 16–24. Includes facsimiles of Salter's covers from 1935.

Schauer, Georg Kurt. "Georg Salter und die jüngste Phase des Schutzumschlags." *Börsenblatt für den deutschen Buchhandel* (Frankfurter Ausgabe) 100 (December 16, 1957): 1525–1532.

———. "Georg Salter: Buchgraphiker hier und drüben/Designer of Books on either Side of the Atlantic." *Gebrauchsgraphik/International Advertising Art* 28:10 (1957): 12–15.

———. "Buchgestalter in zwei Welten." *Form und Technik* 14:12 (December 1963): 689–694. Reprinted in Schauer, *Von den Herbergen des Geistes,* 106–113.

———. "Der Schriftmann Georg Salter." *Der Druckspiegel* 12:10 (1957): 516–525.

———. *Von den Herbergen des Geistes: Eine Anthologie aus Versuchen.* Ed. Kurt Londonberg. Krefeld: Scherpe Verlag, 1976.

Shaw, Paul. "Liberty with a Foundation: Georg Salter as Calligrapher." *The Friends of Calligraphy Newsletter* (San Francisco, Calif.) 6:3 (Spring 1980): 1–7.

[Standard, Paul]. "American Jacketeer." Review of *George Salter: A Third of a Century of Graphic Work. Times Literary Supplement,* January 19, 1962, 48.

Related studies

"Buchgestaltung im Exil 1933–1950: Eine Ausstellung des Deutschen Exilarchivs 1933–45 der Deutschen Bibliothek." *Gesellschaft für das Buch* 9. Wiesbaden: Harrassowitz, 2003.

The Dialogues of Plato: In Tribute to George Salter. 2 vols. Interlaken Designer Award Library. New York: Random House, 1963.

Geddes, Donald Porter. "Hellmut Lehmann-Haupt: Humanist." *Print: A Quarterly Journal of the Graphic Arts* 2:2 (Summer 1941): 73–76.

Hansen, Thomas S. "Berlin Culture in Exile 1933–1945." In *Views of Berlin: From a Boston Symposium*, ed. Gerhard Kirchhoff, 98–111. Boston, Basel, Berlin: Birkhäuser, 1988.

Huttner, Martin and Jerry Kelly, eds. *A Century for the Century: Fine Printed Books 1900–1999*. New York: Grolier Club, 1999.

Salter, Stefan. *From Cover to Cover*. Englewood Cliffs: Prentice-Hall, 1969.

Schoor, Kerstin. *Verlagsarbeit im Exil: Untersuchungen zur Geschichte der deutschen Abteilung des Amsterdamer Allert de Lange Verlages 1933–1940*. Amsterdam and Atlanta, Ga.: Rodopi, 1992.

Archives

Newberry Library (Chicago, Illinois), John M. Wing Collection. *Papers, 1919–1967*.

> The papers consist mostly of art, correspondence, contracts, and printed materials relating to design projects executed in New York. Included are many original works and drafts of unpublished projects. There is also a small file of correspondence between Salter and German colleagues; drafts of articles by Salter; papers relating to the Cooper Union; and a file of articles about Salter. The holdings also include 184 jackets that Salter did in Germany; files of articles about Salter; and letters of condolence to his widow. 66 boxes.

Mortimer Rare Book Room, Neilson Library, Smith College (Northampton, Massachusetts).

> The collection is rich in books designed by Salter and books related to his professional interest, together with proofs, papers, and ephemera relating to his book designs from his German and New York periods. Among these papers are *The Reminiscences of Agnes O'Shea Salter* (Oral History Research Office, Columbia University, 1979), which is a carbon copy of typescript. The interview was conducted by Paul Shaw on January 27, 1979, and has hand-written emendations by Agnes O'Shea Salter (94 pages; Box 5). This archive has fewer pieces than the Newberry Library (only two of original art), and duplicates many of the jacket proofs.

Kunstbibliothek Staatliche Museen zu Berlin (Berlin, Germany).

> A small selection from Salter's work placed there by his family for study purposes. The pieces duplicate material in the two American libraries, including author's proofs from his German and New York periods and some photographs.

Alfred A., Knopf, Inc. 1873–1996. Harry Ransom Humanities Research Center (University of Texas at Austin).

> A repository of documents and correspondence, many of which shed light on the art department at Knopf and refer to Salter's work.

Conversations with the author

Alvin Eisenman (June 22, 2002)
Jeanyee Wong (August 15, 2000; March 13, 2001)
Lili Wronker (March 14, 2002; December 3, 2001)
Janet Salter Rosenberg (March 30, 2001; August 4, 2001; June 17, 2003; August 8, 2003).
Charles Skaggs (August 23, 2002)
Peter Salter (August 26, 2002)
Anita Karl (March 14, 2001)

Index to Text

Index to Plates